D0495451

endorsed for
BTEC

BTEC Tech Award

TRAVEL AND TOURISM

Student Book

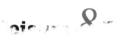

Steve Ingle

Nikki Old

Tom Rock

Pearson

Published by Pearson Education Limited, 80 Strand, London, WC2R 0RL.

www.pearsonschoolsandfecolleges.co.uk

Copies of official specifications for all Pearson qualifications may be found on the website: qualifications.pearson.com

Text © Pearson Education Limited 2019
Typeset by PDQ Digital Media Solutions
Original illustrations © Pearson Education Limited 2019
Cover illustration by Jo Goodberry, KJA Artists

First published 2019

22 21 20 19
10 9 8 7 6 5 4 3 2 1

British Library Cataloguing in Publication Data
A catalogue record for this book is available from the British Library

ISBN 978 1 292 25869 0

Copyright notice
All rights reserved. No part of this publication may be reproduced in any form or by any means (including photocopying or storing it in any medium by electronic means and whether or not transiently or incidentally to some other use of this publication) without the written permission of the copyright owner, except in accordance with the provisions of the Copyright, Designs and Patents Act 1988 or under the terms of a licence issued by the Copyright Licensing Agency, Barnards Inn, 86 Fetter Lane, London EC4A 1EN (www.cla.co.uk). Applications for the copyright owner's written permission should be addressed to the publisher.

Printed in the UK by Bell & Bain Ltd, Glasgow

Acknowledgements
The publisher would like to thank the following for their kind permission to reproduce their photographs:

Text Credit(s):
Amadeus Benelux N.V: Bleisure Travel: Catching Up On A Hot Trend, Amadeus Benelux N.V. 29, **Crown Copyright**: The Countryside Code, © Natural England 2016 43, The future use of the Olympic Stadium and the park is key to the legacy of the games, London 2012 Olympic Park (13 July 2012).jpg 37, Foreign travel advice, gov.uk 9, Foreign travel advice, United Arab Emirates, gov.uk 17, Holiday entitlement 7, **Dundee Press Agency Ltd 2019**: British families spend quarter of annual disposable household income on holidays 8; **Egypt Today**: Bringing Tourists Back: A look at initiatives and policies launched by Lolwa Reda 43; **Euromonitor**: Brexit Requires Radical Rethink to Safeguard UK Travel and Tourism by Lydia Gordon 1, **Freepik Company S.L.**: https://www.freepik.com/free-photos-vectors/background" Background vector created by makyzz - www.freepik.com 20, **International Passenger Survey, Office for National Statistics**: Top towns for 'staying visits' by inbound visitors, 2017 7; **Michigan State University**: Terrorism's Effect on the Global Travel and Tourism Industry, 2015 8; **Office for National Statistics**: Data presented in Maps 1-3 in the Article showing employment by tourism industry at NUTS 3 areas for 2013-2014 by Office for National Statistics 1; **Reuters**: From high season to absolutely nothing': Indonesian quake devastates tourism, AUGUST 8, 2018 3; **Richard Branson**: Richard Branson 39, **Social Care Institute for Excellence**: The Dignity factors, © Social Care Institute for Excellence 5; **The British Tourist Authority**: Annual Survey of Visits to Visitor Attractions: Latest results, 2017 © British Tourist Authority 2016 10; **The Tourism Department of the Welsh Government**: The GB Tourist 2017 Annual Report 7; **UNESCO World Heritage Centre**: UNESCO World Heritage-Sustainable Tourism Online Toolkit, Guide 5 Communicating with visitors 26; **Visitbritain**: Discover England Fund Year 1 Pilot Projects – The first phase of successful applicants to receive year one funding from the Discover England Fund were announced in Autumn 2016. Activities and outputs have been delivered by 31 March 2017 55.

Photo Credits:
123RF: Viktoriia Hnatiuk 6, Amokl 15, ammentor 5; **Alamy Stock Photo**: Westmacott 11, Martin phelps 27, Chris Harris 6, Avpics 34, Greg Balfour Evans 24, Clover 27, peruvianpictures.com 2, Paul Watkins Photography 4, Michael DeFreitas Caribbean 20, Clara Margais 40, John Davidson Photos 46, Bazz 21, Trevor Chriss 30; **Getty Images**: Chris Jackson 49, Pablo Blazquez Domingue 60; Shutterstock: Matthew Jacques 2, Photofusion 13, Tupungato 21, Tupungato 21, Olesia Bilkei 30, Maridav 1, Natalia Sidorova 9, Giovanni Love 26, Maximchuk 27, LightField Studios 29, Olesya Kuznetsova 2, Maciej Czekajewski 15, Dan Burton/Robert Harding 32, Ruben Martinez Barricarte 45, Alberto Atienza/EPA 49, Moia 31 59, BallBall14 17, Pavel Lysenko 25, Tminaz 29, Volodymyr Goinyk 35, Pecold 42, Dancestrokes 52, Jon Stroud 54, Stuart Miles 2, kitzcorne 36, DisobeyArt 40, Stacie C 46, Shutterstock 20, Geoff Moor 30, Mangostar 40.

Websites
Pearson Education Limited is not responsible for the content of any external internet sites. It is essential for tutors to preview each website before using it in class so as to ensure that the URL is still accurate, relevant and appropriate. We suggest that tutors bookmark useful websites and consider enabling students to access them through the school/college intranet.

Notes from the publisher
In order to ensure that this resource offers high-quality support for the associated Pearson qualification, it has been through a review process by the awarding body. This process confirms that this resource fully covers the teaching and learning content of the specification or part of a specification at which it is aimed. It also confirms that it demonstrates an appropriate balance between the development of subject skills, knowledge and understanding, in addition to preparation for assessment.

Endorsement does not cover any guidance on assessment activities or processes (e.g. practice questions or advice on how to answer assessment questions) included in the resource, nor does it prescribe any particular approach to the teaching or delivery of a related course.

While the publishers have made every attempt to ensure that advice on the qualification and its assessment is accurate, the official specification and associated assessment guidance materials are the only authoritative source of information and should always be referred to for definitive guidance.

Pearson examiners have not contributed to any sections in this resource relevant to examination papers for which they have responsibility.

Examiners will not use endorsed resources as a source of material for any assessment set by Pearson.

Endorsement of a resource does not mean that the resource is required to achieve this Pearson qualification, nor does it mean that it is the only suitable material available to support the qualification, and any resource lists produced by the awarding body shall include this and other appropriate resources.

DUNDEE CITY COUNCIL

LOCATION
REFERENCE AND INFORMATION

ACCESSION NUMBER
CO1 023 660X

SUPPLIER
ASK

PRICE
£20.00

CLASS No.
338.4791

DATE
9.1.2020

Contents

CONTENTS

About this book

This book is designed to support you when you are taking a BTEC Tech Award in Travel and Tourism.

About your BTEC Tech Award

Congratulations on choosing a BTEC Tech Award in Travel and Tourism. This exciting and challenging course will introduce you to the travel and tourism sector. The travel and tourism sector is the UK's third largest employer and one of the fastest growing sectors in the UK. It employs nearly 3 million people and contributes nearly £121 billion to the UK'S GDP. There are a host of different and exciting jobs and roles in the sector, and a wide ranging knowledge of the different issues and roles in the sector will help you take advantage of the opportunities in this growing sector.

How you will be assessed

You will be assessed in two different ways. Components 1 and 3 are assessed through internal assessment. This means that your teacher will give you an assignment brief and indicate to you the deadline for completing it. The assignment will cover what you have been learning about and will be an opportunity to apply your knowledge and skills. You teacher will mark your assignment and award you with a grade. Your other assessment (for Component 2) will be an external assessment. This will be a task that is set and marked by Pearson. It will allow you to apply you knowledge and understanding of factors influencing tourism, the impact of tourism on destinations and destination management. You will have a set time in which to complete this task.

About the authors

Steve Ingle is an experienced consultant, teacher educator, and author. He has over fifteen years' experience with outstanding education providers across the learning sector in the UK and overseas. Steve is passionate about vocational education. He has held senior management positions in further and higher education, as well as vocational experience in the leisure and tourism sector. A Fellow of the Higher Education Academy, Steve has significant experience of external assessment, quality assurance, and quality improvement. He is a Qualified Teacher of Learning and Skills (QTLS) and holds a range of postgraduate qualifications, including an MA in Education.

Nikki Old worked in the travel industry for over 10 years and travelled extensively while working for a major tour operator. This was followed by 20 years as a lecturer in travel, tourism and aviation. She has been an assessment associate for a number of years, working as a standards verifier, writer and trainer. She says working in the travel industry has been so exciting. It has provided amazing opportunities for adventure and career progression.

Tom Rock is an experienced secondary school teacher and writer. He holds a BA honours degree in Sport, Recreation and Tourism. Prior to becoming a teacher, Tom worked in the leisure and entertainment sector for a number of years. Tom is currently Head of Geography and BTEC Quality Nominee at an academy; a combined role that allows him to be involved in curriculum planning for subjects including Travel and Tourism and the quality assurance of all BTEC programmes offered by the centre. He has worked with Pearson on several projects, including previous editions of the BTEC Travel and Tourism Student Book.

How to use this book

The book has been designed in a way that will help you to easily navigate through your course. Each component from the course is covered in a separate chapter that makes clear what you are learning and how this will contribute to your assessment. There are opportunities for you to test your understanding of key areas, as well as activities that will challenge and extend your knowledge and skills. You will get the most from this book if you use each feature as part of your study. The different features will also help you develop the skills that will be important in completing your assignments as well as preparing you for your external assessment.

Features of the book

This book is designed in spreads, which means that each pair of facing pages represents a topic of learning. Each spread is about 1 hour of lesson time. Your teacher may ask you to work through a spread during a lesson or in your own time. Each spread contains a number of features that will help you to check what you are learning and offer opportunities to practise new skills.

Getting started A short activity or discussion that will introduce you to what you will be covering in the lesson.

Link it up This indicates where what you're learning about is covered in another part of the course.

Did you know? These include interesting facts that relate to what you're learning about.

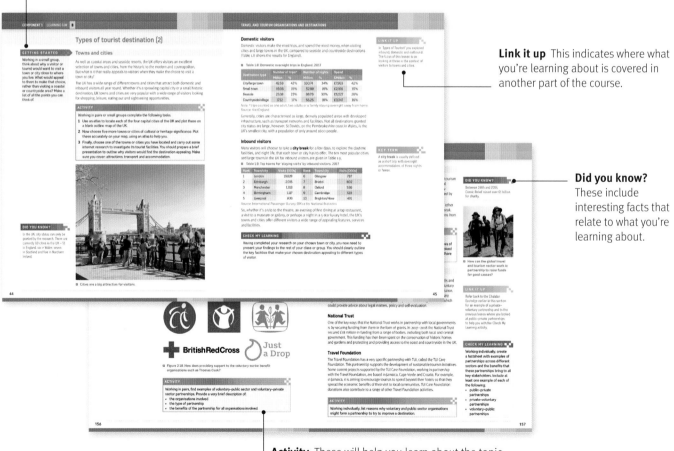

Activity These will help you learn about the topic. You may be asked to work in pairs, groups or on your own.

At the end of each learning aim there is a section that outlines how you will be assessed and provides opportunities for you to build skills for assessment.

Assessment Activity This is a practice assessment that reflects the style and approach of an assignment brief. In Component 3, tasks in the assessment activity features will be similar to those you should expect in your external assessment.

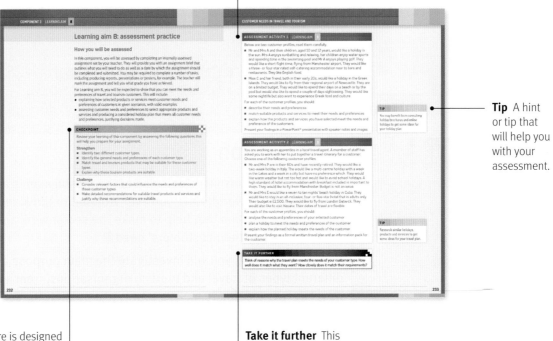

Tip A hint or tip that will help you with your assessment.

Checkpoint This feature is designed to allow you to assess your learning. The 'strengthen' question helps you to check your knowledge and understanding of what you have been studying, while the 'challenge' questions are an opportunity to extend your learning.

Take it further This provides suggestions for what you can do to further the work you've done in the practice assessment.

Travel and Tourism Organisations and Destinations

Introduction

The travel and tourism sector is one of the most dynamic and exciting industries in the world. Have you ever stopped to think about all the different types of organisation that help to make the sector work and how they work together to meet their customers' needs?

In this component, you will investigate the main purpose and aims of different types of travel and tourism organisations, from a privately owned travel agency looking to make a profit, to a publicly funded museum aiming to educate and inform its visitors and local community. You will also investigate how different travel and tourism organisations work together to save money and provide better levels of customer care.

Why do people choose to travel to different destinations? You will explore the different reasons that motivate people to travel, along with the different types of holidays, accommodation and tourist destinations that they choose to travel to.

LEARNING AIMS

In this component you will:

A	Investigate the aims of UK travel and tourism organisations
B	Explore travel and tourism and tourist destinations.

Travel and tourism organisations (1)

GETTING STARTED

Working in pairs, list as many different travel and tourism organisations as you can think of, for example: airline, travel agent. Now compare your list with another pair; how many different types of organisation did you think of?

The travel and tourism sector is made up of lots of different organisations. It is important to understand the different types of organisation, their purpose and how they each contribute to the travel and tourism sector, for example in creating employment opportunities.

Travel and tourism is one of the world's largest and most exciting industries and it continues to grow year on year. Many different organisations are involved with the travel and tourism sector, not just airlines and travel agents (Figure 1.1).

◻ Figure 1.1: How many examples of each type of travel and tourism organisation can you think of?

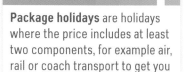

ACTIVITY

Working in a small group, discuss any holidays that you have been on. Think about where you went, what you did when you were there and how the holiday was booked. Did you go on a **package holiday** or were the different components all booked separately? Did you use a tour operator?

Tour operators

Many holidays are organised and provided through a tour operator.

Tour operators have contracts with different travel and tourism organisations, such as hotels, airlines and **ground transport** operators. They are able to contract large numbers of hotel rooms and flights at discounted prices and then assemble a single package containing the transport, accommodation, transfers, excursions and trips. These can then be sold to customers either through travel agents, or directly by the tour operator themselves, for example online or through a call centre.

KEY TERMS

Package holidays are holidays where the price includes at least two components, for example air, rail or coach transport to get you to your destination, plus at least one night's accommodation.

Ground transport moves visitors and travellers when they are not flying between destinations, for example a transfer from the airport to a hotel.

The UK has a large number of tour operators which help to contribute to the UK economy. Some of the largest are shown in Table 1.1.

◻ Table 1.1: Large UK tour operators

Tour operator	Description	Website
TUI UK	One of the UK's leading travel brands	www.tui.co.uk
Jet2holidays	Package holidays to sun destinations from 9 UK airports	www.jet2holidays.com
Thomas Cook	Over 175 years old, is one of the oldest leisure travel organisations	www.thomascook.com
Inghams	One of the UK's leading specialist tour operators	www.inghams.co.uk
Virgin Holidays	Specialising in the USA and the Caribbean	www.virginholidays.co.uk

Some of the larger tour operators also provide their own holiday components. For example, Thomas Cook, TUI and Jet2 operate their own airlines. TUI and Thomas Cook also own and run their own hotels and resorts across the world.

Some tour operators provide a broad range of package holidays and travel options for large numbers of customers, for example summer and winter sun beach holidays and city breaks.

Other tour operators provide more specialist products, designed to appeal to a smaller but more specialist market, for example responsible tourism, adventure travel or health and fitness holidays.

DID YOU KNOW?

Every UK travel company which sells air holidays and flights is required to hold an Air Travel Organiser's Licence (ATOL). This scheme, run by the Civil Aviation Authority (CAA), protects customers financially if the organisation fails and goes out of business, to ensure that they get a full refund. Holidays and flights covered by the scheme are known as ATOL Protected.

ACTIVITY

Working in a small group, use copies of different holiday brochures to explore what goes into the different types of package holiday organised by a tour operator. Now, complete the following tasks.

1 Produce a short definition of a tour operator.

2 Describe the role of a typical tour operator.

3 How might a tour operator help to contribute to the UK economy?

CHECK MY LEARNING

1 Describe to your partner what a tour operator does.

2 Now make a list of as many named tour operators as you can think of.

Travel and tourism organisations (2)

GETTING STARTED

Working in pairs, list as many different organisations as you can think of where you can book a holiday.

Travel agents

When arranging a holiday, chances are that most people have used the services of a travel agent at some point. Travel agents give expert advice and guidance to customers looking to travel, either on a leisure holiday or perhaps as part of a business trip.

Travel agents have several specific roles, including:

- booking flights
- booking package holidays
- arranging and booking trips and excursions
- booking **ancillary services**, such as car hire and travel insurance
- providing foreign exchange.

There are different types of travel agency, for example retail and business.

KEY TERM

Ancillary services are services which support the main travel and tourism components and organisations. For example, when taking a flight, ancillary services could include travel insurance, airport lounge access and transfers.

ACTIVITY

Working in a small group, initially discuss what you might already know about *retail* and *business* travel agents. Now complete the following tasks.
- Carry out some internet research to find a named example of both a retail and a business travel agent.
- Identify one reason why a customer might use the services of a retail travel agent.

Retail travel agents

Retail travel agents offer their products and services to customers looking for holidays and leisure travel. They can often be found in convenient locations, such as on the main high street in a town or city, or within supermarkets or other organisations. Retail travel agents can also be accessed via the telephone through call centres or as web-based agents accessed online.

Retail travel agents are often part of a large chain, with many branches found throughout the country. For example, popular UK brands of retail travel agent include Thomas Cook and TUI. Agencies could also be part of a smaller, or more local chain of branches, often found in a particular area. Independent travel agencies are not part of a chain but sometimes join a group or partnership to access useful services and systems.

As more and more customers now book their own holidays online, there has been a reduction in the number of travel agency branches on the high street. However, not everyone wants, or is able, to book online. Travel agents are able to provide the specialist advice and knowledge that many customers need when faced with too many different options online. As travel agents are often part of large chains, tour operators and partnerships, many good value holidays can be found in-store rather than going online.

Some agents are also exploring new ways to encourage customers to book with them, rather than going it alone. Thomas Cook offers customers its 'Discovery Store' experience, which makes use of modern technology such as virtual reality, video, online booking and free Wi-Fi to help customers research and choose their perfect holiday.

DID YOU KNOW?

The Advantage Travel Partnership is the UK's largest independent travel agent group. It works with independent travel agents to offer a range of support services, for example staff training, online systems and financial services. For more information, go to: www.advantagemembers.com.

LINK IT UP

In Component 3, you will explore how holiday packages are put together to meet the needs of specific customers.

◘ Customers at travel agencies can use VR headsets to 'explore' the destination, accommodation or flight before booking.

Business travel agents

Business travel agents provide many of the same services as retail travel agents but for the business market. This might involve booking travel for employees to attend meetings, events and conferences. Inbound business travellers from overseas can spend large amounts of money in the UK attending conferences and meetings and staying in good-quality hotels. These customers make a significant contribution to the UK economy.

A business travel agent may book and manage all of the travel booking services for a large business, including flights, rail bookings, hotels, transfers and meeting venues and spaces. It may also provide additional services such as arranging chauffeur-driven cars and booking airport parking.

Many of the large business travel agencies also have websites where employees can request and book their travel services as well as dedicated support from travel advisers responding to emails and telephone calls 24 hours a day.

CHECK MY LEARNING

1 In pairs, describe to each other the key definitions of a retail travel agent and business travel agent.

2 Ask a member of your family about a time when they used the services of a travel agent. Why did they choose to use the agent and not book directly themselves? What was the most useful part of the process? Which type of travel agent did they use?

Accommodation, conferences and events

GETTING STARTED

Working in a small group, make a list of the different names of accommodation providers you can think of, for example 'Hilton Hotels'.

Tourists and travellers all need somewhere to stay; whether taking a trip for leisure or business, to visit a conference or an event. Each provider offers different accommodation options, services and facilities.

Accommodation providers

There are lots of different types of accommodation providers, from small guest houses to large hotels. Some venues are dedicated exclusively to hosting conferences and events. As well as these, many of the large hotels also include conference and events facilities. Together, the accommodation sector makes a significant contribution to the UK economy and is a key component of most leisure and business travel arrangements.

ACTIVITY

Working in a small group, think about any trips or holidays that you may have taken. Where did you stay? Was it in a hotel or with a different type of provider? Now, try to identify four different types of accommodation.

Figure 1.2 illustrates the different types of accommodation provider.

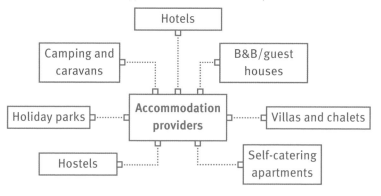

◘ **Figure 1.2: How many different types of accommodation have you stayed in?**

Different types of accommodation provider offer different levels of services, facilities and products to their customers. This is often reflected in the price that customers pay, from hostel accommodation where guests share a basic room and bathroom with other travellers, to 5-star luxury hotels.

KEY TERM

Self-catering apartments, holiday chalets and villas are offered to customers on a self-catering basis, where kitchen and cooking facilities are provided for customers to buy and prepare their own meals.

ACTIVITY

Working in a small group, list all the different facilities and services that might be available at one of the following accommodation providers:

1 5-star luxury hotel
2 campsite
3 **self-catering** apartment
4 small guest house.

Hotels often provide a large range of facilities and services for their guests, for example:

- restaurants and bars
- conference and meeting rooms
- **concierge** service
- business centre
- 24-hour reception
- fitness and leisure facilities
- parking
- entertainment.

Large hotels often provide a range of different rooms for guests, including single, double, twin and triple or family rooms. Some rooms may interconnect, and others may offer executive facilities, such as a large work desk, better views and high-speed internet access.

Rooms may feature a range of facilities and products to meet the needs of guests, including a fridge and mini-bar, tea- and coffee-making facilities, iron and ironing board, trouser press, satellite TV and on-demand movies, and bathroom toiletries.

Conference and events management

Another key type of organisation in the travel and tourism sector is conference and events management companies. These organisations book, or provide, venues and locations for conferences and different types of events. Management companies can also arrange support services such as providing administration, promotion for the conference or event, equipment hire, such as audio-visual facilities, catering, and delegate materials.

Conference and event venues are often located in large hotels but may also be purpose-built venues or part of more unusual locations, for example castles, museums and football stadiums. Many people are employed on a casual basis to meet the demands of a large conference or event. This can provide valuable employment for local people.

KEY TERM

A **concierge** is a member of staff, usually in a hotel, who helps guests by providing directions, recommendations and advice, booking tours, and making reservations at theatres and restaurants.

ACTIVITY

Working in a small group, think about different examples of conference and event providers.

1 On a map of your local area, locate at least three examples of conference and event providers.

2 Now, using the internet to carry out some research, create a list of all the different products and services that each one provides.

3 Discuss the similarities and differences.

CHECK MY LEARNING

Research one local accommodation provider and produce a description of all the different products, facilities and services it provides.

Tourist attractions

GETTING STARTED

Working in a small group, make a list of all the different visitor attractions you can think of. Start with any local examples and then broaden your list to those further away. Now try to categorise the attractions into different groups.

Many people enjoy visiting tourist attractions, such as theme parks and zoos, to have fun, be entertained and spend time with friends and family. Attractions can also provide educational resources as well as other facilities and services for tourists, such as wheelchair hire, cafes and shops.

Attractions are often much busier in the summer months and during school holidays, providing seasonal work for many local people.

Tourist attractions are a significant part of the travel and tourism sector. They attract visitors for a range of different purposes, such as recreation, entertainment and education. Some attractions are educational and provide visitors with information and exhibits to help them learn something new.

Attractions are often grouped into two main types: natural and built. Table 1.2 shows the top five in the UK for each type, ranked by visitor numbers.

Natural attractions

These are natural features of the landscape and environment. They have not been built by man. Many tourists visit natural attractions for recreation, to relax, get some exercise, escape from the city and to connect with nature. Examples of natural attractions include:

- beaches
- caves
- forests
- lakes.

Many natural attractions are free of charge to visit, although sometimes they are managed and maintained by organisations that charge tourists to visit, or to park their cars.

Built attractions

These are not naturally occurring but have been built by man. Many tourists visit built attractions to have fun and to be entertained. Some attractions are purpose-built, for example a theme park, while other attractions have been built for a different reason but now attract visitors, such as stately homes and castles. Other examples include:

- art galleries
- museums
- zoos.

Table 1.2: VisitBritain Annual survey of visits to visitor attractions, 2017

Rank	Most visited paid attractions		Most visited free attractions	
	Name of attraction	Number of visitors in 2016/2017	Name of attraction	Number of visitors in 2016/2017
1	Tower of London	2,842,970	British Museum	5,906,716
2	Chester Zoo	1,866,628	Tate Modern	5,656,004
3	Flamingo Land Theme Park and Zoo	1,691,083	National Gallery	5,229,192
4	Windermere Lake Cruises, Bowness	1,611,491	Brighton Pier	4,684,000 (Estimated)
5	Stonehenge	1,582,532	Natural History Museum	4,434,520

DID YOU KNOW?

Many built attractions have an entrance charge, but some are free. For example, many of London's main museums do not charge visitors but suggest an optional donation.

◨ Many tourists visit built attractions, for example theme parks, to have fun and to be entertained.

ACTIVITY

Working in a small group, think about all the different tourist attractions in a specific area of the UK, for example Cumbria and the Lake District, London or Cornwall.

1 On a map of your chosen area, locate as many different tourist attractions as you can.

2 Now use a code to identify on your map which of the attractions are natural and which are built.

3 Add to your map by indicating which of the attractions are free and which charge for entry.

4 Finally, identify the main purpose of each attraction, for example to entertain or to educate visitors.

LINK IT UP

In Component 3, you will explore how travel and tourism organisations provide different products and services to meet the needs of customers and visitors. How do the visitor attractions you have explored meet the needs of different visitors?

CHECK MY LEARNING

Choose one tourist attraction and carry out some research on the facilities, services and products it provides. Think about the main purpose of the attraction and what type of visitors it attracts. Now design a promotional leaflet to highlight what you have found and to attract new visitors.

Tourism promotion

GETTING STARTED

Working in pairs, think about why tourists might want to visit your local area.
1 Create a list of all the features and facilities that might encourage people to visit.
2 How could your local tourist board encourage more people to visit?

A range of different organisations promote tourism to raise awareness and to encourage more people to travel and visit different destinations. Tourism promotion organisations can also support visitors, providing advice and guidance.

A range of different organisations have a key role in promoting tourism in different areas; some are outlined in Table 1.3.

◻ **Table 1.3: Local, regional and national promoters of tourism**

Type of organisation	Description	Example
Tourist, or visitor, information centres (TICs/VICs)	These centres are often located in key locations in many towns and cities. Their key role is to provide support, advice and guidance to visiting tourists. They often provide a range of key services such as directions, hotel bookings, ticket sales for shows, tours and events. TICs also offer a range of products such as souvenirs, merchandise and gifts, maps and guides.	Located in the old railway station, the Morecambe Visitor Information Centre offers local information for tourists, an accommodation booking service and gifts and souvenirs. http://exploremorecambebay.org.uk/visitor-info/vics/
Regional tourism agencies	Certain areas may also have a regional tourism promotion agency whose aim is to attract more visitors to a specific region, county or geographical area. Regional agencies often manage websites and online promotional campaigns to attract domestic and inbound tourists to their area for leisure and business tourism.	The South West Tourism Alliance is an umbrella organisation run by the private sector to promote tourism in the south-west of England. www.swtourismalliance.org.uk
National tourism agencies	National tourism agencies have a key role in promoting tourism for a whole country. They manage different promotional and marketing campaigns and activities to attract more inbound visitors. They help to raise the awareness and profile of a country and to increase the money generated by tourism.	VisitBritain is the national tourism agency for Great Britain. Funded by the UK government, it promotes Britain as a tourism destination overseas, to encourage more inbound tourists to visit, spend money and grow the British tourism industry. www.visitbritain.org

DID YOU KNOW?

Visit Cornwall is a Community Interest Company (CIC) providing marketing and promotion to attract visitors to all areas of Cornwall in the south-west of England. Find out more at www.visitcornwall.com.

ACTIVITY

Working in a small group, choose one region of the United Kingdom to research: England, Scotland, Wales or Northern Ireland. Carry out research in your chosen region:
• identify the national tourism agency and its key purpose
• identify any examples of regional tourism agencies and what they provide
• locate at least three examples of tourist/visitor information centres and make a list of the services, products and facilities they offer tourists.

◘ Tourist Information Centres provide support, advice and guidance to visiting tourists.

Encouraging visitors

VisitBritain runs a number of different promotional activities and campaigns to encourage more people to travel and visit different destinations. Its 'Join the World – Discover the UK' campaign is aimed at encouraging young people, aged 16–34, to take a holiday at home rather than travelling outside of the UK. The campaign makes use of social media to highlight the different experiences that can only be found on a holiday in the UK. For more information visit: www.visitbritain.com/jointheworld.

Tourism NI is the national tourism agency for Northern Ireland. The agency has been encouraging more tourists to the region through a range of promotional and marketing campaigns and activities. **Screen tourism** has become very popular in the area due to television series such as *Game of Thrones*®. The 2016 *Game of Thrones* marketing campaign reached around 126 million people around the world, generating coverage worth an estimated £11.3 million.

Advice and guidance to visitors

One of the key roles of tourism promotion organisations is to provide information, advice and guidance to visitors to encourage them to visit, stay and spend money in the local attractions, accommodation providers, cafes, bars and restaurants. Tourist and visitor information centres are often the first port of call for visitors looking for key information about a particular destination or region. Staff have to be well trained to deal with all the potential requests for information and advice for all sorts of different visitors, such as:

- guidance on where to stay, visit and eat
- opening times of attractions
- driving routes, directions and parking information
- weather advice
- the location of key facilities, such as toilets, cash machines and transport hubs.

KEY TERM

Screen tourism is a type of tourism where people visit destinations and locations made popular in films and television series.

DID YOU KNOW?

VisitBritain's forecast for spending by visitors in 2018 is £26.3 billion.

CHECK MY LEARNING

Think about how you would promote your local area to attract more tourists to visit. Make a list of all the appealing factors that your local area has to offer. Think about different types of visitor and what would attract them. Now, create a brief presentation to promote your local area to possible visitors looking for a new destination to visit.

Transport facilities and providers, gateways and terminals

GETTING STARTED

Identify as many different types of transport as you can think of. Now with a partner, try to identify an example of a specific provider for each type of transport, for example Virgin Trains.

One of the most important aspects of the travel and tourism sector is of course transport. Tourists and travellers need safe transport from one destination to another as well as access to a range of facilities and services to make their journeys comfortable.

Tourists can use a number of different transport providers to help them complete their journeys safely, for either inbound, outbound or domestic tourism reasons (Figure 1.3).

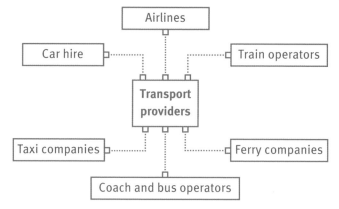

◪ **Figure 1.3: Can you think of any more transport providers?**

Air travel

When travelling further away, tourists may choose to travel by air for speed and convenience. A large number of different airlines provide different flight options for those looking to go away on holiday or a business trip, either **short haul** or **long haul**.

Short haul	A flight time of generally four hours or less and under 1,500 km from the point of departure.
Medium haul	A flight time of generally four to six hours and between 1,500 km and 3,500 km from the point of departure.
Long haul	A flight time of generally longer than six hours and more than 3,500 km from the point of departure.
Ultra-long haul	A term sometimes used to describe very long non-stop flights, for example those lasting over 12 hours.

Full-service airlines, such as Emirates or Virgin Atlantic, often provide customers with a range of products and services onboard their flight, included in the ticket price, for example:

- a choice of food and drink options, including special meals
- entertainment; such as movies, TV shows, music and games
- duty-free shopping opportunities and amenity kits, such as eye masks, travel socks and earplugs.

Full-service airlines often provide different classes of travel, for example economy, premium, business and first, all offering a different level of service and comfort relative to the price paid.

Low-cost airlines, such as Ryanair and easyJet, often offer lower-priced flights but with fewer products and services included. Check-in luggage, choosing a specific seat and food and drinks are all available but at an additional cost.

Terminal facilities

Air travellers benefit from a range of facilities and services at airport **terminals**, such as shops, bars and restaurants, washrooms and executive lounges offering more relaxed seating areas and areas to work. Large international **gateway** airports, such as London Heathrow Airport, may have many different terminals and provide inbound travellers to the UK with a range of onward travel options, for example connections to the London Underground and the Heathrow Express rail service to London Paddington station.

Rail travel

Around 33 train operating companies offer rail transport to customers in Britain, such as Northern and Southeastern rail. Many providers offer customers a choice of first and standard class travel and the opportunity to buy discount tickets if booked in advance. Large rail terminals include Manchester Piccadilly, Birmingham New Street, London Euston and London King's Cross station.

ACTIVITY

1   Working in pairs, complete a table to identify different types of transport provider and key terminals and gateways. An example of each has been provided for you in Table 1.4.

2   Now using blank maps, locate your chosen stations, ports and terminals.

▪   Table 1.4: Examples of providers and gateways by transport type

Transport type	Example provider	Key gateways and terminals
Air	British Airways	London Heathrow Airport (LHR)
Rail	Virgin West Coast	Glasgow Central Station
Sea	P&O Ferries	Hull Ferry Terminal
Road	National Express	Birmingham Coach Station

Sea travel

The UK has a large number of ferry terminals and ports, providing sea travel options for customers. Some ferry services only carry people, but others are able to transport vehicles as well as passengers. Ferry providers, such as Stena Line and Irish Ferries, offer customers a range of facilities and services onboard, from bars and restaurants to cabins for longer journeys. Key seaport gateways include the Port of Dover, where many travellers from Europe enter the UK.

Road travel

Whether travelling in your own car, a hire car or on a coach, road travel is often the most convenient and flexible method of transport for many travellers. Local, regional and national coach operators offer a range of scheduled and charter services for those looking to travel long distances or for special events. A network of motorway service stations provides road travellers with facilities such as toilets, fuel, shops and restaurants.

KEY TERMS

A **terminal** is a location where transport journeys start or end, for example Liverpool Lime Street Station.

A **gateway** is a place where visitors enter or exit the UK and continue their journey, for example a large international airport, such as London Heathrow, or seaport, such as the Port of Dover. Travellers often change from one mode of transport to another at the gateway.

CHECK MY LEARNING

Choose a type of transport; road, rail, air or sea, and research one named provider. Identify all the different facilities and services it offers to customers.

Regulators and travel and tourism trade associations

GETTING STARTED

Working in pairs, discuss with your partner why customers in the travel and tourism sector might need protecting. What are some of the risks involved with taking part in travel and tourism?

Regulators help to protect customers and ensure that organisations meet industry standards. There are a number of regulators in the travel and tourism industry and they play an important role in ensuring that the industry meets set standards and keeps customers safe.

Regulators and trade associations have a number of key roles and responsibilities; Table 1.5 outlines some of these.

▣ **Table 1.5: Roles and responsibilities of regulators and trade associations**

Role/Responsibility	What does it involve?
Ensuring that organisations meet set industry standards, including enforcement and prosecution	Regulators often have specific powers to ensure that travel and tourism organisations meet the necessary industry standards. Where standards are not being met, they may take legal action to ensure that organisations comply.
Giving customers advice and support	Customers are able to contact regulators and trade associations for advice and guidance on related issues. Most offer customer helplines or respond to email enquiries.
Representation	Trade associations are able to represent their members when campaigning and liaising with the UK government or the European Commission for example. They provide a voice when campaigning on travel industry issues.
Repatriation	Regulators can help to provide repatriation assistance to return someone to their own country if things go wrong when overseas.
Licensing	Many transport providers require a licence to operate. For example, train operators require a European Passenger Licence to operate passenger rail services and a Station Licence to run and manage train stations. Taxi operators require a licence to operate, often granted by the local council or authority.
Dealing with customer complaints	If a customer complaint has not been resolved directly with an airline or tour operator for example, many regulators and trade associations offer customers an alternative complaint-handling service.
Arbitration and dispute resolution	Trade associations sometimes provide an arbitration service – a process to settle disputes with the support of an impartial third party.

Regulators

Civil Aviation Authority (CAA)

The CAA is a public corporation and the UK's specialist aviation regulator. It helps to ensure that the aviation industry meets strict safety standards and to ensure that customers are protected.

The CAA works closely with other aviation regulators around the world. These organisations include the International Civil Aviation Organization (ICAO) and the European Aviation Safety Agency (EASA). The CAA regulates all UK airports to ensure that they comply with relevant international and UK safety standards.

The CAA also runs and manages the Air Travel Organiser's Licence (ATOL) holiday financial protection scheme. The scheme applies to every UK company that sells air package holidays and some flights. If the company collapses, customers receive a full refund for their holiday if they have not yet travelled. If they are already on holiday, the ATOL scheme ensures that they can finish their holiday and return home.

Office of Rail and Road (ORR)

The ORR is an independent statutory body that regulates railways and highways. It regulates the different train operating companies (TOCs) and Network Rail, the company that runs the railway infrastructure. The ORR has a range of enforcement powers which it can use if safety and operating standards are not being met.

ORR also provides advice and guidance to passengers on station and platform safety and produces a number of publications and guidance documents. The ORR also monitors serious railway incidents.

ORR monitor Highways England, the organisation that operates, maintains and improves England's motorways and major A roads.

Maritime and Coastguard Agency (MCA)

The MCA is an agency sponsored by the Department for Transport. It produces legislation and guidance on maritime (relating to the sea) matters, and is responsible for a range of monitoring and inspection functions, including:
- the safety of passengers and crew in vessels in UK waters
- making sure all equipment on UK vessels is fit for purpose.

ACTIVITY

Railways and highways are carefully regulated in the UK but sometimes things can go wrong. Working in pairs or small groups, think about what might go wrong in the travel and tourism sector and how regulators could help protect the travelling public.

Travel and tourism trade associations

Travel and tourism trade associations represent their members and provide guidance and support. They can often help to represent the views of their members to the government. Customers can get help, advice and support from them if the member organisation they used did not meet their expectations.

Examples of travel and tourism trade associations include:
- ABTA (formerly, the Association of British Travel Agents), www.abta.com
- AITO (Association of Independent Tour Operators), www.aito.com
- ATTA (Adventure Travel Trade Association), www.adventuretravel.biz
- ITT (Institute of Travel & Tourism), www.itt.co.uk.

ABTA

ABTA is the UK's largest travel association, representing both travel agents and tour operators. Customers often prefer to book with an ABTA-registered travel agent as they are protected under its financial protection scheme. If the travel agency was to fail, customers would be entitled to a refund or financial help to get home.

CHECK MY LEARNING

Carry out some research on one other travel and tourism regulator and prepare a short description of its purpose. Think about bus, coach and taxi providers.

LINK IT UP

In Component 2, you will explore different types of legislation and regulations that are used for visitor security, health and safety, and financial protection.

LINK IT UP

Further on in this component, you will learn more about ABTA and about how meeting regulatory standards is a key aim of many travel and tourism organisations.

ACTIVITY

Choose one key travel and tourism regulator, or travel and tourism trade association, and create a small leaflet outlining its key roles and responsibilities.

Ownership of travel and tourism organisations (1)

GETTING STARTED

Working in pairs, briefly discuss what you already know about the ownership of travel and tourism organisations. Think about public, private and voluntary organisations. Can you give any examples of specific organisations that have these different ownership types?

Just like any business sector, travel and tourism organisations have different types of ownership. The ownership type affects the way an organisation works as well as its aims and values.

Private sector organisations

Travel and tourism organisations in the private sector are owned or controlled by private individuals, or by shareholders for limited companies. Ownership of a limited company is divided into shares. An owner of one or more of these shares is called a shareholder.

There are two types of limited company; a private limited company (ltd) and a public limited company (plc). Public limited company shares can be traded on the stock market to any member of the public. Private limited company shares cannot.

Private sector organisations include travel agencies, accommodation providers, many visitor attractions and transport providers (Table 1.6). The main aim and objective of private sector organisations is to make a profit by selling their products and services to tourists and travellers. The private sector can be very competitive and organisations need to ensure that their products and services continue to attract new and repeat customers. Private sector organisations make an important contribution to the UK economy through taxation and by providing a range of employment opportunities.

◻ Table 1.6: Examples of different types of private sector organisations

Type of travel and tourism organisation	Example of private sector organisation
Tour operators	Trailfinders Limited – an independently owned tailor-made tour operator. www.trailfinders.com
Travel agents	Alpha Holidays Limited trades as alpharooms.com – an award-winning online travel agent established in 1999.
Accommodation providers	The Principal Hotel Company Limited is a collection of hotels in city centre locations. www.phcompany.com
Tourist attractions	Founded in 1896, Blackpool Pleasure Beach Limited is a family-owned company. www.blackpoolpleasurebeach.com
Transport providers	FlyBe Limited is the largest independent airline in Europe. www.flybe.com
Conference and events management	chooseyourevent.com Limited offers a range of online services to help clients find meetings and event venues. www.cye-group.com

Common ownership

Large private sector companies may also own and control several different smaller organisations, or brands. For example, many tour companies are umbrella organisations for a range of smaller specialist travel organisations. The TUI Group owns a number of travel companies in the UK and overseas including hotels, airlines, tour operators, travel agencies and cruise companies. In the UK, TUI airlines and First Choice Holidays are popular brands owned by the TUI group.

ACTIVITY

In small groups, carry out some research into a large private sector travel and tourism organisation that has common ownership of different organisations and brands. You might like to choose one of the following organisations:

- Virgin Group – www.virgin.com
- Merlin Entertainments – www.merlinentertainments.biz
- Arriva – www.arriva.co.uk
- Intercontinental Hotels Group – www.ihgplc.com
- Thomas Cook – www.thomascook.com.

Now complete the following activities.

1 Describe the organisation's aims and purpose.

2 Give two ways your chosen organisation helps to contribute to the UK economy.

3 Outline three possible benefits of the common ownership of different organisations and brands.

Merlin Entertainments

Merlin Entertainments is a public limited company which owns and runs many different well-known attractions and entertainment brands. In the UK, these include:

- Alton Towers Resort
- THORPE PARK Resort
- Chessington World of Adventures Resort
- The Dungeons
- Madame Tussauds
- LEGOLAND Windsor Resort
- Warwick Castle
- SEA LIFE Centres
- Seal Sanctuaries.

Stagecoach Group

Stagecoach Group plc is a public limited company that provides bus, coach, tram and train services across the UK. As well as bus and coach services, such as megabus.com, the company also operates East Midlands Trains, and has part ownership of the Virgin Trains West Coast franchise. Stagecoach also operates Sheffield's tram network. As well as UK services, Stagecoach also operates services in the United States and Canada.

LINK IT UP

In Component 2, you will explore private sector partnerships and new tourism developments funded by the private sector.

 Some large transport companies provide services in more than one area.

CHECK MY LEARNING

Working with a partner, discuss the advantages and disadvantages of being a travel and tourism organisation operating in the private sector.

Ownership of travel and tourism organisations (2)

GETTING STARTED

Working with a partner, check your understanding of public and voluntary ownership. What are the key differences?

Carry out some research into tourist attractions in your local area. Can you identify a public tourist attraction in your local area?

As well as private sector ownership, organisations in the travel and tourism sector also include those in public and voluntary sector ownership. The type of ownership affects how these organisations are funded and often their main aims and objectives.

Public sector

Travel and tourism organisations in the public sector are funded, and sometimes owned, by central and local governments. Often the main aim and objective of public sector organisations is to provide a valuable service to customers and users. This could be to offer advice and support, to educate and inform, to raise awareness or to preserve and protect. In this way, public sector organisations often make an important contribution to their local community. Increasingly, public sector organisations in the travel and tourism sector also have an objective to raise funds and revenue from the sale of products and services, to ensure that they can continue to provide a good level of service.

Public sector organisations often include tourist and visitor information centres, which are funded by local councils and authorities as well as through the sale of products and services, such as souvenirs and tickets. Tourist information centres aim to support visitors to the local area and encourage them to spend money in local hotels, shops and restaurants, creating jobs and generating income for the local area.

As well as visitor centres, some visitor attractions such as museums, galleries and parks are often publicly owned and controlled. Their main aim is to provide facilities for recreation and education.

Tropical World Leeds

Tropical World Leeds is owned and managed by Leeds City Council. This popular visitor attraction aims to educate, conserve and provide a fun experience for visitors. Funding is generated through entrance tickets as well as sales in the shops and cafe, and through special events.

ACTIVITY

Working in a small group, carry out some research into a specific public-sector organisation in the travel and tourism industry. Find out:
- the organisation's key aims and objectives
- sources of funding and revenue.

Voluntary sector

Voluntary organisations are independent organisations usually funded by membership donations, grants and sometimes through the sale of products and services, such as tickets, food, drink and merchandise.

The main aims and objectives of voluntary organisations are often to provide a service to the public or local community, to protect and conserve the environment and local heritage, or to raise awareness and promote a particular cause, rather than to make a profit. Voluntary organisations are often run by volunteers.

Examples of voluntary organisations in the travel and tourism sector include charities and trusts that look after visitor attractions such as heritage railways, ancient monuments, parks and nature reserves.

The East Lancashire Railway

The East Lancashire Railway Preservation Society (ELRPS) is a voluntary membership organisation whose volunteers help to run and maintain the heritage steam railway. Volunteers pay a membership fee and can get involved in a range of different ways, for example:
- administration
- engineering
- events
- sales and retail
- stations and signalling.

The National Trust

Founded in 1895, the National Trust is Europe's largest conservation charity that looks after and conserves historic houses, castles, ancient monuments, coastline, forests, gardens, parks and nature reserves across England, Wales and Northern Ireland. Over five million people are members of the National Trust, which is governed by a board of twelve trustees who come from a variety of different backgrounds, for example business or conservation.

The National Trust relies on income from membership fees, donations and legacies, as well as money raised from commercial activities, such as retail and catering through gift shops, cafes, restaurants and parking charges. Over 60,000 volunteers help to run over 500 properties and sites.

Popular National Trust sites include:
- Giant's Causeway, County Antrim
- Cliveden House, Buckinghamshire
- Attingham Park, Shropshire
- Belton House, Lincolnshire
- Larrybane, County Antrim
- Waddesdon Manor, Buckinghamshire
- Fountains Abbey, North Yorkshire.

LINK IT UP

In Component 2, you will explore public and voluntary sector partnerships and their role in destination management.

ACTIVITY

Working in pairs or small groups, investigate an example of voluntary funded local or regional attraction. Use the website to find out information on the different ways the attraction receives its funding.

CHECK MY LEARNING

1 Explain to a partner the difference between private, public and voluntary sector organisations

2 Now, identify a range of different publicly funded organisations for each of the following categories:
- museum
- national tourism agency
- tourist information centre
- tourist attraction.

Aims of travel and tourism organisations (1)

GETTING STARTED

Working in pairs, think of *two* reasons why a travel and tourism organisation might be in business. Think about one financial reason and one non-financial.

Different types of organisation in the travel and tourism industry often have different aims but what are these differences and why are they important? In this lesson, you will explore the key financial and strategic aims of many travel and tourism organisations and how they interrelate.

Financial aims

Travel and tourism organisations may have a number of key financial aims.

Selling of goods and services to make a profit

For most private organisations, their main priority is to stay in business and to make money. This is achieved by selling goods and services to customers. The travel and tourism sector is very competitive, however, with many different organisations trying to attract the same customers. Organisations must work hard to keep encouraging customers to buy their goods and services. Most organisations will have specific financial targets linked to the amount of goods and services they hope to sell in each financial period.

Increasing sales and maximising sales revenue

In order to remain competitive, many organisations will have a key financial aim to increase sales, for example by attracting new customers and making sure they receive the most revenue possible from the sales of goods and services. This is known as maximising revenue. One way to maximise revenue is to reduce costs, increasing the amount of profit made. For example, a hotel chain may be able to negotiate better deals on toiletries and bathroom supplies by buying large amounts in bulk.

Increasing market share

Market share is the percentage of sales an organisation has in a particular market or industry. A private sector organisation may aim to expand its business in order to control a larger share of the market. For example, a tour operator which specialises in selling beach holidays to Spain for UK outbound tourists, may wish to sell more holidays to tourists who currently use a competitor organisation.

Reducing losses

Organisations aim to minimise any financial losses in order to maintain or maximise revenue. Losses could occur when a customer has a legitimate complaint and the payment of compensation is necessary. Losses could also occur when products expire or go out of date before they are sold, for example food and beverages, which are then wasted.

Breaking even

A new organisation may initially be spending more money than it is making, in order to grow its customer base and promote its products and services. For an organisation to break even they must make as much money as they spend. A key financial aim for a new organisation may be to reduce losses and reach a break-even point, so it can focus on making a profit in the near future.

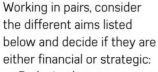
ACTIVITY

Working in pairs, consider the different aims listed below and decide if they are either financial or strategic:
- Reducing losses
- Diversifying
- Breaking even
- Providing value for money
- Raising brand awareness
- Generating customer loyalty
- Managing assets

Controlling costs

One way to at least achieve the break-even point, or ideally to make a profit, is to control costs. Staffing costs are often a very large part of an organisation's expenditure. Many travel and tourism organisations try to control staffing costs by using casual or seasonal workers during periods of higher demand. A theme park, for example, will employ ride attendants and customer service staff on casual contracts during school holidays and the peak summer season, so that costs can be reduced during the low season when there are fewer visitors.

Managing assets

Assets are something of value owned by an organisation, for example premises, vehicles and stock. Organisations may have an aim to carefully manage their assets, so they don't increase their risk of making a loss. For example, a visitor attraction may need to carefully manage its souvenir stock to make sure it has enough products to sell but doesn't over buy items that customers don't want or need.

Strategic aims

Figure 1.4 displays the strategic aims that are common to most travel and tourism organisations.

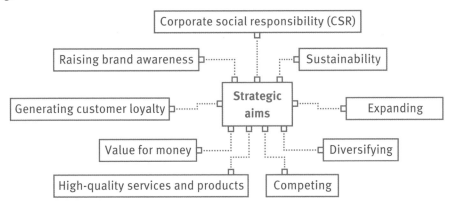

◘ Figure 1.4: Can you think of an advantage for the customer or company for each of these strategic aims?

LINK IT UP

You will learn more about corporate social responsibility, and sustainability in the travel and tourism sector, in the next lesson.

Expanding

One way to grow and develop an organisation is to expand, offering more products and services to more customers. The accommodation industry has seen a large expansion in the number of budget hotels. For example, the hotel chain Travelodge has been steadily expanding its number of properties and now operates 44 hotels across Scotland and more than 560 across the UK, Ireland and Spain. In June 2018, the chain announced plans to open 20 more hotels in Scotland, creating around 385 new jobs.

Diversifying

Diversifying is where a business starts to sell products and services in a different market from what it currently does. For example, many farms have struggled to make a profit with increasing competition from overseas organisations and falling revenue from the sale of food and produce. In order to survive, many farms have turned to tourism to diversify their income and raise more revenue.

CHECK MY LEARNING

With a partner, discuss, compare and check your understanding of the following financial terms: market share, break even, sales revenue, profit.

Aims of travel and tourism organisations (2)

GETTING STARTED

Working in pairs, discuss the difference between financial and strategic aims. What are the key differences between the two?

Farm tourism, or 'agritourism', has been a great success for many providers who attract tourists to countryside areas to stay in converted barns and to take advantage of country living, walking, cycling and adventure activities. Many providers offer their guests organic food and products straight from the farm.

◻ **Agritourism has seen great growth in recent years.**

DID YOU KNOW?

'Open Farm Sunday' is the farming industry's annual national open day. Visitors are encouraged to visit a farm and discover the world of farming. Read more about it at https://farmsunday.org/.

Competing

The travel and tourism sector is very competitive, with many different organisations providing similar products and services, all competing to attract customers and the all-important sale. A key strategic aim for many organisations is to remain competitive. In order to gain the 'competitive edge', organisations need to work hard to ensure that their products and services are the first choice for customers. Gaining the competitive edge could be through a number of different business activities:

- providing consistently excellent customer service
- gaining good-quality customer reviews on online review and comparison websites
- ensuring that the price for products and services offers good value and is not too high
- having a unique or unusual product which other organisations cannot provide
- offering excellent quality for which customers are happy to pay a premium price.

Brand awareness and customer loyalty

Brand awareness relates to how well known a particular brand, product or organisation is with new and potential customers. Having a strong, well-known brand can give customers confidence about using the brand's products and services and provide customers reassurance that they will receive a similar level of quality and service each time.

Many brands operate loyalty schemes to encourage repeat business, offering higher levels of discounts, savings and perks to customers who use their products and services regularly.

Intercontinental Hotels Group (IHG) includes a number of well-known brands in the accommodation sector, both in the UK and also across the world. The IHG Rewards Club is the world's largest hotel loyalty programme. Members gain points for each stay they make when booked directly with the hotel. Customers can redeem points for free 'reward nights' and a range of other benefits.

IHG brands include:

- InterContinental Hotels & Resorts
- Holiday Inn
- Holiday Inn Express
- Hotel Indigo
- Crowne Plaza
- Staybridge Suites.

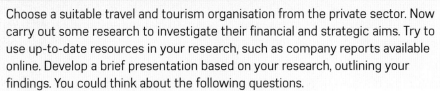

ACTIVITY

Choose a suitable travel and tourism organisation from the private sector. Now carry out some research to investigate their financial and strategic aims. Try to use up-to-date resources in your research, such as company reports available online. Develop a brief presentation based on your research, outlining your findings. You could think about the following questions.
- Does your chosen organisation have a strategic plan?
- What is the organisation's key strategic priorities?
- Are the aims short term, medium term or long term?
- How will the organisation measure the progress in meetings its aims?

Value for money

For many public-sector organisations, a key strategic aim may be to provide value for money for the products and services they provide to the local community. For example, many publicly run visitor attractions, such as zoos, galleries and museums, offer visitors discounted rates on entrance tickets to ensure that they can be enjoyed by everyone. Many offer visitors who are unemployed, or in receipt of financial benefits, free entrance, so they can benefit from the attraction too. In this way, many public organisations make a contribution to their local communities.

LINK IT UP

In Component 2, you will explore public and voluntary sector partnerships and their role in destination management.

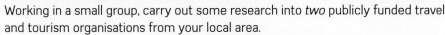

ACTIVITY

Working in a small group, carry out some research into *two* publicly funded travel and tourism organisations from your local area.
- What are the organisation's key aims and objectives?
- What sources of funding and revenue do they have?
- What contribution do they make to their local communities?

CHECK MY LEARNING

Now that you have prepared your presentation on a chosen travel and tourism organisation, it's time to present your findings. Be prepared to clearly present your organisation's specific financial and strategic aims.

You should peer review each other's presentations. Be prepared to offer some useful feedback to the presenter. What could they have done differently to improve their presentation? Think about the presentation content and the style and method of delivery. Be prepared to communicate your feedback in a clear and supportive way.

Corporate social responsibility and sustainability

GETTING STARTED

Working in pairs or small groups, create a mind map listing anything that you think might relate to corporate social responsibility in the travel and tourism sector. Start by thinking about the people and places involved in travel and tourism.

We all love going on holidays and taking day trips but is the travel and tourism sector good for everyone? The impacts of tourism may not always be positive and travel and tourism organisations, like any business, have a responsibility to ensure that their activities are carried out in a fair and sustainable way.

Corporate social responsibility (CSR)

Most organisations recognise that they have a responsibility to carry out their corporate (business) activities in a way which is fair, ethical and sustainable, reducing the negative impacts on people and the environment.

Corporate social responsibility (CSR) is particularly important in the travel and tourism sector, as most business activities involve a range of different people, places and communities, including tourists and travellers as well as host communities and the natural environment. Many travel and tourism organisations have a CSR policy, which outlines their specific strategic aims and objectives.

ACTIVITY

Choose a suitable travel and tourism organisation and carry out some research to explore its CSR and sustainability policy.
- What does the organisation do to operate fairly and ethically?
- How does the organisation contribute to the local community?
- How does the organisation look after the environment?

Now create a poster which summarises the main findings of your research.

Making a positive contribution

As well as achieving their financial aims, many organisations in the travel and tourism sector wish to make a positive contribution to their local communities. This could involve supporting local projects financially through sponsorship or grants or setting up charities to help specific groups. Organisations may have specific strategic aims not just to make money but to give something back to the communities where they work and operate.

Virgin Trains takes its social responsibilities seriously. It has a number of initiatives to try to make a positive contribution to the communities it works in such as: working with local schools, staff volunteering and mentoring, and free places for local people at its 'Talent Academy'. For more information, go to: www.virgintrains.co.uk/about/social-responsibility.

British Airways operates a number of projects to help make a positive contribution. Its Flying Start programme is a global charity partnership with Comic Relief, which aims to raise money to help children living tough lives in the UK and around the world. British Airways aims to raise in excess of £20 million by 2020.

Sustainability

Tourism provides a lot of fun and entertainment for visitors, travellers and tourists but there can be a cost, often to the environment. For example, large numbers of people travelling to a national park or visitor attraction can cause delays, noise and pollution. Hundreds, or even thousands, of people visiting natural attractions, such as parks and lakes, can cause congestion and erosion of footpaths.

Large tourism organisations can use significant amounts of power and water, putting a strain on natural resources and creating tons of waste to dispose of. Many travel and tourism organisations have a strategic aim to operate more sustainably, reducing the negative impact that their business has on the natural environment.

Merlin Entertainments is the largest entertainment company operating in Europe. Merlin runs 124 attractions in 25 countries across four continents. In the UK, Merlin operates well-known attractions such as Alton Towers Resort, SEA LIFE Centres, the Blackpool Tower and Thorpe Park Resort. Merlin Entertainments recognises that its operations impact on the environment and it has a strategic business goal to try to reduce any negative impacts. Their environmental policy outlines how it plans to achieve its goals, for example:

- using renewable technologies
- reducing carbon emissions
- providing more opportunities for recycling
- reusing resources where possible.

DID YOU KNOW?

The National Trust often works in partnership with other businesses to try to raise funds for its conservation and preservation work. This fundraising partnership is one way that a business might help to meet its corporate social responsibilities and help to protect the natural environment for visitors.

◘ Water at the SEA LIFE London Aquarium is reused as part of water conservation.

CHECK MY LEARNING

You should now have created a poster which summarises your chosen organisation's CSR and sustainability policy. Now choose a poster created by one of your peers and carry out a review. Be prepared to provide some feedback. Think about the following.

- Are the aims clear and easy to understand?
- What are the similarities and differences between their organisation's policies and the ones of your selected organisation?
- What might the reasons be for any differences?

Meeting regulatory standards

GETTING STARTED

Explore the website of a travel and tourism regulator and investigate the different areas of regulation that it looks after. Make some notes and be prepared to provide feedback.

LINK IT UP

Refer back to 'Regulators and travel and tourism trade associations' to refresh your memory about these important organisations and their key roles.

DID YOU KNOW?

All new cabin crew staff are required to pass an initial medical examination and have ongoing medical assessments every five years. Assessments can only be carried out by authorised medical examiners and practitioners.

A key aim for travel and tourism organisations which are regulated, for example airlines and airports regulated by the CAA, and train operators regulated by the ORR, is to meet the regulator's standards.

If these standards are not met, the regulator may impose fines or sanctions which can seriously impact on other financial and strategic aims of the organisations.

Aviation standards

As you explored in Regulators and travel and tourism trade associations, the Civil Aviation Authority (CAA) is the UK's specialist aviation regulator which helps to ensure that the aviation industry meets strict safety standards and that air travel customers are protected. The CAA ensures that different travel and tourism organisations in the aviation industry comply with a range of different regulations.

- UK airlines must ensure that they comply with relevant international safety standards, including those set by the European Aviation Safety Agency (EASA).
- Airlines must comply with consumer laws, such as providing support to passengers who have had their journeys delayed or cancelled and those with mobility needs.
- UK airports must ensure that they comply with relevant international and UK safety standards and security arrangements, including airport rescue and firefighting services.
- Aviation providers must ensure that professional flight crew, private pilots, air traffic controllers and cabin crew meet strict medical requirements and regulations.
- Airports must enforce strict restrictions on what items passengers can take in their hand luggage and hold (check-in) luggage when boarding a plane in the UK. For example, liquids in containers larger than 100ml generally cannot go through security.

Rail standards

Train operating companies and Network Rail, the company which runs the railway infrastructure, must meet certain regulatory standards. These standards are regulated by the Office of Rail and Road (ORR). Rail regulatory standards include the following.

- Train operating companies, and train station operators, must meet strict health and safety laws and regulations relating to passenger safety and overcrowding on trains and platforms.
- Network Rail must meet regulations relating to track, signalling, bridges and tunnels, including the Channel Tunnel, and the High Speed 1 (HS1) network.

ACTIVITY

Working as a group, carry out some research into the Civil Aviation Authority (CAA) or the Office of Rail and Road (ORR). Be sure to look at what specifically is regulated and how it enforces its regulations.

Now compare your findings with another group which has explored the other regulator.

What are the similarities and differences in its regulation activity?

Road standards

Coach providers and taxi drivers must also meet a range of regulatory standards and laws to ensure the safety and security of the passengers they transport. Different organisations, such as local authorities and councils, enforce these regulations, which can include the following.

- Drivers must undergo regular medical checks to ensure that they are fit to drive.
- Taxi drivers may need to produce their identify badge and licence when requested.
- Coach operators must meet regulations for public service vehicles (PSV), for example access for people with disabilities and the fitting and wearing of seat belts.

Health and safety regulations

As well as specific regulatory standards relating to transport providers, most travel and tourism organisations will need to meet more general standards relating to the health and safety of customers. Depending on the type of organisation, these could include the following.

- Theme parks must meet the Health and Safety at Work Act (1974) regulations that require fairground equipment be designed, manufactured, supplied, constructed, operated, maintained and inspected so that it is safe.
- Hotels must meet a range of health and safety regulations, such as ensuring that appropriate fire safety and prevention systems are in place, food safety and hygiene regulation in kitchens, and regulations relating to the safe storage and controls of substances hazardous to health, for example those related to swimming pools and spas.

CHECK MY LEARNING

Produce a brief 'code of practice' for a chosen regulator and outline its regulatory standards and how it aims to protect travellers and tourists.

Contribution of travel and tourism organisations to the UK economy

GETTING STARTED

Working in pairs, make a list of all the travel and tourism jobs you can think of which are related to either an accommodation provider, such as a local hotel, or a tourist attraction in your local area.

1 Discuss what you think the terms 'direct' and 'indirect' mean in the context of employment.

2 Now, consider if the jobs you have identified provide direct or indirect employment. Make two columns and list each job in the most appropriate place.

Travel and tourism is not just about going on holiday and staying in hotels. The sector makes an important contribution to the UK economy and employment. In this lesson, you will explore how the sector provides a range of exciting direct and indirect employment opportunities for people like you.

Providing employment

Travel and tourism directly supports around 1,600,000 jobs, which is around 4.6 per cent of total UK employment. The total contribution of travel and tourism to employment, including jobs indirectly supported by the industry, was around 12 per cent of total employment, just over 4 million jobs (Source: WTTC, 2016).

Some people are employed in job roles created by travel and tourism organisations themselves. This is known as direct employment. Examples of direct employment jobs are shown in Table 1.7.

▣ Table 1.7: Examples of direct employment opportunities in travel and tourism

Travel and tourism organisation	Direct employment opportunities
Accommodation provider	• Front of House Manager • Receptionist • Housekeeper • Food and Beverage Assistant • Concierge
Tourist attraction	• Guest Relations Manager • Shows and Attractions Host • Sales Assistant • Ride Operator • Retail Assistant
Transport providers	• Train Manager • Ticket Examiner • Cabin Crew Member • Dispatcher • Platform Assistant
Conference and events management	• Conference Producer • Events Coordinator • Convention and Conference Assistant • Banqueting Assistant • Steward
Travel agent	• Regional Manager • Store Manager • Travel Sales Consultant • Foreign Exchange Cashier
Tourism promotion	• Tourism and Development Officer • TIC Manager • Marketing and Events Manager • Visitor Information Assistant

As well as a range of direct employment opportunities, there are a number of jobs which supply and support travel and tourism organisations. This is known as indirect employment.

Examples of indirect employment includes jobs in other sectors such as:

- retail
- hospitality and catering
- engineering and logistics
- information technology and media
- cleaning and laundry.

Customers travelling on a long-haul flight with an airline provider would need onboard food and beverages. Meals would be prepared by chefs and food preparers employed by specialist catering companies. These employees are indirectly employed in the travel and tourism sector, as they supply products to the airline industry.

A large hotel may offer its clients a range of rooms and venues to stage conferences and events. They may use the services of a sound and vision company to provide the technical support, sound and audio facilities needed for large events. Technicians supporting the event are indirectly employed in the sector as they are supporting the function.

ACTIVITY

In small groups, carry out some research to explore travel and tourism employment statistics in the UK. Focus your research on one particular industry in the sector, for example visitor attractions, accommodation providers or travel agencies.

- Are employment rates increasing, decreasing or remaining static in your chosen industry?
- Are job roles mainly full-time, part-time, seasonal or casual?
- What are the average earnings for entry-level positions in your chosen industry?

Think carefully about the sources of information and try to find the most up-to-date statistics you can find. Summarise your findings and get ready to present back to the whole class.

Economic multiplier effect

When visitors, travellers and tourists buy travel and tourism products and services, the income received does not just stay with travel and tourism organisations, but also circulates throughout the economy on indirect products and services. This flow of revenue has an impact on both direct and indirect employment.

For example, a tourist staying at a guest house will require fresh towels and bed linen. The guest house may use the services of a local laundry, which employs workers to clean, press and deliver the linen required regularly by the guest house. The laundry is benefiting from the travel and tourism industry, and the demand for its services enables it to employ more staff.

CHECK MY LEARNING

Select an industry in the travel and tourism sector that you might like to work in, in the future. Carry out some research, using the internet or trade magazines, to find a current job vacancy within that industry.

- What is the salary and other benefits on offer?
- What are the main roles and responsibilities?
- What are the main entry requirements and qualifications needed to apply?

Contribution of tourism to gross domestic product (GDP)

GETTING STARTED

Working in pairs, think about where you might be able to find statistics on both inbound and domestic tourism. Create a list of the possible sources of statistical data and information.

How would you make sure that the data you find is both valid and reliable?

The travel and tourism sector makes a major contribution to the UK economy in terms of **gross domestic product (GDP)**. In this lesson, you will explore this contribution and why the development of travel and tourism is so important.

Both domestic and inbound tourism contribute to the UK's GDP. Outbound tourism does not contribute, as most of the money spent by these travellers and tourists will be in another country. For example, a group of students from Newcastle travelling to Ibiza for a week is an example of outbound tourism. They will spend most of their money on this trip when they are in Ibiza on hotels, transport, food and drink, and socialising.

A family coming to the UK from the USA to travel around England and Scotland on a sightseeing trip is an example of inbound tourism. They will spend money while visiting the UK on accommodation, travel and sightseeing for example. The money spent by the family helps contribute to the UK's GDP.

In 2017 the UK had the fifth biggest GDP in the world (Source: IMF, 2017). The direct contribution of travel and tourism to the UK was £66.3 billion in 2016, which is around 3.4 per cent of GDP. Total contribution of travel and tourism was £209 billion, which is around 11 per cent of GDP (Source: WTTC, 2017).

KEY TERM

Gross domestic product (GDP) is the value of a country's economy. GDP measures the value of all goods and services over a specific time period (usually one year).

Infrastructure development

The development of tourism can impact on the development of infrastructure, for example the building of new roads and transport links. An expected increase in tourism can often lead to rapid infrastructure development, as seen in the preparations for the 2012 Olympic Games in London.

In preparation for the 2012 Olympic Games and the large number of tourists heading to London, Transport for London invested £6.5 billion in its transport network. Infrastructure developments included ten railway lines, 30 new bridges and a range of projects to promote greener travel, including upgrades to pedestrian and cycling routes across London.

Another example of infrastructure development is the construction of the high-speed rail network across England. The new 'HS2' high-speed line will connect eight out of Britain's ten largest cities, reducing travel times, increasing capacity and improving connections. It is hoped that the HS2 project will create over 28,000 jobs in both building the new network and running it once complete.

DID YOU KNOW?

Britain's tourism industry is predicted to be worth over £257 billion by 2025 – supporting almost 3.8 million jobs, which is around 11 per cent of the total UK number (Source: VisitBritain, 2018).

DID YOU KNOW?

HS2's budget is £55.7 billion but it is predicted that for every £1 invested in HS2 the UK will receive £2.30 in benefits. To find out more, visit www.hs2.org.uk.

ACTIVITY

Working in pairs, or small groups:

1 choose a tourist destination in the UK and make a list of all the infrastructure that tourists might need;

2 using the internet, for example the Office for National Statistics website www.ons.gov.uk, investigate tourist numbers and visitor spend of inbound tourism and domestic tourism in the UK.

◪ The HS2 route will connect eight of Britain's largest cities.

Tourism decline

When a destination is no longer as popular with tourists, the lack of visitors, and the income they generate, can cause a decline in infrastructure development. In the UK, seaside resorts were once the place to go on holiday for most families. However, with the introduction of affordable package holidays to European destinations, such as the Spanish coasts, many families turned their backs on British seaside resorts and took to the skies in search of guaranteed sunshine overseas.

Many once popular UK seaside resorts have struggled to cope with the decline in visitor numbers and are now some of the country's most deprived towns, with high levels of unemployment and a lack of investment. Busy hotels and guest houses have often been converted into shared accommodation for residents on benefits and welfare support. Many visitor attractions, shops and restaurants have closed down due to a lack of customers, leaving large gaps in high streets and shopping centres and fewer facilities for residents.

Clacton-on-Sea was once a popular seaside town in Essex, England, attracting hundreds of thousands of holidaymakers each year. Like many similar towns, however, it became one of the UK's most deprived areas as visitor numbers declined. More recently, infrastructure developments, such as the refurbishment of the pier to include exciting indoor and outdoor attractions, and new marketing campaigns, have encouraged tourists to return. Visitor numbers are up and employment in the sector has been steadily increasing.

CHECK MY LEARNING

Carry out some research to find out how many UK tourism trips and visits your friends and family have made in the last year. Estimate how much they may have contributed to the UK economy through their visits.

How travel and tourism organisations work together

GETTING STARTED

Working in pairs, carry out some internet research to explore what 'vertical' and 'horizontal' integration could mean. Make a mind map of your initial thoughts and findings and be prepared to feed back your ideas to the whole class.

Think about the last time you went on holiday or took a day trip. How many different travel and tourism organisations did you use? Did any of these organisations work together to make your experience better? In this lesson, you will explore how travel and tourism organisations work together to better meet the needs of their customers and to meet their organisational aims.

Different travel and tourism organisations might work together in different ways, such as integration, partnerships or interdependencies but what are the key differences between these approaches?

Integration

Travel and tourism businesses may decide to integrate with other organisations, either horizontally or vertically.

Vertical integration

Vertical integration is where an organisation owns different companies at different levels of the supply chain, for example a tour operator might also own and control its own travel agencies, airlines and hotels (Figure 1.5). This level of control helps the organisation to meet customer demand, control quality and provide savings, and to assemble holiday packages.

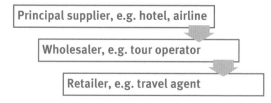

■ Figure 1.5: An example of vertical integration

Horizontal integration

Horizontal integration is where a business takes control of another business at the same level of the supply chain, for example one travel agent taking over another travel agent to increase its market share or access a new customer market.

There are lots of examples of horizontal integration in the travel and tourism sector, as organisations try to increase their presence and become the number one choice for tourists and holidaymakers.

TUI, the German travel company, is an example of a large travel organisation that is both vertically and horizontally integrated. TUI is a tour operator but also with its own high street travel agency branches. In 2000, TUI took over the British Thomson Travel Group but the Thomson name was kept. However, in 2017, Thomson was re-branded as TUI on the high street and online. TUI also has its own airline, TUI Airways and hotels resorts, such as Sensatori, Sensimar and Iberotel.

ACTIVITY

In pairs or small groups, carry out some research into how different travel and tourism organisations have integrated, both horizontally and vertically.

1 Draw a diagram, or flow chart, showing an example of horizontal integration for a hotel company.

2 Draw a diagram or flow chart, showing an example of a vertical integration for a tour operator or travel company.

Partnerships

Rather than taking over another business, organisations in the travel and tourism sector may choose to work together in partnership. Partnerships can exist between public, private and voluntary organisations.

Organisations may choose to work together in a number of different ways, for example providing discounts and deals to customers if they buy products from both companies in the partnership.

One example of partnership working is VisitBritain, the UK's national tourism agency, which runs a range of promotional campaigns with different private sector organisations such as easyJet, British Airways and Virgin Atlantic, to encourage visitors in overseas destinations to visit the UK.

Virgin Trains works in partnership with Uber, the online taxi booking service, to provide customers with a smooth and seamless journey from door to door. Virgin Trains customers are provided with a link to book their onward Uber journey from the train station, receiving a discount off their first booking.

ACTIVITY

In the same pairs or small groups, investigate how a tourist attraction works in partnership with other travel and tourism organisations, for example hotels and transport providers. Prepare a short summary of your findings to share with the rest of your class.

Interdependencies

As well as partnerships, travel and tourism organisations may work together more closely, interdependently or as part of an alliance. Working closely together in this way can help all organisations involved to share resources and provide a better service to customers. Different airlines often work together as part of interdependent alliances to offer customers more routes, more services and greater benefits and rewards.

One example is the 'oneworld' alliance between 13 of the world's leading airlines. Working together, they can offer their customers access to 1,000 destinations in more than 150 countries worldwide. For more information, see: www.oneworld.com.

CHECK MY LEARNING

Test your friends! Working in small groups, set five questions for another group to answer that will really test their knowledge on how travel and tourism organisations work together.

The reasons travel and tourism organisations work together

GETTING STARTED

Working in pairs, discuss all the different reasons a travel and tourism organisation might want to work together with other organisations. Think about the advantages and disadvantages of organisations working together in relation to the organisations themselves and the customers that buy their products and services.

You have now explored different ways that travel and tourism organisations can work together but why do these organisations want to work together? What are the advantages? In this lesson, you will investigate the different reasons why, and the advantages for both organisations and their customers.

Travel and tourism organisations will often work together for a number of different reasons (Figure 1.6).

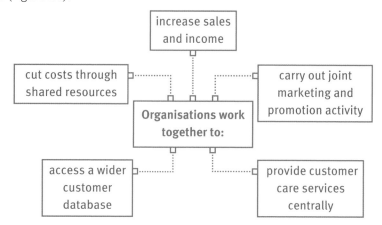

☐ Figure 1.6: Why else might organisations choose to work together?

Increase sales and income

By working together, travel and tourism organisations can better meet their customers' needs, leading to more sales and increased income. For example, many airlines have partnerships with car hire companies, as they recognise that many travellers will need to continue their journey from the airport by road. By providing discounts and information, the two companies can mutually benefit from this partnership working.

The airline Flybe has a partnership with car hire company Avis. Customers booking a flight with Flybe can also book their car hire online at the same time, benefiting from special rates and deals, such as 15 per cent off or seven days hire for the price of five.

Carry out joint marketing and promotion

One common way of working together is for travel and tourism organisations to offer deals, discounts and promotions to their customers, if they use the products and services of partners. Customers benefit from cost-saving deals as they are encouraged to book with preferred providers. For example, the London Transport Museum works with the MBNA Thames Clippers ferry company to promote a special joint ticket to customers. Visitors buying the package can benefit from discounted rates.

Provide central customer care

Some small organisations may not have the resources to provide good levels of customer care support, such as helplines and online advice and guidance facilities, such as 'live chat'. By working together, smaller organisations can share resources to provide a central customer support service to deal with enquiries from all of the organisations involved.

In recent years, many councils have had to review their funding and spending on public services, for example providing tourist information. In a bid to save money and reduce costs, many tourist information centres are now located alongside other council services such as inside libraries, sharing staff and resources. Visitors to Birmingham can access tourist information services from the city's main library six days a week. Gifts and souvenirs can also be purchased from the library shop.

Access a wider database

By working together, organisations are able to share key information on customers and their buying behaviours. They can then target these customers with deals and offers which may appeal to them, leading to more sales and more revenue.

Organisations need to be careful when sharing personal information. Data protection laws, such as the General Data Protection Regulation (GDPR), have strict guidelines for how customers' personal information can be stored, used and shared.

Cut costs through economies of scale

When organisations work together, they are often able to benefit from 'economies of scale'; this is a cost advantage when organisations expand and benefit from lower unit costs for their products, as output increases. For example, working together, larger organisations have greater buying power. They are able to place larger orders and often receive discounts for buying in bulk.

ACTIVITY

In pairs or small groups, prepare a short presentation to be delivered to the rest of your class. In the presentation, you should:

- give an example of a travel and tourism organisation which works with other organisations in the sector
- explain how they work together – giving examples to illustrate your findings
- assess the reasons why they are working together – what are the advantages?
- evaluate how effectively the organisations are working together – what is the impact?

CHECK MY LEARNING

Get Set – Present! Now that you have carried out your research on how travel and tourism organisations work together, it's time to deliver your presentation. Make sure you are well prepared.

- Check your spelling, punctuation and grammar – is your presentation professional and easy to follow?
- Don't just read from your slides – have prompt cards and key notes prepared in advance.
- Use images – they help to keep your audience interested and engaged.

Learning aim A: assessment practice

How you will be assessed

In this component, you will be assessed by completing an internally assessed assignment. You may be required to complete a number of tasks, including producing reports, presentations or posters, for example.

Your teacher will set the assignment. They will provide you with an assignment brief that outlines what you will need to do as well as a date by which the assignment should be completed and submitted. The teacher will mark the assignment and tell you what grade you have achieved.

For Learning aim A, you will be expected to show that you know about different types of travel and tourism organisations, their aims and ownership and understand how they work together. This will include:

- describing the type, ownership, purpose and main aims of a travel and tourism organisation
- assessing the extent to which an organisation meets its purpose and aims through working with other organisations.

CHECKPOINT

Review your learning of this component by answering the following questions; this will help you prepare for your assignment.

Strengthen

- Identify a named example for each type of travel and tourism organisation.
- Compare the key differences between public, private and voluntary organisations.
- Explain what the main aims of a large, privately owned travel and tourism organisation might be.
- Explain the differences between vertical and horizontal integration.

Challenge

- Explain what is meant by 'economies of scale'.
- Assess how travel and tourism organisations can benefit from working together.

ASSESSMENT ACTIVITY 1 | LEARNING AIM A

Choose a specific travel and tourism organisation from the private or voluntary sector and describe:

- the organisation type and ownership
- the purpose of the organisation
- the aims of the organisation.

Now go on to explain how the organisation works with other organisations to meet its purpose and aims.

- What type of organisations does it work with?
- How do they work together?
- How effectively does it meet its purpose and aims by working together with other organisations?

Present your findings in a blog or a magazine article format. Use relevant images and statistics to support your findings.

TIP

Many organisations outline their main vision, values, aims and objectives on their websites. Look for the 'About Us' link on the homepage of most internet sites as a starting point.

ASSESSMENT ACTIVITY 2 | LEARNING AIM A

Frontier Adventureland is a small, privately owned theme park providing a range of rides and attractions for children and adults.

The general manager is reviewing the main aims and objectives of the park and is considering ways that working with other organisations might be helpful.

You have been lucky enough to secure a work placement at the park over the summer period. The manager has asked you to complete a project while on your placement, investigating examples of other similar organisations, their aims and how they work together with other travel and tourism organisations.

Your manager has asked you to put together a presentation. You will need to choose a named travel and tourism organisation from the private sector to investigate, such as a visitor attraction.

Your presentation should:

- describe the ownership, type and purpose of your chosen organisation
- explain the organisation's aims
- explain, with examples, how the organisation works with other organisations to meet its purpose and aims
- assess how working with other organisations helps the organisation to meet its purpose and aims.

You will present your findings, supported by a copy of your presentation and any supporting notes you have made.

TIP

Try to make sure you use clear and relevant examples to support the main points in your presentation.

TIPS

In this assessment, make sure you provide details about a real travel and tourism organisation.

Make sure you include details of how it works with at least **two** other travel and tourism organisations, for example accommodation providers, transport providers and tourism promotion agencies.

TAKE IT FURTHER

Have you identified **all** the different organisations that your chosen travel and tourism business works with? Make sure you have considered organisations that indirectly provide support and supplies to your chosen organisation.

Types of tourism

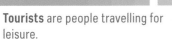

GETTING STARTED

Working in pairs, describe each of the following terms, in your own words, for different types of tourism:
- domestic
- outbound
- inbound.

People travel for all sorts of different reasons. Have you ever wondered about the different types of tourism and what attracts different **tourists** and **visitors** to different destinations?

Tourism is not just about taking a day trip to the local theme park or zoo; there are different types of tourism.

KEY TERMS

Tourists are people travelling for leisure.

Visitors are people making a visit to a main destination outside their usual environment and for less than a year, for any main purpose, including holidays, leisure, business, health and education.

◻ **At the heart of tourism are the attractions that cause people to travel.**

ACTIVITY

Working in small groups, create a blog for **two** of the following types of traveller:
- visitor
- tourist
- domestic
- outbound
- inbound.

Create names for them, give them a home town/city and country, and the destinations they have travelled to. Describe the kind of activities they may have engaged in while at their destination.

Domestic tourism

Domestic tourism is when visitors and tourists take holidays within their own country. Examples of domestic tourism could include the following:
- a group of college students travelling from Carlisle to Liverpool to visit the Albert Dock and the Beatles Museum
- a retired couple from Bradford taking their grandchildren to Morecambe for the weekend.

Outbound tourism

Outbound tourism is when visitors and tourists travel to a different country from their own, to visit or take a holiday. Examples of outbound tourism could include the following:

- an independent traveller from Leeds travelling to Peru to walk the Inca Trail to visit Machu Picchu
- a family from Bristol flying to Turkey for a week in an all-inclusive holiday resort.

◧ Nearly 10 million inbound visitors arrived at Heathrow in 2017.

Inbound tourism

Inbound tourism is when visitors and tourists from overseas travel into a different country. Examples of inbound tourism could include the following:

- a group of students from China visiting the UK to tour historic cities, such as London, Oxford, York and Edinburgh
- a couple from Italy visiting the Lake District in Cumbria, England, for a romantic long weekend.

DID YOU KNOW?

UKinbound is a trade association that represents the interests of almost 400 businesses that contribute to the UK's inbound tourism sector. For more information, go to: www.ukinbound.org.

CHECK MY LEARNING

You should now understand the differences between different types of tourism. Perhaps review the United Nations' World Tourism Organization's definitions of 'tourism' and a 'tourist', which you can find on its website.

Types of tourist destination (1)

GETTING STARTED

Working in pairs:

1 make a list of all the different types of visitor you can think of, for example, 'families'

2 now choose one type of visitor from your list and write a description of their characteristics and what they might *want* and *need* from a tourist destination.

The UK offers visitors and tourists a great variety of different types of destination, from fun seaside resorts to picturesque countryside areas and bustling cities. When working in the travel and tourism industry, it is important to understand how destinations attract different types of visitor through their features and services.

Types of visitor

It is sometimes useful to categorise visitors into different types, as they share similar wants and needs. Different types of visitor include those outlined in Figure 1.7.

◘ Figure 1.7: Examples of types of visitor. Did you come up with any others?

Certain visitors might have a range of specific needs that must be met when taking a day trip or a holiday. These visitors could include:

- speakers of other languages
- customers with different cultural needs
- visitors with disabilities and impairments, for example wheelchair users and those with hearing and visual impairments.

Types of destination

The UK has a broad range of different destinations. These can be categorised into different destination types:

Coastal areas	These include destinations along the UK's thousands of kilometres of coastline, including popular seaside resorts.
Countryside areas	These include destinations in National Parks, Areas of Outstanding Natural Beauty (AONB), lakes, forests, wilderness and mountains.
Towns and cities	These include the UK's four capital cities: London, Cardiff, Edinburgh and Belfast, as well as historically and culturally rich towns and cities.

Coastal areas and seaside resorts

The UK is an island nation and has many kilometres of outstanding coastline, from flat, sandy beaches to steep cliffs and jagged headlands. Coastal areas are very attractive destinations for many visitors looking to walk, surf, relax or to be entertained at one of the many seaside resorts found along the coast.

Seaside towns and resorts were once the most popular destinations in the UK. The arrival of steam train travel in the Victorian era meant that, for the first time, many people were able to afford to travel. Seaside towns boomed as people from polluted and crowded towns and cities wanted to escape to the coast for fresh air and fun. Attractions such as pleasure piers, donkey rides and Punch and Judy shows kept visitors returning year after year.

ACTIVITY

Working in pairs or small groups complete the following tasks.

1 Carry out some internet research to identify the five most visited seaside destinations in the UK.

2 Use an atlas to locate each of the five seaside destinations on a blank outline map of the UK.

3 Finally, choose one of the seaside destinations and create a brief presentation that outlines the facilities available there. Think about why visitors would want to go there.

The huge popularity of seaside towns was not to last forever, however. As air travel became more popular and cheaper in the 1970s and 1980s, many visitors swapped Blackpool and Margate for Benidorm and Majorca and guaranteed sunshine. UK seaside towns and resorts began to decline rapidly, leading to high levels of unemployment and the closure of many attractions and hotels.

Fortunately, UK seaside resorts are increasing in popularly once more. Visitors are returning, in search of a traditional experience and good value for money. Many domestic visitors are visiting coastal areas and seaside resorts as a **staycation** alternative to going abroad.

CHECK MY LEARNING

Carry out some research with a friend or a family member on their favourite seaside destination. Why have they chosen that destination as their favourite? What is it that made them want to visit?

KEY TERM

A **staycation** is a holiday spent in a person's home country rather than abroad, quite often at home with day trips out to visit local attractions.

DID YOU KNOW?

The Blue Flag award scheme recognises beaches that meet four criteria: water quality, environmental awareness and information, environmental management and safety, and services. In 2018, there were 124 Blue Flag beaches across the UK.

Types of tourist destination (2)

Towns and cities

GETTING STARTED

Working in a small group, think about why a visitor or tourist would want to visit a town or city close to where you live. What would appeal to them to make that choice, rather than visiting a coastal or countryside area? Make a list of all the points you can think of.

As well as coastal areas and seaside resorts, the UK offers visitors an excellent selection of towns and cities, from the historic to the modern and cosmopolitan. But what is it that really appeals to visitors when they make the choice to visit a town or city?

The UK has a wide range of different towns and cities that attract both domestic and inbound visitors all year round. Whether it's a sprawling capital city or a small historic destination, UK towns and cities are very popular with a wide range of visitors looking for shopping, leisure, eating out and sightseeing opportunities.

ACTIVITY

Working in pairs or small groups complete the following tasks.

1 Use an atlas to locate each of the four capital cities of the UK and plot these on a blank outline map of the UK.

2 Now choose five more towns or cities of cultural or heritage significance. Plot these accurately on your map, using an atlas to help you.

3 Finally, choose one of the towns or cities you have located and carry out some internet research to investigate its tourist facilities. You should prepare a brief presentation to outline why visitors would find the destination appealing. Make sure you cover: attractions, transport and accommodation.

DID YOU KNOW?

In the UK, city status can only be granted by the monarch. There are currently 69 cities in the UK – 51 in England, six in Wales, seven in Scotland and five in Northern Ireland.

◻ Cities are a big attraction for visitors.

Domestic visitors

Domestic visitors make the most trips, and spend the most money, when visiting cities and large towns in the UK, compared to seaside and countryside destinations (Table 1.8 shows the results for England).

▣ Table 1.8: Domestic overnight trips in England, 2017

Destination type	Number of trips*		Number of nights		Spend	
	Million	%	Million	%	£Million	%
City/large town	42.58	42%	100.74	34%	£7,963	42%
Small town	19.06	19%	52.88	18%	£2,901	15%
Seaside	23.38	23%	88.79	30%	£5,027	26%
Countryside/village	17.12	17%	55.25	18%	£3,047	16%

Note: *trips counted as one adult, two adults or a family staying overnight away from home.
Source: VisitEngland

Generally, cities are characterised as large, densely populated areas with developed infrastructure, such as transport networks and facilities. Not all destinations granted city status are large, however. St Davids, on the Pembrokeshire coast in Wales, is the UK's smallest city, with a population of only around 1600 people.

Inbound visitors

Many visitors will choose to take a **city break** for a few days, to explore the daytime facilities, and night life, that each town or city has to offer. The ten most popular cities and large towns in the UK for inbound visitors are given in Table 1.9.

▣ Table 1.9: Top towns for 'staying visits' by inbound visitors, 2017

Rank	Town/city	Visits (000s)	Rank	Town/city	Visits (000s)
1	London	19,828	6	Glasgow	787
2	Edinburgh	2,015	7	Bristol	602
3	Manchester	1,319	8	Oxford	536
4	Birmingham	1,117	9	Cambridge	519
5	Liverpool	839	10	Brighton/Hove	491

Source: International Passenger Survey, Office for National Statistics

So, whether it's a trip to the theatre, an evening of fine dining at a top restaurant, a visit to a museum or gallery, or perhaps a night in a 5-star luxury hotel, the UK's towns and cities offer different visitors a wide range of appealing features, services and facilities.

LINK IT UP

In 'Types of Tourism' you explored inbound, domestic and outbound. The focus of this lesson is on looking at these in the context of visitors to towns and cities.

KEY TERM

A **city break** is usually defined as a short trip with overnight accommodation, of three nights or fewer.

CHECK MY LEARNING

Having completed your research on your chosen town or city, you now need to present your findings to the rest of your class or group. You should clearly outline the key facilities that make your chosen destination appealing to different types of visitor.

Types of tourist destination (3)

Countryside areas

GETTING STARTED

Working in a small group, think about why a visitor or tourist would want to visit a countryside area local to you. What would appeal to them to make that choice, rather than visiting a coastal resort or a large town or city? Make a list of all the points you can think of.

After the hustle and bustle of the busy city, many visitors may choose to take a visit to the range of countryside destinations the UK has to offer. But what is so appealing about the British countryside?

From National Parks to mountains, farms and forests, the UK countryside offers visitors a huge range of appealing features. Getting out into the great outdoors, and exploring some of the UK's amazing geographical features, is what attracts many different types of visitor, from walking groups to those seeking remote romantic getaways.

National Parks

The UK has 15 National Parks. National Parks are areas protected because of their beautiful countryside, wildlife and cultural heritage. For more information, go to: www.nationalparks.gov.uk. The UK's National Parks are:

Brecon Beacons	Lake District	Peak District
Broads	Loch Lomond & The Trossachs	Pembrokeshire Coast
Cairngorms	New Forest	Snowdonia
Dartmoor	Northumberland	South Downs
Exmoor	North York Moors	Yorkshire Dales

Areas of Outstanding Natural Beauty (AONB)

The UK has 46 Areas of Outstanding Natural Beauty, known as AONBs. The AONB designation is unique to the UK and aims to conserve and enhance the natural beauty of the UK's countryside areas. The National Association for AONBs is a registered charity, made up of AONB partnerships and conservation boards, local authorities and environmental organisations, which aims to promote the conservation of the protected areas as well as educate the public. For more information, please see: www.landscapesforlife.org.uk.

LINK IT UP

In Learning aim A, you explored the key aims and objectives of the voluntary organisations and charities that own and manage many National Parks and AONBs.

Forests

The UK has a range of forests and woodland areas for visitors to explore. Many visitors are attracted to these by the opportunities for walking, mountain biking and orienteering. In recent years, forests have also been used as the setting for live music concerts and other events. Some of the most popular forests include Delamere, Grizedale, New Forest and Sherwood Pines. For more information, explore the Forest England website: www.forestryengland.uk.

DID YOU KNOW?

Forest Live is an annual live music event across seven of England's forests. Income made from ticket sales is reinvested in conserving the forests for everyone's enjoyment.

Wilderness and wild areas

When thinking about wilderness, most people will probably think about destinations such as Australia or Canada and their large areas of unspoilt, uninhabited land. The UK does still have some areas of wilderness, or wild land, however, such as areas of north and west Scotland. Scottish Natural Heritage has identified 42 wild land areas, rugged parts of the country that show few signs of human influence, such as buildings, roads, train stations or electricity pylons. Visitors looking to really get away from it all might be attracted to areas of wilderness for walking and wild camping.

 Wild open areas attract visitors looking to get away from busy modern life.

Lakes and mountains

Visitors can enjoy lakes and mountains across the UK. Whether it's for open water swimming or boating, with over 40,000 lakes, there's plenty to choose from. Lake Windermere in the Lake District National Park is England's largest lake, but Lough Neagh in Northern Ireland is the UK's biggest at over 38,000 hectares. The UK Lakes Portal provides key data on lakes across the UK: https://eip.ceh.ac.uk/apps/lakes.

The UK landscape also provides visitors with many hills and mountains to climb. Hills become mountains after 2,000 feet (610 metres). Three of Britain's highest mountains are Snowdon in Wales, Scafell Pike in England and Ben Nevis in Scotland. Over 30,000 people each year challenge themselves to travel between and climb all three peaks in 24 hours!

ACTIVITY

Working in pairs, use an atlas as a guide to locate each of the following on a blank outline map(s) of the UK: a National Park; an AONB; a lake; a forest; a mountain; and an area of wilderness or wild land.

Then choose one and create a promotional poster of a chosen countryside area, focusing on why tourists would visit it.

CHECK MY LEARNING

Choose a countryside area that you have not visited before. Carry out some research into the features and facilities in the area and identify **two** specific reasons why you would want to visit. Be prepared to share your findings.

Features of destinations (1)

GETTING STARTED

Choose a tourist destination local to you. Think about all the different reasons why tourists and travellers would want to visit. Make a list of as many different reasons as you can.

Visitors and tourists, when deciding when and where to visit, will consider their needs, what they want from their visit and which destinations appeal to them the most. They will consider the range of features at destinations before making their final choice, but what are these features and how important are they?

Most visitors find certain key features, such as geographical and natural attractions, visitor attractions, the facilities available and the climate, important when considering different tourist destinations, whether a city, coastal or countryside location.

ACTIVITY

Select one UK destination – this could be a coastal location or seaside resort, a countryside area or a large town or city.

1 Carry out some research into the geographical and natural features, and visitor attractions available at your chosen destination.

2 Now produce a written summary, with appropriate images, as either a report or a presentation.

Geographical features and natural attractions

Different types of visitor will often have very different reasons for choosing a tourist destination. The range of geographical features and natural attractions available could be a key deciding factor for many, especially those looking to relax, get active or get outdoors. Specific geographical features of a destination could include:

oceans	seas	rivers	canals	caves	waterfalls	lakes
mountains	hills	woodland	parks	coastal areas	islands	nature reserves

Cumbria, in the north-west of England, is a very popular destination for both domestic and inbound visitors because of the unique geographical features on offer (Table 1.10). To protect and preserve these features, a large part of the county is a designated National Park. In 2017 47.3 million people visited Cumbria, attracted by its mix of appealing features and facilities.

☐ **Table 1.10: Geographical features and natural attractions in Cumbria**

Feature	Examples
Lakes	Many visitors are attracted by the 16 lakes in the National Park. Visitors can enjoy trips on the lake ferries or on the steamer.
Caves	Cumbria has several caves to explore but some are only accessible to those with climbing experience. The Honister Slate Mine is also a popular attraction where visitors can climb around the inside of a Lake District mountain.
Mountains	Walkers and climbers flock to the Lake District to take advantage of some of the highest peaks in the country, including England's highest, Scafell Pike.
Parks	Fell Foot Park is owned by the National Trust and offers visitors views of the nearby mountains, a running route and a range of water activities, such as paddling, open water swimming and boating.
Woodland	Whinlatter Forest is England's only mountain forest and offers visitors a range of activities including walking trails, mountain bike routes and play areas.

Nature reserves	Cumbria offers over 40 nature reserves for visitors interested in trees, flowers, wildlife spotting, bird watching and walking.
Waterfalls	Cumbria and the Lake District offer visitors access to a range of waterfalls, including Scale Force, the National Park's highest waterfall with a drop of 170 feet.
Coastal areas	Cumbria has a long coastline featuring a number of popular coastal towns. The Solway Coast is an Area of Outstanding Natural Beauty (AONB). Many walkers are attracted to the area to walk the 150 miles of the Cumbria Coastal Way, which can take around 10–14 days to complete.

Visitor attractions

In Learning aim A, you learned about the difference between natural attractions – the natural features of the landscape and environment – and built attractions, those which are not naturally occurring but have been built by man. Visitor attractions, both built and natural, are often a key appealing feature for many tourists in deciding where to visit and where to spend their money. Different visitor attractions could include:

- theme and water parks
- historical sites, such as castles, stately homes, walls, ruins
- wildlife and nature sites, such as marine worlds, safari parks and zoos
- arts and entertainment venues such as sports stadiums/events, theatres, art galleries, museums, festivals, exhibitions and local events.

As well as popular natural attractions and appealing geographical features, Cumbria also attracts visitors through the wide range of built visitor attractions on offer. Table 1.11 lists some examples.

DID YOU KNOW?

The Lake District National Park is England's largest National Park and a **World Heritage Site**.

KEY TERM

World Heritage Sites are landmarks or areas selected by the United Nations Educational, Scientific and Cultural Organization (UNESCO) as having significance (cultural, historical or scientific) and are legally protected by international treaties.

LINK IT UP

Theme parks, a major type of built attraction, were looked at in Learning aim A. Table 1.2 shows that the third most visited attraction in 2016/2017 was Flamingo Land Theme Park and Zoo.

▣ Table 1.11: Built visitor attractions in Cumbria

Feature	Examples
Arts and entertainment	Threlkeld Quarry and Mining Museum Derwent Pencil Museum Abbot Hall Art Gallery Dove Cottage and the Wordsworth Museum The World of Beatrix Potter Attraction Lakeland Motor Museum The Rum Story Windermere Steamboat Museum
Wildlife and nature	The Lake District Wildlife Park Lakes Aquarium Lakeland Bird of Prey Centre Lakeland Wildlife Oasis
Historic sites	Muncaster Castle Carlisle Castle Wray Castle Furness Abbey Heron Corn Mill

CHECK MY LEARNING

Using the examples in Tables 1.10 and 1.11 as a guide, identify **two** key features (one natural and one built) for your chosen destination and create a poster advertising their merits.

Features of destinations (2)

GETTING STARTED

Think about a destination you and your family visited recently. What were the main features that attracted you?

Facilities

The range of facilities and services available, alongside tourist attractions, attract many visitors to a destination. There are four key groups: sports facilities, shopping, catering, and activity and adventure centres.

Sports facilities

Many visitors may choose to visit a destination because of its sporting facilities, whether to watch as a spectator or to take part as a competitor (Table 1.12). The UK is perhaps most famous for football, but also plays host to a wide range of other major sporting events and has many famous sporting venues. With London as the host of the 2012 Olympic Games, and Glasgow as the host of the 2014 Commonwealth Games, the UK is well known globally as a sporting nation. England's 'second city', Birmingham, will take on the role of host for the 2022 Commonwealth Games.

☐ Table 1.12: UK top sporting facilities and venues

Sport	Facilities
Cycling	The popularity of British cycling has soared in recent years with world-leading performances at the Olympics and in major road events, such as the Tour de France. Visitors can head to Manchester to see the UK National Cycling Centre and velodrome or head over to Yorkshire to watch the annual road race, the Tour de Yorkshire, which in 2017 was watched on the roadside by over 2 million spectators, boosting the local economy by £64 million. The 2012 Olympic velodrome in London now hosts prestigious Six Day Series meetings.
Football	Home to the Premier League, many of the UK's football teams are known the world over and attract thousands of inbound visitors each year to watch games and visit stadiums such as Manchester United at Old Trafford, Liverpool at Anfield and Manchester City at the Etihad Stadium. One of the most famous sporting venues in the world, Wembley Stadium attracts hundreds of thousands of visitors and sports fans each year.
Rugby	Twickenham Stadium is the largest dedicated rugby union venue in the world, seating 82,000 spectators and is considered the home of England Rugby. Visitors can take part in a stadium tour and visit the World Rugby Museum.
Tennis	Wimbledon is home to one of the world's most famous 'Grand Slam' competitions and the oldest tennis tournament in the world. It is host to the annual Championships competition each year. Visitors at other times can also visit the Wimbledon Lawn Tennis Museum.

Shopping

Many destinations are famous for their shopping facilities, whether they be specialist retailers, local shops, outlets or markets. London compares well to overseas locations, such as Dubai, Paris, Milan and New York, which are famous for their department stores, boutique shops and modern malls, with famous names such as Harrods, Fortnum & Mason, Liberty London and Harvey Nichols. As well as high-end stores, visitors are also attracted to London's markets and quirky venues, such as Camden Lock Market, Carnaby Street, Covent Garden and Portobello Road Market. Outlet shopping centres, such as Bicester Village, have become quite common and are popular with day trippers.

DID YOU KNOW?

The new Wembley Stadium has 90,000 seats with no obstructed views. The rows of seating, if placed end to end, would stretch 54 kilometres.

Catering

From fine dining to cheap eats, many visitors are attracted to a destination based on the catering options available. For many visitors, having a great selection of bars, restaurants and cafes to experience is a major appealing factor when deciding on a new destination to visit. The 'Northern Quarter' in Manchester attracts hundreds of thousands of visitors each year looking to find a hip and trendy new spot for a meal or drink with friends. Located in London's West End, the popular Rainforest Cafe is designed as an exotic jungle that recreates the sights and sounds of the Amazon rainforest; great for keeping the kids entertained! Founded in 1919, Betty's Café Tea Rooms in Harrogate is a famous destination for shoppers looking to take the weight off their feet and fill up on a traditional afternoon tea and scones. The world-famous Michelin Guide is a useful road map to the world's best restaurants. In 2018, the UK had five 3-star Michelin rated restaurants, placing it seventh in the world. Japan had the most with 28, closely followed by France with 27 and the USA in third place with 14.

Activity and adventure centres

The geographical features of the UK make it an ideal place for outdoor activities and adventure, as well as a growing range of indoor centres, offering tourists a variety of thrilling experiences (Table 1.13).

KEY TERM

Seasonal variations are the changes in weather, temperature and climate at different times of the year, for example in summer or in winter.

Table 1.13: Selection of key activity centres

Activity provider	Description	Website
Chill Factore	The Manchester-based snow centre for indoor skiing and snowboarding.	www.chillfactore.com
Zip World	Located in north Wales, Zip World Penrhyn Quarry is home to Velocity 2, the world's fastest zip line.	www.zipworld.co.uk
Ryze	With locations across Scotland, Ryze trampoline parks provide visitor with an 'Xtreme Air Sports' experience.	www.ryze.co.uk

Climate

The weather and climate of a destination can significantly affect its appeal for different types of tourist. **Seasonal variations** in weather and climate can also impact on the activities available and the length of the peak and off-peak seasons, which in turn affects how many tourists visit. For example, Aviemore, a town in the Cairngorms National Park, has two peak seasons: in the winter months, it is a very popular destination for visitors interested in skiing and snowboarding, and in the summer months, the destination is popular with visitors interested in walking, biking and climbing. During the off-peak late autumn and early spring periods, when there is unlikely to be snow and the weather is less good for walking, visitor numbers are much lower.

CHECK MY LEARNING

You have now researched the different geographical features, natural and built visitor attractions, facilities and climate of your chosen UK destination. For each of the following visitor types, write a brief summary explaining why they would or would not chose your destination:

- families with small children
- a retired couple
- a group of college students.

Be prepared to justify your choice for each type of visitor.

ACTIVITY

Returning to your chosen destination from the previous lesson, complete the following.

1 Investigate the facilities available at your destination and the typical climate at different times of the year.

2 Add this information to your written summary.

Reasons for travel

GETTING STARTED

Pick **two** reasons for travel from Figure 1.8 and, with a partner, list two or three specific features of each of your choices and compare them.

When was the last time you travelled? What was the reason for your journey? We all like to go on holiday but taking a vacation may be only one reason for travelling. In this lesson, you will explore all the different reasons why people may travel (Figure 1.8).

▣ Figure 1.8: Can you think of any different reasons to travel?

Leisure travel

Leisure travel can be defined as travel that is not for work or business purposes. When travelling for leisure, people are often taking a holiday, or day trip, or travelling to visit a friend or relative (VFR). Leisure travel can be domestic, inbound or outbound. Consider the examples of leisure travel listed in Table 1.14.

▣ Table 1.14: Examples of leisure travel

Scenario	Reason for travel
Kunal and Steve decide they would like to go and visit the world-famous Blackpool Illuminations. They take the train from Manchester to Blackpool and stay overnight in a hotel for the night, before returning home the next day.	This is an example of leisure travel as they are taking a short break to enjoy the Illuminations and the seaside attractions. This is an example of domestic tourism.
Stuart, Louise, Kalpesh and Dan are a group of friends travelling from Luton to Barcelona for a week. They want to see all the famous sights, eat in nice restaurants, visit the beach and party in clubs in the evening.	This is an example of leisure travel. The group of friends are taking a holiday to visit a new European destination, popular with tourists. This is an example of outbound tourism.
Kieran is travelling from Dublin to Glasgow to stay with his sister for the weekend. The rest of the family are arriving from England to celebrate the 50th birthday of Kieran's uncle.	This is an example of leisure travel to VFR. Kieran is travelling from Ireland to Scotland to celebrate a family birthday. For Kieran, this is an example of inbound tourism to the UK, and for the rest of the family it is domestic tourism.

DID YOU KNOW?

In 2017, British residents took 100.6 million overnight trips in England. Of these, the number of VFR trips taken was 36.6 million and the number of overnight business trips was 14.2 million.

Business travel

Business travel can be defined as any travel to locations and venues for work purposes, but usually excludes a person's normal commute from home to work. Business travel is usually paid for by the employer and could be for a number of reasons, for example to attend a meeting, conference or training event. Business travel could be domestic or overseas, an example of outbound tourism. Travellers entering the UK for work purposes would be classed as inbound business travellers.

Business travellers may often take advantage of business class facilities and services, for example on planes or trains, or when using business lounges and business centres in hotels and airports. These facilities often provide additional spaces to work and connect online. Table 1.15 provides two examples.

▣ **Table 1.15: Examples of business travel**

Scenario	Reason for travel
Claire needs to travel from Cambridge to Hong Kong to make a presentation to some potential new clients. Her office makes the airline and hotel reservations and arranges the transfer from work to the airport.	This is an example of business travel as Claire needs to travel overseas to secure new business for her employer. As she is travelling from the UK to another country, this is an example of outbound business travel.
Marcus has been asked by his manager to present at a large international conference in Belfast. The conference includes overnight accommodation the night before his presentation, in a 5-star hotel. Marcus must leave from his home in Cardiff and would prefer to fly to Belfast in business class.	This is an example of business travel as Marcus has been directed to attend the business conference by his manager. This is an example of domestic tourism, as Belfast is part of the UK.

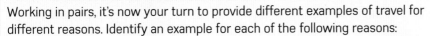

ACTIVITY

Working in pairs, it's now your turn to provide different examples of travel for different reasons. Identify an example for each of the following reasons:

1 VFR

2 holiday

3 conference.

Try to include examples of domestic, inbound and outbound tourism.

CHECK MY LEARNING

Choose one of the visitor profiles below and put together a brief itinerary for their trip.

1 Mikey needs to go from Leeds to Birmingham to attend a training course for his employer. He must arrive in the city centre before 9am. The course finishes at 4pm, a few minutes' walk away from the Birmingham New Street train station.

2 Naila lives in Peterborough and needs to get home to Carlisle to attend her parents' anniversary party, which starts at 7pm. She would prefer to drive. Ideally, she would rather not have to take a whole day off work but is unsure of the latest time she can start her journey.

Modes of transport

Planes, trains, cars, coaches, taxis and trams; visitors often have a range of transport options available to them, but different visitors might find different models of transport better suited to their needs. In this lesson you will explore the advantages and disadvantages of different types of transport (summarised in Table 1.16), and why visitors may choose one form over another.

GETTING STARTED

Working in pairs, think back to what you learned in Learning aim A about the different types of transport provider. Test your knowledge on the following terms:
- medium-haul flight
- transport gateway
- terminal
- full-service airline.

ACTIVITY

In small groups, you should discuss the advantages and disadvantages of different modes of transport for each of the following scenarios.

1 Teresa needs to travel from Plymouth to central London to attend a business meeting. The meeting starts at 10am and finishes around 4pm. Her business is paying her travel expenses and she is allowed overnight accommodation the night before the meeting if necessary.

2 Paul works for a charity and is travelling from Lancaster to a university in Nigeria to run three days of training sessions. He would like to keep costs to a minimum as the charity has limited funds.

3 Divanka would like to travel from Lincoln to Skegness with his two young nieces for the day. They only have a small budget. He has a Family and Friends Railcard but is wondering if there are any cheaper options.

4 Adi and Rich, and their two-year-old son, need to travel from Crewe to Galway in Ireland to spend Christmas with their family. What transport options do they have, and which would be the best?

LINK IT UP

In Learning aim A you explored different transport facilities and providers, gateways and terminals. Go back and refresh your memory of different types of air, rail, sea and road travel.

DID YOU KNOW?

The UK has over 40 airports, many of them regional. Carlisle Lake District Airport is the latest airport to offer commercial and business passenger flights, doing so for the first time since 1993.

Air transport

Air transport is a popular choice for many outbound tourists as travel times are often very quick. This might be a good option for business travellers who are looking to minimise the time spent travelling, even if the travel costs are higher.

As well as large, international airport gateways, offering both long- and short-haul outbound flights, such as London Heathrow and Manchester, the UK has an increasing number of smaller, regional airports, making it easier to get away, not just for short-haul outbound but for domestic travel around the UK too.

Rail transport

Business and outbound

For many business travellers, rail transport is often the most convenient and affordable method of transportation. Passengers can avoid the time taken to be processed through airport security checks and long check-in queues, making rail travel times reasonable. The introduction of high-speed rail lines has also helped to make train travel a viable competitor to flights, for those who need to get to their destination quickly.

The Channel Tunnel, opened in 1994, between Folkstone in Kent and Calais, France, provides high-speed Eurostar passenger rail services, which travel on to Paris and Brussels (in Belgium), freight services and the Eurotunnel Shuttle for road vehicles; a good alternative to ferries.

Leisure and domestic

For leisure travellers who can book in advance, rail fares can be good value, with big discounts available for railcard holders. Six different railcards are available to different types of travellers, often leading to a third off most rail fares. Railcards include those for people aged 16–25, Family and Friends, Seniors, Disabled Persons and the Two Together Railcard. More information can be found at: www.railcard.co.uk.

With refreshments, large windows, and at-seat entertainment systems, travelling by train is often a more convenient method of transport than driving. For very long distances, the UK has two sleeper train services available between London and Scotland and London and the south-west of England. Passengers are able to hire a bed, known as a sleeping berth, to get a good night's sleep before arriving at their destination.

Sea transport

Travellers to and from the UK also have the option of sea travel to a limited number of destinations. Travel by ferry can offer a slower but more leisurely form of transport and includes access to a great range of facilities and services. For example, the daily overnight crossing between Hull and Rotterdam in the Netherlands takes 12 hours but passengers can take advantage of onboard cabin accommodation, a small cinema, live shows and a disco, as well as a range of restaurants, bars and even a kids' club. For other travellers, the limited number of ports and sailings may not meet their needs.

As well as large passenger ferries, visitors might also be attracted to destinations to ride on pleasure boats and small ships. For example, the Lake District in Cumbria has a number of ships and pleasure boats that tourists can travel on to see the picturesque scenery of the lakes and mountains. The *Lady of the Lake* transports tourists on Lake Ullswater and is believed to be the oldest working passenger vessel in the world, having been launched on the 26 June 1877!

Road transport

Travellers choosing road transport have the option of private cars, hire car, coaches and taxis to get from A to B. For many travellers, travelling by road in a car offers the ultimate flexibility; set off when you like and take whichever route that you like. For others, the prospect of roadworks and unpredictable traffic jams make car travel less desirable.

Coach travel is popular with travellers looking to keep costs down. Excellent value fares can often be found when booking in advance, often much cheaper than rail or air but usually taking longer. Megabus is one coach provider famous for low-price deals, for example London to Manchester from only £3.

◻ **Table 1.16: Advantages and disadvantages of different types of transport**

Transport mode	Advantages	Disadvantages
Air	Often the quickest way to travel	Prices can be very expensive
Rail	Frequent services from most towns and cities	Services may often be overcrowded
Sea	Lots of services and facilities for all the family	Bad weather may disrupt services
Road	Often the most flexible transport option	Could be delayed by roadworks and jams

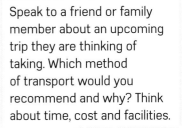

CHECK MY LEARNING

Speak to a friend or family member about an upcoming trip they are thinking of taking. Which method of transport would you recommend and why? Think about time, cost and facilities.

Types of holiday (1)

GETTING STARTED

Working in pairs, think back to Learning aim A and check your understanding of the definition of a package holiday. What does a package holiday include?

When did you last go on holiday and what kind of holiday was it? People choose to go on all sorts of different types of holiday for many different reasons. It is important for those working in the travel and tourism sector to understand why the features of different types of holiday appeal to different types of visitor.

Visitors can choose a wide range of different holiday types to meet their needs and preferences. Some examples are presented in Figure 1.9.

□ Figure 1.9: Think about the most important features for these types of holiday.

ACTIVITY

Choose one of the visitor types below and carry out some research on a UK holiday that might be suitable to meet their needs.

- An email from a customer interested in an all-inclusive UK holiday for a family of four with two children aged 6 and 8 years old. They would ideally like lots of indoor and outdoor activities to keep the children entertained.
- A face-to-face enquiry in a travel agency from someone looking to take a short break for themselves and their pet dog. They would like to take the train and would need pet-friendly accommodation. They can only take a few days holiday from work.
- A couple looking to research online to find a coach touring holiday. They have a limited budget and would like to stay near the sea if possible.

When you have found a suitable option, complete a brief summary of your choice and explain why it would be suitable.

Package holidays

A package holiday is one where the different travel services are put together by the travel company and offered to customers at a single price. Packages must include at least two different types of travel services, for example air, rail or coach transport to get you to your destination, plus at least one night's accommodation. Other travel services in a package holiday could include car hire or a tourist service, such as excursions and guided tours.

Package holidays became very popular with UK visitors throughout the 1960s to the 1990s with Spain and other Mediterranean destinations the first choice for British holidaymakers looking to find summer and winter sunshine at an affordable price. Tour operators and high street travel agents provided attractive deals and discount packages to holidaymakers. Operators were able to offer large numbers of package flights, hotels, transfers and excursions together in one attractive price.

Although the popularity of the package holiday declined, more and more visitors are now returning to package holidays. In 2017, just over half of UK holidaymakers took a package holiday abroad. Older travellers and families are particularly attracted to booking package holidays. According to ABTA (formerly, the Association of British Travel Agents), the three most common reasons for choosing a package holiday are:

1 having everything taken care of
2 receiving good value for money
3 saving time when booking.

All-inclusive holidays

All-inclusive holidays are package holidays but often with all food, selected drinks and leisure activities included in the one price. An all-inclusive package helps visitors to manage their budgets, as the total cost of their holiday experience is included in the one price paid. Many companies offer different levels of all-inclusive packages, with different terms and conditions relating to the type of products and services included, for example standard or premium food and drinks packages.

Independent and tailor-made holidays

Tailor-made holidays are a collection of different travel services chosen and booked independently. Visitors often use the internet and online booking sites to select the specific travel options and services that will build the holiday experience they want. Independent, tailor-made holidays give visitors much more choice and freedom to choose the transport, accommodation and activity options that meet their particular needs.

In 2003, the popularity of online booking and budget flights meant that independent travel overtook package holidays for the first time, with 53 per cent of holidaymakers organising their own trips abroad rather than using a tour operator. For those looking to avoid the crowds at busy resorts popular with package holiday tourists, a tailor-made option offers a more unique and personalised experience, however this can be much more expensive.

LINK IT UP

In Learning aim A you explored the role of tour operators and what goes into different types of package holiday.

DID YOU KNOW?

In 2012, tour operator First Choice became the first mainstream holiday company to offer all its holiday packages as all-inclusive, providing flights, in-resort transfers, hotel accommodation, three meals a day and unlimited local drinks as standard.

CHECK MY LEARNING

Looking back at the holiday option you selected for your chosen customer, how would you adapt that choice to meet the needs of a different visitor type, for example a family with children or a visitor with specific needs?

Types of holiday (2)

GETTING STARTED

Working in pairs, describe the following types of holiday:
- multicentre
- fly-drive
- self-drive
- short break.

As well as traditional package holidays and more individual tailor-made options, there is a wide range of other holiday options available to visitors looking to get away from it all. It is important for those working in the travel and tourism sector to understand all the different options available to meet customers' needs.

Multicentre

DID YOU KNOW?

Visiting two different destinations in one holiday is sometimes called a 'twin-centre' holiday.

A multicentre holiday is where travellers visit two or more different destinations or resorts as part of one trip. Multicentre holidays help visitors to see more of the world in a short space of time and can often offer good value for money. Long-haul destinations are often popular with visitors taking a multicentre holiday, taking advantage of just one long flight but getting to experience more than one destination. This type of holiday is also popular with people looking to have different experiences on one holiday, for example spending some time exploring an exciting city and some time to rest and relax by the beach before coming home.

Figure 1.10 illustrates some examples of popular multicentre holidays.

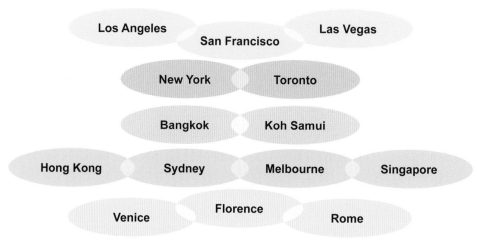

Figure 1.10: Which two or more destinations would you put together in a multicentre holiday?

Fly-drive

DID YOU KNOW?

Car hire companies often charge a 'one-way drop-off fee' if you need to return the car to a different location from the one you picked it up. This can increase the holiday cost.

A fly-drive holiday involves travel by air to a new destination, followed by car hire to allow visitors to explore further afield themselves. Travellers often pick up their hire car at the airport and return it to the same airport, or a different airport location, before flying home again. The cost of the flight and car hire are included in the price of the holiday and it may also include pre-booked accommodation along the planned route, satellite navigation equipment and roadside breakdown assistance.

Fly-drive holidays are often popular with visitors looking to explore famous road routes and stunning scenery at their own pace. This type of holiday provides visitors flexibility on how much time they want to spend travelling or exploring different towns and attractions along the way.

Self-drive

Self-drive holidays often include car or motorhome hire and pre-booked accommodation for visitors following a specific route or tour. They can form part of a fly-drive holiday experience or be closer to home without the need for air travel. Visitors benefit from suggested driving routes and itineraries, which guide them to interesting destinations and attractions. Like a fly-drive holiday, they give travellers some flexibility in the duration of travel, how much time is spent at each stop and opportunities to explore the scenery and facilities along the way. Rather than staying in expensive hotels or motels, visitors on self-drive holidays often choose a motorhome, which combines a fully equipped living and sleeping space with road transport all in one.

◪ The freedom offered by hiring a motorhome is a big attraction for many visitors.

Short breaks

Holidays don't need to be for a week or two, nor do they have to involve leaving the country. With lots of cheap flight options from budget airlines and more regional airports than ever before, and with the rise in staycation options, many visitors are taking advantage of regular short breaks, both in the UK and abroad. A short break is often considered to be a trip of between one and three nights, with a minimum of one night's stay in paid accommodation. City breaks, spa breaks and activity breaks are all very popular as visitors try to get the most from a long weekend. Many hotels offer special deals and discounts for visitors booking a two-night stay over a weekend. Alongside trendy European city destinations, such as Paris, Berlin, Stockholm and Rome, domestic city breaks, such as to the vibrant 2008 European Capital of Culture, Liverpool, or long weekends in the country are often very popular for UK travellers taking a short break. The short travel times ensure that visitors can get to their destinations quickly to take advantage of their time away and to explore the sights and attractions.

ACTIVITY

Choose one of the visitor types below and carry out some research to find a type of holiday that might be suitable to meet their needs.

- A couple looking to experience the theme parks of Florida, along with its coastal attractions and a visit to the Everglades.
- A group of five friends looking to visit San Francisco and Las Vegas.
- A family wishing to spend two weeks in the Scottish Highlands, staying in a mixture of bed and breakfasts and remote motorhome sites.
- A retired person hoping to spend two or three days at the Cambridge Literary Festival.

When you have found a suitable option, complete a brief summary of your choice and explain why it would be suitable.

CHECK MY LEARNING

Looking back at the multicentre, short break, fly-drive or self-drive holiday option you selected, how could your chosen option be adapted to meet the needs of a different type of visitor?

Types of holiday (3)

GETTING STARTED

Working in pairs, describe **three** different holidays that are linked to an activity or area of special interest, for example: sport, culture or adventure.

While most visitors might opt for a package holiday or a short break, sometimes travellers are looking for something a little bit more unusual. Touring and specialist holidays provide a range of different options for those looking to experience something really special.

Touring holidays

While sometimes it can be fun to plan and arrange every aspect of your holiday, some people would like to see different places but are happy to let someone else do all the planning. Touring holidays offer travellers the chance to experience different destinations in one trip, fully organised by the travel company. Touring holidays follow a set route and itinerary, taking in a range of different destinations along the way. They offer visitors a chance to relax while still experiencing new places and attractions.

There is a range of different touring holiday options available, including ocean or river cruises, and rail or coach tours.

Cruises

Cruises are increasingly popular, not just with older travellers but also with younger visitors and families. Cruise ships are now bigger and feature more activities than ever before, all helping to appeal to people of all ages. Cruise itineraries can last for just a couple of days to many weeks, ensuring that there's an option to fit most travellers' needs. Visitors benefit from regular stops at exciting destinations plus onboard accommodation and facilities to enjoy the journey in between locations.

◻ **Cruise ships offer an amazing array of activities to suit all ages and interests.**

Royal Caribbean International is one of the world's leading cruise operators. Their ships visit around 250 different destinations around the world. Launched in 2018, *Symphony of the Seas* became the world's largest cruise ship, carrying over 6,500 passengers at a time, with 18 decks, 22 restaurants, 42 bars and lounges, a theatre, surf simulator, waterslides, rock climbing wall, ice rink and even its own zip line.

River cruises take a gentler pace, usually aboard smaller boats with large windows to allow passengers to watch the world go by before the next stop.

DID YOU KNOW?

Research carried out by ABTA revealed that 53 per cent of 18–24-year-olds who have not been on a cruise would like to go on one.

Rail and coach tours

For those who prefer to stay away from the water, touring holidays are also popular, by rail or by coach. Following a pre-set itinerary, these tours also allow visitors the opportunity to stop off at lots of different exciting destinations, while enjoying the scenery and facilities along the way.

On coach tours, hotel accommodation is likely to be pre-booked, either overnight or for a few nights if being used as a base to explore the local region. Many rail tours include different accommodation options on board, with travellers enjoying fine dining options and large windows to watch the changing landscape.

Specialist and niche holidays

For those visitors looking for something a little different, a number of holiday companies offer more specialist, or niche, holiday options. These could include trips to attend a major sporting event, to experience different cultures, or to take time out to focus on health and wellbeing (Table 1.17).

◘ Table 1.17: Examples of specialist holidays and some of the leading companies that provide them

Specialist area	Holiday option	Travel company
Sport	Take a 'learn to dive' holiday in the Red Sea and explore the corals and marine wildlife.	www.regal-diving.co.uk
Culture	Explore ancient Greece and its key archaeological sites with a guided tour from an expert guide.	www.culturaltravel.co.uk
Education	Take a holiday to Italy to learn the language. Stay in a villa and receive tuition to learn to cook an authentic meal.	www.golearnto.com
Wellbeing	Attend a specialist yoga retreat weekend. Relax and unwind with regular classes and healthy food.	www.yogaweekends.co.uk
Adventure	Embark on a trekking holiday all the way to Mount Everest Base Camp.	www.exodus.co.uk
Eco-holidays	Reduce your carbon footprint and give something back on a residential volunteering holiday in the UK with the RSPB.	www.rspb.org.uk/get-involved

ACTIVITY

Choose one of the visitor types below and carry out some research to find a type of touring or specialist holiday that might be suitable to meet their needs.
- A solo traveller looking to improve their drawing and painting skills.
- A group of friends looking for a winter activity holiday including snowboarding.
- A family looking to take an environmentally friendly safari holiday.
- A couple wanting to spend a week playing golf in the sun.

When you have found a suitable option, complete a brief summary of your choice and explain why it would be suitable.

CHECK MY LEARNING

Looking back at the touring or specialist holiday option you selected, how could your chosen option be adapted to meet the needs of a different type of visitor?

Types of holiday (4)

GETTING STARTED

Working in pairs, discuss why someone might choose to volunteer as a holiday choice. Make a list of your ideas and share with the whole class.

Taking time off to have fun and recharge your batteries is great but sometimes it's good to give something back and use our free time to help others and protect the environment. Volunteering and conservation holidays can help travellers to do just that.

Voluntary work

For many people, spending their leisure time helping others is an important part of any holiday, particularly when visiting countries and destinations that are less well developed and where local people do not have access to the basic facilities that we often take for granted.

A volunteering holiday is often popular with younger travellers, helping them to gain experience while on a gap year for example, or those with more time to spare to help improve the lives of others. A number of specialist travel companies help to connect visitors with volunteering opportunities. Examples of volunteering holidays include those in Table 1.18.

■ **Table 1.18: Examples of volunteering holidays**

Type of activity	Reason for doing so
Teaching English	Help educate some of the world's poorest children to improve their life chances
Animal care	Help to protect the habitats and improve the living conditions of animals
Healthcare awareness	Train local people on how to stay safe and protect themselves from important health risks
Sports coaching	Work with groups of children to promote exercise and teamwork as well as having fun in difficult circumstances
Construction projects	Help to build, renovate and maintain basic facilities, such as classrooms and toilets, in less developed communities

Conservation work

For those looking to help protect the environment, a number of conservation holiday options are available, both in the UK and further afield. Travellers on these holidays will spend part of their holiday helping to restore and protect the natural environment, for example building and repairing trails, maintaining dry stone walls, planting trees and wild flowers, and cleaning lakes and ponds.

Wild Days Conservation Holidays is a private travel company offering different conservation holidays in the UK. Visitors stay in different types of accommodation and meet like-minded people, while completing different conservation projects each day, such as carrying out wildlife surveys. Visit https://wilddaysconservation.org for more information.

■ **Many visitors choose to help protect or repair the very natural attractions they would normally seek out.**

ACTIVITY

- Working in small groups, carry out some research into different voluntary and conservation holidays available in the UK.
- Working together, create a brief presentation which explores your chosen holiday, what it involves and how it helps local people. You should make sure you explain why your chosen holiday would be appealing to different types of visitor.

LINK IT UP

In Learning aim A you explored the work of the National Trust. The National Trust also offers a range of volunteering opportunities to help conserve many of the countryside areas it looks after.

Holiday parks

Holiday parks can be a very appealing option to many visitors looking for lots of different activities all in one place. Holiday parks were once incredibly popular in the UK, providing families and friends with a range of indoor and outdoor entertainment and accommodation, including live shows, swimming pools, rides and competitions.

One of the most well-known brands of holiday park is Butlin's. Founded by Billy Butlin, the first park opened in 1936 in Skegness. The unpredictable British weather meant that many parks became less popular when package holidays to the Mediterranean became popular in the 1970s. More recently, holiday parks have re-invented themselves with more indoor activities and facilities to cope with all weathers, including spas and shopping facilities.

Butlin's still has three popular seaside resorts in Skegness, Minehead and Bognor Regis. Other popular holiday park brands include Haven, Pontins, Hoseasons, Parkdean Resorts and Center Parcs.

ACTIVITY

- Working in small groups, carry out some research into different types of holiday park in different regions of the UK. Try to find an example of a traditional seaside holiday park and one other example.
- Working together, complete a mindmap to highlight the similarities and differences in the products and services the two parks offer to their customers.

CHECK MY LEARNING

Having completed your own presentation on a selected voluntary and conservation holiday available in the UK, you should now watch a presentation from some of your peers. Review the presentation and make a list of the positive aspects and anything you would change. Did the presentation make it clear why the holiday would appeal to different types of visitor?

Types of accommodation (1)

GETTING STARTED

Pick **two** types of accommodation from the diagram and, with a partner, list two or three specific features of each of your choices and compare them.

LINK IT UP

Refer back to Learning aim A to refresh your understanding of different types of accommodation provider and the range of facilities and services provided by many hotels.

From luxury hotels to basic campsites and everything in between, the travel and tourism sector has a full range of accommodation options to meet the needs, preferences and budgets of different visitor types. It is important to understand how the different accommodation options on offer can impact on the appeal of destinations to different types of visitor.

Tourist destinations often provide visitors with a range of different accommodation types, including those illustrated in Figure 1.11.

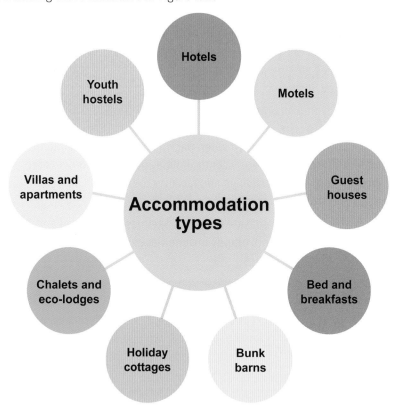

◫ Figure 1.11: How many of these accommodation types have you stayed in?

Serviced and non-serviced accommodation

Different types of accommodation are often categorised as serviced or non-serviced. Serviced accommodation includes a number of guest services in the price, for example housekeeping services to clean and make up the room, to change the bed linen and towels and to refresh the facilities, such as the mini-bar. There is often a range of meal services available too, such as breakfast and dinner. Serviced accommodation is usually provided in hotels, guest houses and bed and breakfasts. Non-serviced accommodation provides less services to visitors. Often referred to as self-catering, non-serviced accommodation is often cheaper, but visitors will need to cook and clean for themselves for the duration of their stay. Non-serviced accommodation often includes self-catering apartments, chalets and villas, and camping and caravan sites.

DID YOU KNOW?

QuirkyAccom.com (www.quirkyaccom.com) provides a list of more unusual accommodation options for visitors looking for something a little bit different, including yachts, tree houses, castles and even former prisons. The Landmark Trust rescues buildings of historic merit and turns them into unusual holiday accommodation.

All-inclusive and self-catering accommodation

When staying in accommodation on an all-inclusive basis, visitors get all their meals (breakfast, lunch and dinner) and selected drinks included with the price of the holiday. This is appealing to visitors looking to manage how much they spend as there should be no hidden surprises. Different accommodation providers often have different levels of all-inclusive rates, offering premium packages for those who prefer to pay a little more.

Self-catering accommodation is often found in apartments, holiday cottages, villas and chalets. They are usually equipped with kitchen and dining facilities to allow visitors to make their own meals. This can be appealing to those travelling on a budget.

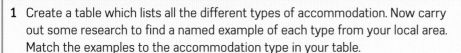

ACTIVITY

1   Create a table which lists all the different types of accommodation. Now carry out some research to find a named example of each type from your local area. Match the examples to the accommodation type in your table.

2   In a second table, make a list of all the different visitor types you can think of and match each one to a type of accommodation that would appeal to them.

Youth hostels

Not just for younger travellers, youth hostels provide affordable accommodation often in very central or scenic locations. Visitors often share a large room, or dormitory, with other people, and share a bathroom, kitchen and social areas with the other guests. Youth hostelling can be a great way to meet fellow travellers, sharing stories and swapping notes on the best places to visit. Many hostels also offer some private rooms at higher prices for visitors looking for more privacy and peace and quiet.

DID YOU KNOW?

The Youth Hostel Association (www.yha.org) was founded in 1930. The charity now provides over 150 hostels and 45 campsites for visitors across England and Wales.

▣ Visitors to youth hostels will often share a room, or dormitory.

CHECK MY LEARNING

Choose an example of a local accommodation provider and make a list of all the facilities and services they offer to their customers.

Types of accommodation (2)

GETTING STARTED

Working in a small group, design a quiz for another group to test their knowledge of different types of accommodation and accommodation providers. Make sure you know the answers too!

While some visitors like to book a hotel for their visit to a new city or resort, visitors looking to explore a wider area, or more destinations, might choose a different type of accommodation. But what are these options and why would they appeal to different visitors?

Touring accommodation

Campsites

Visitors pay a fee to place their tent on a given 'pitch' or area of the site. Some camping sites are very basic and offer little more than the pitch and a toilet block. Other campsites include a range of visitor services and facilities, such as hot showers and shops to buy essential supplies.

More recently, up-market camping options have become more popular. Glamorous camping, or 'glamping', offers visitors larger and more secure tents, such as yurts, along with other useful facilities, such as mobile phone charging points and Wi-Fi. Glamping options are appealing to those attending music festivals who can afford to pay for a little more luxury.

Touring caravans

For travellers with their own caravan or motorhome, touring caravan sites provide individual pitches for hire and additional services, such as connections to electricity and gas supplies. Larger sites also have additional services, such as an on-site shop, bar and restaurant and maybe even a pool, leisure and social facilities to appeal to families.

Boats

DID YOU KNOW?

The city of Birmingham has 35 miles of canals, that's nine miles more than Venice!

An alternative form of touring accommodation can be found on boats, such as barges and narrowboats for example. Travelling the waterways can be a relaxing holiday option for many visitors, who take the time to wind their way along canals, through locks and across aqueducts. Boats offer compact accommodation, often including a small kitchen area, bathroom and seating and sleeping areas. Boats can be moored at specific sites for a small fee, often with access to showers and refreshment areas.

Motels

Motels (a combination of motor and hotels) provide accommodation close to major roads and motorways for travellers on long journeys. Very popular in the USA, motels are also found in the UK, often at larger motorway service stations with ample car parking space. Along with the basic accommodation provided by the motel, the service stations often provide additional facilities for travellers looking to break their journey when touring on a long trip, for example an on-site restaurant and basic shopping facilities.

ACTIVITY

In small groups, choose a specific destination and **two** different visitor types from the list below. Carry out some research to explore the range of accommodation options in that area that would appeal to your chosen visitor types.

Visitor profiles	Destinations
Solo traveller looking to make friends	Lake District National Park
Family looking for activities to keep the kids entertained	Glasgow
A group of friends travelling on a tight budget	Margate
A couple looking for a romantic short break to celebrate an anniversary	Isle of Man
A visitor with restricted mobility taking a short city break	Belfast

Create a summary of your chosen options and get ready to present your reasons as to why your chosen accommodation options would appeal to your selected visitor type. Try to list as many reasons as possible.

 Motels are normally very basic; just a bed for the night for those breaking a journey.

CHECK MY LEARNING

Having completed your own presentation on your chosen accommodation option, you should now watch a presentation from some of your peers. Review the presentation and consider if the option selected was appropriate to meet the needs of the visitor.

Learning aim B: assessment practice

How you will be assessed

In this component, you will be assessed by completing an internally assessed assignment set by your teacher. They will provide you with an assignment brief that outlines what you will need to do, as well as a date by which the assignment should be completed and submitted. You may be required to complete a number of tasks, including producing reports, presentations or posters, for example. The teacher will mark the assignment and tell you what grade you have achieved.

For Learning aim B you will be expected to show that you know about different types of travel and tourism destinations and the different features that would appeal to different types of visitor. You should understand the different reasons why people travel and the types of holiday and accommodation they choose to meet their specific needs. This will include:

- describing the types of visitor who visit a UK tourist destination
- discussing how the features of a chosen UK tourist destination contribute to its appeal for visitors
- evaluating the appeal of the chosen UK tourist destination for different types of visitor.

CHECKPOINT

Review your learning of this component by answering the following questions; this will help you prepare for your assignment.

Strengthen

- Identify different types of tourism and the different reasons why people travel.
- Describe the features of a named UK seaside, countryside and city destination, explaining some of the features of each and why they would appeal to visitors.
- Compare the key differences between package and tailor-made holidays.
- Explain the differences between serviced and non-serviced accommodation, giving examples for each.

Challenge

- Explain how climatic conditions and seasonal variations affect the appeal of a UK destination.
- Evaluate how the geographic features of a UK destination appeal to different types of visitor.

ASSESSMENT ACTIVITY 1 | LEARNING AIM B

Choose a specific travel and tourism destination in the UK and investigate the features affecting the appeal of the destination, such as the transport links, attractions and types and range of holidays available there.

- Identify the *type* of destination.
- Describe the *types* of visitor at the destination.
- Describe their *reasons* for travel.
- Explain how the main *features* of the destination appeal to visitors.

Now go on to discuss and evaluate how the features increase the appeal of your chosen destination for different types of visitor.

Present your findings in a magazine article format, using relevant images and statistics to support your findings.

TIP

Each year, ABTA produces a report which explores the holiday habits of UK visitors. Check the latest report to explore attitudes to planning and booking holidays over the last year. Look on the ABTA website for the 'ABTA holiday habits reports'.

ASSESSMENT ACTIVITY 2 | LEARNING AIM B

You have secured a work placement at your local tourist information centre run by the local authority. Visitor numbers to the area have been declining recently and the authority is looking to launch a new marketing campaign to highlight the appealing features of the destination to different types of visitor.

Your supervisor has asked you to put together a presentation to highlight these appealing features, so they can choose the main ones to focus on as part of the new campaign.

Your presentation should:

- explain the main features of the destination that appeal to visitors
- describe the types of visitors who currently visit the destination and some of their reasons for travel, with examples
- discuss and evaluate how the features of the destination appeal to different visitor types.

You will present your findings, supported by a copy of your presentation and any supporting notes you have made.

TIP

In this assessment, make sure you provide detailed examples of different types of visitor who visit the destination and the reasons that they travel.

TIP

Try to be specific when evaluating which aspects of the destination are appealing for different visitor types. For example, when exploring types of accommodation, what are the features of specific hotels that might appeal to a couple looking to celebrate a significant anniversary or their honeymoon?

TAKE IT FURTHER

Have you identified **all** the different features of your chosen destination? Make sure you have considered all the different features that contribute to the appeal of your chosen destination for different visitor types, not just the ones that appeal to you personally.

02 Influences on Global Travel and Tourism

Introduction

You will be aware that the travel and tourism sector is affected by many different factors. These factors range from naturally occurring events such as earthquakes and tsunamis, to human events such as major terrorist incidents and global economic recession. Did you know that how destinations respond to such factors often depends on how economically developed they are?

Tourism can have a positive effect on destinations and their host communities; the way a destination is managed is of critical importance. Sustainable tourism management can amplify the positive benefits of tourism while reducing or eliminating the negative impacts. What do you think the benefits of more destinations engaging with the principles of sustainable tourism could be?

LEARNING AIMS

In this component you will learn about:

A	Factors that influence global travel and tourism
B	Impact of travel and tourism and sustainability
C	Destination management.

Factors influencing global travel and tourism

GETTING STARTED

Working with support from your teacher, define the following key terms: 'disposable income', 'recession'/'boom', 'exchange rates'. Now compare your definitions with another student.

There is a wide range of factors that can have a massive impact on travel and tourism organisations and destinations. These factors influence visitor choice about which destinations to travel to and also require organisations to respond and adapt their products and services.

Economic factors

It is important to understand that economic factors are dynamic and change all the time; for example, fluctuations in exchange rates can affect the cost of outbound holidays and an economic recession can make people less willing to spend a lot of money on a holiday.

Recession

A recession is a slowdown in economic activity, measured by looking at economic output over two successive quarters (six months). A major global recession began in late 2007 and ended in 2013 in the UK. This caused issues for travel and tourism organisations as people had less **disposable income**. Even when the UK came out of recession, by 2013, tourism industry research found that in the UK, 18 per cent fewer people were visiting global destinations than before the recession (Figure 2.1).

Boom

An economic boom or 'boom time' is when the economy of a country experiences medium- or long-term periods of growth. The tourism sector can benefit hugely during a boom period because people are more willing to spend their disposable income on luxury products such as holidays.

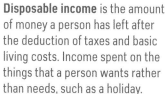

KEY TERM

Disposable income is the amount of money a person has left after the deduction of taxes and basic living costs. Income spent on the things that a person wants rather than needs, such as a holiday.

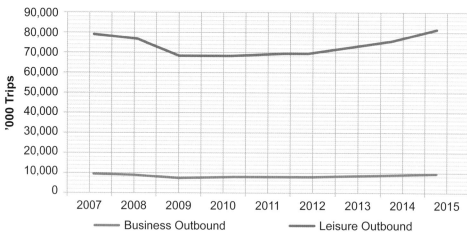

▣ Figure 2.1: How did the global recession impact on travel and tourism organisations and destinations?

Levels of employment

Employment levels measure how many people of working age are in employment at any one time. One impact of the 2007 global recession was higher unemployment. By 2010, an estimated 1.3 million people in the UK had lost their jobs due to the recession. As the economic recession initially led to a fall in employment levels within countries such as the UK, this led to fewer people taking both domestic and outbound holidays.

Fuel costs

Fuel costs change all the time, usually depending on the wholesale price of oil. Fuel costs are a significant expense for organisations that operate within the transport sector. Rising fuel prices can affect the profitability of organisations, such as airlines and coach operators. Sometimes organisations pass on the increase in fuel prices to customers by increasing the prices of their products. In July 2018, Delta Airlines announced that they expected to regain US$2 billion in higher fuel costs partly by increasing ticket prices.

In the UK fuel prices rose 50 per cent between June 2017 and August 2018. Along with passing on fuel price increases to customers, many airlines often consider reducing the number of flights they operate in order to save costs and make the operation of each flight as profitable as possible.

Currency exchange

This is the value of the currency of one country against another; rates of currency exchange are constantly changing. This will affect how much a tourist's money is worth when they exchange it to another currency. The exchange rate is important because it can affect the amount of money that tourists have available to spend on products and services, such as accommodation, meals out, entertainment and gift shopping.

ACTIVITY

Working in a small group, select an economic factor to think about. Discuss how this economic factor affects tourism. Could this economic factor have a negative impact on tourism? Could this economic factor have a positive impact on tourism?

Find any data that might support your research. For example, you could find employment data linked to tourism at: https://www.ons.gov.uk/peoplepopulationandcommunity/leisureandtourism/datasets/tourismemploymentsummaries.

	% main and second jobs in tourism industries (2013–2014)	% main and second jobs in accommodation and food and beverage-serving activities (2013–2014)	% main and second jobs in passenger transport, culture, sport and recreation services (2013–2014)
Blackpool	16.36	9.25	7.10
Orkney Islands	15.49	8.42	7.08
Brighton and Hove	14.69	7.77	6.92
Shetland Islands	12.02	5.91	6.10
Isle of Anglesey	14.00	8.13	5.87
Outer London – South	9.88	4.08	5.79
Edinburgh, City of	12.42	6.92	5.50
York	14.71	9.44	5.28

Do some parts of the UK rely on tourism industries for employment more than others?

The UK voted to leave the European Union (EU), an economic and political union of member states, in June 2016. In the following month the value of the pound against the euro fell by 10 per cent and against the dollar by 13 per cent. This meant that inbound travellers visiting the UK would find that they had more money to spend. Flight bookings to the UK increased by 4.3 per cent in the month that followed. Hotels.com reported that hotel searches by Americans for UK destinations had increased 50 per cent year on year since the referendum.

ACTIVITY

Select a global destination to explore. Find at least one example of data that highlights an increase or decrease in tourism within that destination over the last ten years. This data could include visitor numbers, visitor spending, numbers of attractions etc. Check out the European Commission website, and the website of tourism agencies in your chosen destination.

Write a conclusion about whether or not tourism in your selected destination has increased or decreased, in which you refer to the data. Create a PowerPoint® presentation summary of your research findings.

LINK IT UP

Staycations are defined and discussed in Component 1. Have you recently taken a holiday 'at home'?

CHECK MY LEARNING

Work in groups to present your Power Point® presentations created in the previous activity, then make notes on each group's presentations. Can you answer the following questions?

- How does economic recession affect employment?
- How do changes to fuel costs impact on visitors?
- How do exchange rates impact on visitor spending?

Political factors influencing global travel and tourism (1)

GETTING STARTED

In pairs, look at the following list, which includes examples of different legislation and regulations:
- visitor security
- equality
- customer financial protection
- developing services and facilities
- controlling development
- health and safety laws
- employment laws
- planning laws.

Identify any examples of the above that you are already aware of. Why is the legislation or regulation used? How is it important for the travel and tourism sector?

KEY TERMS

Legislation means laws made by a government, e.g. UK Health and Safety at Work etc. Act 1974.

Regulations are rules set and monitored by an administrative body, such as the UK Trading Standards Institute.

Political factors affect global organisations and destinations in a wide range of ways. For example, different countries have different legislation and regulations that can affect how a tourist gains entry to that country. Furthermore, factors such as political instability can affect how desirable a country is to visit.

Legislation and regulation

Legislation and **regulations** in global destinations can affect visitors in a number of ways (Table 2.1). Certain laws are put in place to try to ensure visitor security or protect the destination. For example, according to foreign travel advice, tourists visiting the USA will be required to prove that they have enough money to support them during their visit.

Some countries have legislation and regulations that are influenced by religion and culture. For example, in Dubai it is forbidden to eat and drink in public during daylight hours during Ramadan, however, hotels are often exempt from such rules. Other expectations in Dubai including dressing appropriately in public; for women this includes covering exposed skin from the shoulders to the knees. Popular public locations such as The Dubai Mall often broadcast announcements reminding visitors to dress appropriately.

 Table 2.1: Examples of how legislation and regulation are used

Legislation	Example	Advantages	Disadvantages
Visitor security	National identity proof laws – all foreign visitors to France must carry a passport or national identity card.	Can help police and security forces monitor people using airports and railway stations.	Security checks can increase waiting times at airports and railway stations.
Equality	Australian Human Rights Commission Act 1986 – ensures equal rights for all people in Australia, including visitors.	It is illegal to discriminate against people based on a range of factors including race, colour, sex, religion and sexual orientation.	The laws are not always applied consistently across different Australian states and territories.
Customer financial protection	Package Travel Regulations – protect consumer rights when booking a package holiday.	Customers are able to claim a refund or compensation if the holiday doesn't match the description given when booked.	Customers who have booked the components of their holiday separately and not as a package holiday are unlikely to have legal or financial protection.

Legislation	Example	Advantages	Disadvantages
Developing services and facilities	Tourism Act 2011 (Kenya) – an act of parliament to provide for the development of sustainable tourism and tourism-related activities in Kenya.	Such an act can encourage the development of tourism in a country like Kenya. One of the main benefits is generating income and creating employment for Kenyan people through tourism.	Many tour operators, such as Kuoni Travel, offer all-inclusive holidays to Kenya. However, visitors on all-inclusive holidays are often less inclined to spend money in the local area.
Controlling development	Barcelona's licensing laws – in 2017, local government banned new hotels and visitor apartments from opening in Barcelona city centre.	This law may help to preserve the character of Barcelona's historic city centre by preventing over-development of the area.	Fewer hotels and apartments may lead to a shortage of accommodation for visitors to Barcelona.
Health and safety laws	UK Health and Safety at Work etc. Act 1974 – ensures that both employees and guests in travel and tourism facilities are kept safe.	This act helps to ensure that visitors are kept safe when visiting UK travel and tourism facilities.	How well organisations follow health and safety procedures can vary.
Employment laws	USA Equal Employment Opportunity Commission (EEOC) – the EEOC ensures employees, including those working in the travel and tourism sector are protected by federal laws.	The EEOC ensures that employees are protected against discrimination, harassment and unfair treatment by managers, co-workers and others in the workplace.	Not all organisations are subject to EEOC laws; smaller businesses with fewer than 15 employees are not liable for discrimination complaints.
Planning laws	UNESCO – locations that are designated World Heritage Sites by UNESCO are discouraged from planning tourism development that detracts from the character of the site.	Strict planning regulations can help to preserve the character of historic locations and attractions. This approach can help to preserve World Heritage Sites for the future.	Many World Heritage Sites are located in poor countries that would benefit from tourism development. Developing World Heritage Sites carefully could help to encourage tourism in such locations.

DID YOU KNOW?

Unique planning and building regulations in Dubai have helped to encourage the development of some of the most amazing structures in the world, such as the Burj Khalifa, which, in 2019, is the world's tallest building at over 800 metres high.

Political factors influencing global travel and tourism (2)

Passport and visa entry requirements

To travel from the UK, a tourist needs to have a valid passport in order to leave the country and gain entry to outbound destinations. Some countries also require a valid visa or special application to travel there. For example, in order to travel to the USA from the UK a tourist will need to apply to travel through the Visa Waiver Programme, which allows a 'British Citizen' to enter the USA for up to 90 days. The Electronic System for Travel Authorisation (ESTA) is an automated system used to determine if visitors who apply to visit the USA via the Visa Waiver Programme pose a security or law enforcement risk.

Governments promote tourism through funding and tax incentives

Tourism can benefit host destinations in a number of ways; for example, by providing employment in tourism-related jobs. Therefore, governments are keen to encourage tourism development in any way they can. In the UK, VisitBritain reported that in 2017/18 for every £1 the government had invested in VisitBritain for domestic and international marketing, visitors spent an additional £25 in Britain.

In Kenya, the government has tried to stimulate domestic tourism by using tax incentives, such as removing VAT charges on air tickets and park entrance fees and allowing employers to deduct the cost of providing paid holidays to employees from their taxes.

> **ACTIVITY**
>
> Working in pairs, research the entry requirements for British citizens with a full UK passport travelling to one chosen destination using www.gov.uk/foreign-travel-advice.
> - Can you identify the passport/visa requirements?
> - Do these apply to all visitors or just to those from certain countries?
> - Does this country charge a departure tax when visitors leave?

Trade and taxes

Some countries impose departure taxes when people leave the country. For example, the UK has an Air Passenger Duty (APD) charge on all aircraft that weigh 5.7 tonnes or have more than 20 seats for passengers. The APD charge is usually added to the flight cost. Other countries such as Australia, China and Egypt charge a similar departure tax when a person uses one of their airports to leave the country.

ACTIVITY

Working in small groups, discuss the question: do airport taxes affect visitor numbers? There are useful videos available on Dubai airport and Queensland in Australia. To help you answer this question think about the following.
- Which countries apply airport taxes?
- What is the opinion of key **stakeholders** about these taxes? Look for newspaper articles and other sources.

Write down your answers and share them as a class.

Political instability

Civil unrest

Over the years, there has often been political turmoil in some tourist-receiving countries in North Africa and the Middle East. This most recent political instability began with the 'Arab Spring' uprising, which originated in Tunisia in December 2010. The 'Arab Spring' uprisings brought about much civil unrest in these places; initially many tour operators cancelled holidays to affected destinations. For example, TUI cancelled all holidays to Egypt in order to protect the safety of their customers. Events like this can affect the reputation of destinations; Tunisia suffered a loss in tourism due to the civil unrest triggered by the 'Arab Spring.' However, tourism in Tunisia was further damaged in 2015 when a terrorist attack occurred in the destination of Sousse. Thirty-eight people were killed in the attack, including 30 British tourists.

In 2018 there were widespread protests against fuel price rises in France. Some of these protests turned violent and led to the disruption of travel, as major motorways and roads were blocked. As a result, the Foreign and Commonwealth Office (FCO) advised that visitors to France from the UK do everything possible to avoid areas where protests might be happening and check advice issued by travel operators before visiting.

War

The threat of the outbreak of war can have an impact similar to civil unrest on tourism. Mainly, visitor safety cannot be guaranteed and therefore the FCO advises against all travel to affected areas. For example, as of November 2018, the FCO was still advising against all travel to Syria, a country that was devastated by a civil war. The main reason for this travel advice is that the situation in the country remains unpredictable and dangerous, partly due to the presence of terrorist organisations.

ACTIVITY

Working in pairs, discuss the different political factors that you have studied.
- List the positive impacts that these factors have had on global tourism.
- List the negative impacts that these factors have had on global tourism.
- Predict how these factors might impact on tourism in the future.

CHECK MY LEARNING

Review the notes that you have made over the last two lessons. Create at least five revision questions about the impacts of tourism from your notes. For example, 'How does political instability and war impact on tourism?'

KEY TERM

A **stakeholder** is a person or organisation that has an interest in the business or project. This can include the local community, customers, suppliers and businesses. Stakeholders can include organisations from the public, private and voluntary sectors.

DID YOU KNOW?

The French Retail Federation estimates that French retailers lost about €1 billion in the first two weeks after the protests began on November 17th 2018, with restaurant trade declining by up to 50 per cent.

LINK IT UP

Further on in this component, you will learn more about the roles that local and national government play in setting entry requirements, including passport and visa requirements. Why do you think this is such an important issue?

Natural disasters influencing global travel and tourism

GETTING STARTED

Working in pairs, list examples of natural disasters you can remember that have affected tourism; for example, the 2018 California wildfires. For one natural disaster from your list, think about the following.
- Where did the disaster happen?
- What damage was caused to affected destinations?
- What were the impacts for tourism?

Natural disasters are dramatic, unpredictable and can have a huge impact on the travel and tourism industry. Many of the world's most popular tourist destinations are located in areas that are affected by natural disasters. Would you be happy to take a holiday in a destination that had previously experienced a natural disaster?

Natural disasters – geological hazards

Recent natural disasters have had a dramatic impact on global travel and tourism destinations. In July and August 2018, a series of earthquakes struck Lombok in Indonesia, killing over 550 people in total. Lombok is a popular holiday destination with tourism an important source of income for the area. A lot of the **infrastructure** that was important to the tourism industry was damaged or destroyed during the earthquakes.

It was estimated by Indonesian authorities that the total value of destroyed infrastructure and facilities could be as high as US$342 million. However, it is believed that impacts on tourism from the earthquake will be temporary; a local business owner commented that 'History shows that even after the worst scenarios... tourists will always come back. Lombok is such as beautiful place.'

Table 2.2 gives examples of other recent natural disasters.

KEY TERM

Infrastructure is the structures and facilities, such as roads, buildings and power supplies, that enable a tourist destination to function properly.

◻ **Table 2.2: Examples of recent natural disasters**

Natural disaster	Example	Impacts upon tourism
Volcanic eruption	In 2018, Volcán de Fuego, Guatemala erupted.	At least 159 people were killed and volcanic ash forced the closure of La Aurora International Airport in Guatemala City.
Tsunami	In 2018, a 7.5 magnitude earthquake triggered a tsunami that hit the city of Palu in Indonesia.	Over 1000 people were killed in the tsunami. The FCO advised that British visitors to the area exercise caution and stay away from collapsed buildings. The FCO went on to advise that certain areas such as the Gili Islands were especially vulnerable.
Sink holes	In 2018, a sinkhole appeared in Lewisham in south London.	The sinkhole trapped a coach full of tourists. The London Fire Brigade helped 40 tourists to escape from the coach, which was carrying 90 passengers.

ACTIVITY

Find a video online that discusses the effects of a natural disaster on tourism. Then working individually, make notes on this disaster by answering the following questions.
- Where was affected?
- What were the short-term impacts for tourism businesses?
- What were the longer-term impacts for tourism infrastructure?
- How did this natural disaster influence people's choice of the location as a tourist destination?

Severe weather events – weather hazards

Severe weather events affect certain parts of the world on a regular basis (Table 2.3). The eastern coastline of the USA is regularly hit by hurricanes. In October 2012, Hurricane Sandy devastated the city of New York, causing billions of dollars' worth of damage. Many tourist-hosting facilities within the city, such as the New York City Subway, were shut down.

◘ **Table 2.3: Examples of recent severe weather events**

Severe weather event	Example	Impacts on tourism
Flooding	In August 2017, a series of floods in South Asia struck India, Nepal and Bangladesh.	Over 1200 people were killed in the floods. Lots of infrastructure, such as roads and electricity towers, which support tourism in India, Nepal and Bangladesh, was destroyed.
Drought	Since 2014, Kenya has been suffering from an ongoing drought.	Many of the country's natural visitor attractions, such as game reserves and national parks, have been suffering as dozens of wild animals living in the parks have died due to a lack of water.
Fires	In 2018, a series of destructive wildfires burned across northern California and southern Oregon in the USA.	The fires caused more than US$2,975 billion damage and killed over 100 civilians and six firefighters. Many major tourist-receiving areas were damaged, including Yosemite National Park.
Landslides	In 2017, there was a series of deadly landslides in three hilly districts of Bangladesh.	The landslides killed at least 150 people and damaged tourism infrastructure, such as telecommunications systems and caused power cuts.
Tornados	Between January 21st and January 23rd 2017, a series of tornados stuck the south-eastern USA.	In total, 20 people were killed during the outbreak of tornados. In Georgia alone, an estimated US$400 million damage was caused to facilities, infrastructure and housing.
Avalanches	Between November 2017 and March 2018, a series of deadly avalanches occurred in the French Alps.	In total, 25 people were killed in the series of avalanches. In response to this, the Minister of the Interior for France warned those participating in winter sports to take the utmost caution.
Snowstorms	During the winter of 2017–2018, many parts of Europe were affected by freezing conditions and heavy snow caused by a Siberian weather system.	As many as 55 people died as a result of the extreme cold and snow. The weather system called 'the beast from the east' even caused snow in parts of southern Europe, such as on the beaches of the French Riviera. Many European airports, such as Dublin airport, were forced to cancel flights.

ACTIVITY

Working in small groups, discuss how a severe weather event from Table 2.3 might affect a destination and the tourists that visit. You will need to consider the short-, medium- and long- term impacts of this event on business, infrastructure and visitors.

Possible effects

Poorer countries tend to rely on income from tourism more than richer countries, as a proportion of their GDP. Therefore, the impact of natural disasters can be even more devastating for poorer countries. Many individuals and smaller businesses offering tourist products and services in poorer countries do not have the same levels of protection from insurance and government support as those in wealthier countries. Furthermore, when infrastructure such as roads become damaged this can cut off access to the areas that are popular with visitors.

Flight cancellations are often a precaution when an area has been hit by a natural disaster; this can result in the **repatriation** of affected tourists being delayed. In some cases, airports are temporarily shut, which can also further delay repatriation.

LINK IT UP

Understanding how tourism contributes to a country's Gross Domestic Product (GDP) is an important part of Component 1. Can you explain how tourism can benefit a country's economy?

KEY TERM

Repatriation is the return of a person to their country of origin.

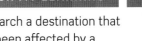

CHECK MY LEARNING

Research a destination that has been affected by a natural disaster in the last five years and make notes about it. Include answers to the following.

- What was the name of the destination?
- What type of natural disaster affected the destination?
- What were the impacts for tourism in the destination?

Media, publicity and image influencing global travel and tourism

GETTING STARTED

Working in pairs, think about the influence that media and publicity have on the image of destinations.
- List five ways that the media and publicity can have a positive effect on the image of a destination.
- List five ways that the media and publicity can have a negative effect on the image of a destination.

The media has a powerful role in the promotion of global tourism. The images portrayed can have a big impact on the popularity of destinations and the numbers of visitors that go there.

Types of media

Over the last few years new forms of media, such as social media, have grown increasingly in popularity. Traditional printed media (newspapers and travel books) is in decline compared with online media, partly due to the increase in popularity of handheld technology, such as tablets and smartphones. When using such technology, people now have instant access to online review sites such as TripAdvisor, travel blogs, Expedia destination guides available via YouTube and online news reports.

The use of locations in film and TV programmes brings exposure, as does coverage of international events and sporting competitions.

Negative effects on destinations

A number of European summer sun destinations, such as Magaluf, Faliraki and to some extent Benidorm, all have reputations as 'wild party' resorts, fuelled by negative media coverage.

The BBC series *Stacey Dooley Investigates* portrayed a range of destinations, such as Sunny Beach, Bulgaria, as cheap, cheerful and rowdy party locations popular with young adults. However, at the same time, each episode highlighted the negative impacts of tourism in such locations. For example, episodes exposed the pressures that dealing with drunk holidaymakers places on the emergency services in tourist destinations.

Positive effects on destinations

Coverage of special events can show places in a really positive light. For example, an article on BBC News commented that the 2018 World Cup was a public relations triumph for Russia. Similarly, the 2012 Summer Olympics in London was widely praised as having generated valuable positive publicity for the UK.

ACTIVITY

Working in pairs, list the ways in which a travel review website such as TripAdvisor may be useful for tourists. Think about the following questions.
- What sort of information does the website contain?
- Are the comments made in the reviews fair?
- Are they a reliable source of information?

How media exposure of global destinations can affect visitor numbers

Favourable exposure of global destinations can have a positive effect on visitor numbers. For example, visiting locations used in films and TV shows is popular with tourists. Destinations featured in the HBO series *Game of Thrones* have seen a dramatic growth in visitor numbers. Locations used in the series include Spain, Croatia and Northern Ireland.

◪ **Dubrovnik in Croatia is one of many filming locations featured in the HBO TV series** *Game of Thrones* **– would you like to visit here?**

One of the most popular locations that is frequently featured in television and films is Times Square in New York. Times Square is a popular movie location and has been featured in the likes of *Spiderman*, *Superman*, *Captain America* and *Annie*. Times Square receives approximately 50 million visits per year, making it one of the most visited locations in the world.

However, unfavourable media exposure of global destinations can have a negative impact on visitor numbers. In 2018, www.travelmarketreport.com commented that negative media coverage and US State Department warnings impacted on the number of travellers looking to book holidays in the Mexican resorts of Cancun and Los Cabos.

ACTIVITY

Working in small groups, research a location from a popular TV show. For example, Majorca was used as the location for *Love Island 2018*. Create a PowerPoint® presentation that looks at the following questions.
- What have the positive impacts of this publicity been for the location?
- What have the negative impacts of this publicity been for the location?
- What do you think the impact has been on the people that live there?

DID YOU KNOW?

According to TripAdvisor, visits to Castle of Zafra in Spain have increased 488 per cent since it was featured in *Game of Thrones*. Why has being featured on a TV show had such a huge impact on visitor numbers?

LINK IT UP

Further on in this component, you will study how health risks can impact on the image of the destination. Why do you think this is?

CHECK MY LEARNING

Share your presentation from the previous activity with the whole class. Make notes on the other groups' examples. Can you answer the following questions?
- How can the media affect the image of a destination?
- How can the media influence visitors' choices?
- Why are some locations more popular with the media than others?

Safety and security concerns influencing global travel and tourism

GETTING STARTED

Working in pairs, make a list of safety and security concerns that tourists might:
- have before they decide to travel
- experience once they are on their holiday.

A tourist in an unfamiliar environment may naturally feel vulnerable when visiting a destination for the first time. Safety and security is one of the most important factors to be considered when planning a visit, especially for a family with young children or for a solo traveller. If a destination has a reputation for crime, including against tourists, this can affect the image of the place.

Risks relating to personal safety

Staying safe makes the difference between a dream holiday and a nightmare experience. Being in an unfamiliar area can be an intimidating experience, especially if a language barrier prevents communication with other people. Risks relating to personal safety may include:
- theft of personal belongings, such as wallets and handbags
- getting lost in a new environment, particularly if signage is in a foreign language
- accidents relating to not understanding the local area; for example, chaotic road traffic systems.

ACTIVITY

Working in pairs, select a destination and use https://www.gov.uk/foreign-travel-advice to research Foreign and Commonwealth Office (FCO) advice on safety and security for that destination.

Create a poster to advise visitors of the main issues and precautions that they should take when visiting the destination. Include:
- a heading for the poster that highlights the name of the destination
- information about any FCO advice that has been issued about the destination
- a summary of the main precautions that visitors to the destination should take.

Safety measures

In order to keep tourists safe on holiday, authorities and travel providers will often use a range of safety measures. These are not only designed to stop problems arising, but they also provide visual reassurance that the authorities or travel providers are taking security seriously. An example of a safety measure that is routinely used is bag checks when entering museums, theatres and attractions; this is in response to the threat of terrorism.

DID YOU KNOW?

In 2018, the UK government announced that it was committing £1.8 million to fund innovation in airport security. The aim of the initiative is to develop new technology that improves airport security while speeding up the screening process for passengers.

Airport safety

Airports tend to have the most stringent safety measures of any organisation in the travel and tourism sector. These include individuals and/or luggage being screened by a security scanner. Furthermore, most airports publicise a list of items banned from hand luggage, including acid, snooker balls, explosives, knives, scissors and toy guns.

Security checks can be time-consuming, particularly during busy periods, and can be a cause of delays and inconvenience, particularly at airports.

Safety guidance

Some organisations, such as the Foreign and Commonwealth Office (FCO), will issue very specific safety and security advice to tourists about which areas of the world are not safe for them to travel to. For example, in September 2018 the FCO advised against all travel to the North Sinai area of Egypt due to criminal activity and continued terrorist attacks on police and security forces in the area.

More general guidance may be issued by travel companies, such as Trivago, which offer specific travel safety tips for staying safe in destinations such as New York. These include times to avoid certain areas, areas to avoid entirely and how to keep possessions safe. Advice can also cover awareness of the risks of being in an unfamiliar area and those posed by the natural environment, such as venomous animals or poisonous plants.

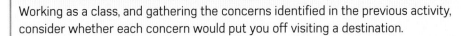

ACTIVITY

Working as a class, and gathering the concerns identified in the previous activity, consider whether each concern would put you off visiting a destination.

Effects of safety and security on the appeal of destinations

If a destination is no longer seen as safe, this can be devastating for the tourism industry. After a gunman attacked the Tunisian resort of Sousse in 2015, British tour operators cancelled holidays to Tunisia. As the FCO warned against travel to Tunisia, tour operators were unable to operate holidays to the country. Such warnings invalidate travel insurance to countries that the FCO warns against visiting. This travel advice from the FCO was effectively a travel ban to Tunisia. It was lifted in 2017.

After the 2015 Sousse shootings and a number of other incidents that occurred in places such as Tunisia, Turkey and Egypt, holiday firms reported that bookings to 'safer' destinations such as Spain and Portugal increased. However, the economic impacts for Tunisia, Turkey and Egypt have been quite severe. In 2014, the year before the Sousse attack, 430,000 people from Britain visited Tunisia. In 2017, the number was just 28,000.

In order to persuade tour operators and visitors that Tunisia is a safe country to visit, the Tunisian government introduced a series of 'exceptional measures', including extra security around tourist sites, along with financial support for tourist organisations, reduced taxes and relaxed visa requirements for visitors.

LINK IT UP

In Component 1, you will have looked at how different features contribute to the appeal of destinations in detail. How much of an effect do you think safety and security issues have on the appeal of a destination?

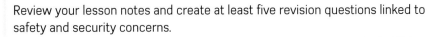

CHECK MY LEARNING

Review your lesson notes and create at least five revision questions linked to safety and security concerns.

Health risks and precautions influencing global travel and tourism

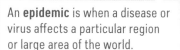

GETTING STARTED

Working individually, follow your teacher's instructions to create a mind map that outlines health risks and possible prevention methods from around the world. This could include research using FCO advice from www.gov. uk/foreign-travel-advice.

KEY TERMS

An **epidemic** is when a disease or virus affects a particular region or large area of the world.

A **pandemic** is the worldwide spread of a disease.

In 2013, there was a terrible Ebola **epidemic** in West Africa that claimed many lives. As the disease is spread by human contact, travel restrictions were put in place for people travelling to and from the area. How do you think such epidemics impact on global travel and tourism? How could travel between countries contribute to a new global **pandemic**?

Infectious diseases and illnesses

A wide range of infectious diseases and illnesses can affect tourists. The symptoms associated with some of these diseases can be extremely unpleasant, sometimes resulting in death if not treated properly. Table 2.4 outlines some of the main diseases and their symptoms that affect tourists.

◻ **Table 2.4: Some diseases and illnesses that affect tourists**

Disease/ illness	Symptoms	Vaccination available?
Malaria	High fever, sweating, nausea, vomiting, abdominal pain	Yes
Yellow fever	Jaundice, internal bleeding, vomiting blood, organ failure	Yes
Cholera	Diarrhoea, vomiting, dehydration	Yes
Tetanus	Stiffness in the jaw muscles, painful muscle spasms, high temperature	Yes
Typhoid	Loss of appetite, abdominal pain, high fever, lethargy	Yes
Norovirus	Nausea, vomiting, abdominal cramps, fever, muscle pain	No

ACTIVITY

Working in pairs, use the same destination as last lesson and research health risks and travel advice using www.gov.uk and www.travelhealthpro.org.uk. Create a factsheet that outlines your findings. You could use the following headings.

- Risk – name of illness or disease.
- Symptoms – the effects of the illness or disease.
- Precautions – information about vaccinations that are available.

Precautions and preventative measures

There are many common-sense approaches that travellers can take to limit the possible risks of different diseases and illnesses. Wearing insect repellent, insect-repelling clothing, keeping exposed parts of the body covered and using special bed netting made of tightly woven mesh can help protect against diseases, such as malaria, which is carried by mosquitoes.

Other precautions include taking the required medical vaccine before, and sometimes during, travelling; these are usually administered in the form of an injection or tablets. Another common-sense method of protection is for travellers to wash their hands before eating and to carefully select food and drink. Many cases of food poisoning can be traced to the *E. coli* bacteria, which is found in faeces. The NHS issues special advice about making sensible food and drink choices when abroad; for example, not drinking tap water, but instead opting for bottled water. Alternately, if no bottled water is available, it recommends boiling tap water to kill bacteria and viruses.

Travel insurance

It is important to have appropriate insurance cover for a number of reasons; firstly, medical care bills can be very expensive and build up quickly. Secondly, if a tourist were to get ill; for example, suffer from norovirus on a cruise, then being appropriately insured may mean that they can claim money back against the cost of the holiday. Third, in the very worst cases, insurance can help them get home if they are very ill or in the case of a death.

ACTIVITY

Working as a class, discuss the question 'how do health risks influence visitors and bring bad publicity to a destination?' Think about:
- the effects of health risks on visitors
- the effects of health risks on organisations and destinations.

How health risks could lead to bad publicity

Bad publicity often follows whenever there are health concerns about a destination or organisation. For example, in September 2018, a number of newspapers reported on a potential health hazard in Barcelona, Spain. Street vendors were found to be selling mojito cocktails that contained traces of *E. coli*. If ingested, *E. coli* can cause serious food poisoning and even death.

Other serious health risks that can result in death, such as malaria, can result in bad publicity that can linger for years. The economic impact of malaria in Africa is estimated to be US$12 billion every year due to a number of factors, including loss of investment and tourism.

How health risks can influence choice of destination

Health risks can influence people's choice of destination as some people may be reluctant to take the necessary precautions before they travel. This may include people being unwilling to receive the necessary vaccinations before travel, due to the time required or the cost. Therefore, people may be encouraged to opt for a destination that doesn't require visitors to have specific vaccinations.

Specific, but sometimes unexpected, health risks should be considered when choosing a suitable destination for a holiday. For example, pregnant women travelling abroad have been advised by the FCO in the past not to travel to countries that have been affected by the Zika virus, including Indonesia and Brazil. The Zika virus can cause harm to unborn babies; one symptom is severe brain damage.

CHECK MY LEARNING

Working individually, create 12 revision questions based on your learning about the six different factors that you have studied so far (two questions per factor). These factors include:
- economic factors
- political factors
- natural disasters
- media, publicity and image
- safety and security concerns
- health risks and precautions.

Travel and tourism organisations' responses to factors (1)

GETTING STARTED

Working in pairs, research and list how organisations, such as the FCO and tour operators, have responded to different factors and events such as: political unrest, economic issues (such as recession), natural disasters, safety and security incidents (such as terrorist attacks) and health issues (such as epidemics). For example, how did the FCO respond to the 2018 Paris riots?

LINK IT UP

In Component 1, you studied different types of travel and tourism organisations in detail, including the products and services that they offer. How many different types of organisation can you recall?

Travel and tourism organisations have to ensure the safety of their customers above all else. Not doing so can have dramatic impacts for organisations, such as facing legal action and compensation claims, poor publicity and, in extreme cases, collapse of the organisation. Therefore, it is in the interests of organisations to anticipate risks and problems, and continually respond to different factors.

Adapting and developing new products and services

Market research will often dictate how new products and services are developed and existing ones adapted in response to real-world situations. Following the principles of 'supply and demand', the success of products and services is often dependent on there being a demand from consumers.

Table 2.5 gives some examples of a range of factors and the adaptations and responses of travel and tourism organisations.

◻ Table 2.5: Examples of factors and responses

Factor	Example	Adaptation/response
Political	2018 – Paris riots	French tourist organisations issued statements at the time to reassure visitors that the riots only affected a small area of the city and the main attractions in Paris were still safe to visit.
Economic	2010 – Economic crisis in Venezuela (ongoing as of 2019)	Travel Republic promoted Venezuela as a 'cheap destination'. According to the *Telegraph*, Caracas, Venezuela is the second cheapest city in the world; since the beginning of the economic crisis the Venezuelan Bolivar has lost 99 per cent of its value against the dollar.
Natural disaster	2017 – Hurricane Maria in the Dominican Republic	British Airways grounded or rescheduled numerous flights to the affected areas.
Media, publicity and image	2017 – Media reports of Magaluf trying to shed its 'party town' image	A five-year regeneration plan launched with the Palmanove-Magaluf Hotel Association was adopted in 2015, with the aim of making the resort appeal more to the family market.
Safety and security	2015 – Terrorist attacks in Sousse, Tunisia	From July 2017 onwards, tour operators such as Thomas Cook and TUI offered cut-price deals to encourage the recovery of Tunisian tourism.
Health risks	2013–2016 – The West African Ebola virus epidemic	A number of airlines, including British Airways, Emirates Airlines and Kenya Airways, cancelled flights to the affected areas.

As the threat of terrorism looms over many European destinations, further afield destinations, such as the US, are becoming more desirable. Research conducted by Travelzoo highlighted that before the Sousse, Tunisia attacks in 2015, 12 per cent of consumers surveyed wished to travel to the US, whereas after the attacks, in 2016, 31.7 per cent of consumers surveyed wished to travel to the US. In comparison, only 0.5 per cent of consumers surveyed wished to travel to Tunisia in 2016.

Economic investment is helping to drive improvements in technology that are making long-haul destinations more accessible to visitors. In 2018, Qantas offered the first-ever non-stop 17-hour flight from the UK to Australia. This highlights how products and services that are new to the tourism industry may influence customer choices in the future.

ACTIVITY

Working in a small group, you will be allocated a factor, such as economic; political; natural disaster; media, publicity and image; safety and security; or health risks. You will also be allocated a type of organisation, such as a hotel, tour operator, travel agency or airline.

Create a list that outlines how the factor might cause the organisation to review the destinations that it offers and change operational procedures.

◘ Do you agree that holiday reps should be given extra training to help prevent future terrorist attacks?

Adapting operational procedures

Political issues and safety and security

It is sensible for travel and tourism organisations to constantly review their operational procedures given that there are multiple global threats to security. By reviewing operational procedures, travel and tourism organisations can identify any areas where they could improve their current practice, thus helping to ensure the safety and security of customers against global threats.

Airports have adapted their operational procedures over recent years to improve the quality of security for passengers. This has been in response to terrorist attacks and attempted terrorist attacks that have targeted aircraft to either destroy or use as a weapon against other targets. However, some passengers consider such security checks an inconvenience that add to the amount of time taken to board the aircraft.

To support travel and tourism organisations against the threat of global terrorism, in 2017 the government launched an initiative with the National Counter Terrorism Security Office (NaCTSO). This initiative involved training holiday reps working abroad in how to recognise and respond to suspicious behaviour in order to help prevent future terrorist attacks. Although this was a government idea, the scheme involved holiday reps from tour operators such as Thomas Cook, Jet2 and TUI.

Table 2.6 provides some examples of how organisations adapt operational procedures in response to influencing factors, other than political issues and safety and security.

◘ Table 2.6: Adapting operational procedures

Factor	Response
Economic	When faced with economic issues, such as falling profitability, travel organisations may adapt operational procedures to try to save money. For example, in 2015 Thomas Cook announced plans for a staffing restructure in its retail business.
Natural disasters	In the event of natural disasters, travel organisations will often adapt their operational procedures. In 2018, Air New Zealand cancelled a number of flights to Bali due to hazardous volcanic activity.
Media, publicity and image	Positive media coverage can lead to increased visitor numbers in destinations. Organisations may have to adapt operational procedures to deal with this; for example, offering more flights to a destination that has grown in popularity, such as Croatia. In 2018, it was reported that over 70 new flights were being offered to Croatia.
Health risks	During the Ebola epidemic (2013–2016), British Airways adapted their operational procedures by cancelling flights to Liberia and Sierra Leone.

ACTIVITY

Working in a small group, explore one destination of your choice. Find out if there is any advice relating to factors including economic, political, natural disasters, media and publicity, safety and security concerns and health risks.

This could be safety and security advice issued by the tour operators or the FCO.

Think about how an organisation might change the destinations that it offers based on FCO travel advice about factors such as safety and security.

Create a PowerPoint® presentation of your findings.

CHECK MY LEARNING

Identify a destination that is 'new' to UK tour operators. Explain why it is becoming popular, including how this destination is affected by factors such as natural disasters, safety and security concerns or health risks.

Travel and tourism organisations' responses to factors (2)

GETTING STARTED

Working individually, create a list of ways in which travel and tourism organisations could adapt the products and services that they offer, in response to influencing factors such as:
- natural disasters, such as an earthquake or tsunami
- terrorist attacks
- health risks, such as a global pandemic.

Travel and tourism organisations need to be able to adapt constantly the products and services that they offer. At the same time, travel and tourism organisations need to review the provision that they offer and be prepared to listen to customer concerns about safety and security.

Reviewing destinations offered

It is sensible for travel and tourism organisations to continually review the destinations that they offer. Factors such as perceived safety and security can play a big part in affecting the demand for holidays in certain destinations.

Changing products and services at existing destinations

After the Sousse, Tunisia attacks of 2015, Thomas Cook adapted to tourists' fears of further terrorist attacks by amending the range of holidays that it offered. Initially, tourists' perceptions of North African and Eastern Mediterranean destinations, such as Turkey, Egypt and Tunisia, were damaged by a number of well-publicised terrorist incidents over recent years. As a response, Thomas Cook initially moved holiday capacity to 'safer' destinations in the Western Mediterranean and USA.

However, more recently, as the FCO lifted the travel warnings to Tunisia in 2017, Thomas Cook was the first tour operator to resume holidays to the country in 2018 and experienced a large surge in demand from consumers. This highlights that destinations can fall in and out of favour, due to the influence of a range of factors, such as security concerns and media coverage about the safety of destinations.

New destinations

Thomas Cook Airlines continually reviews the destinations that it offers and added a number of new destinations to its flight programme for 2019. These locations include Varna, Seattle, Girona, Thessaloniki, Marsa Alam and Dubrovnik. Dubrovnik in particular has benefitted from positive media exposure as it has been featured in a number of movies and TV shows, such as *Star Wars*, *Robin Hood* and *Game of Thrones*.

Reviewing pricing structures

Many organisations perform a cost risk analysis and adjust prices in order to maintain visitor numbers. People are willing to travel to destinations that may be considered 'risky' if they consider the price of the holiday to be excellent value for money. Simon Calder, travel editor of the *Independent*, commented that 'A very good way to get people to go to destinations which have suffered at the hands of terrorists is to cut prices.' However, as the price cuts are often passed on to the hotels, this can impact on the profitability of such organisations.

Despite the FCO warning that terrorist attacks in Tunisia were 'still very likely', in February 2018 Thomas Cook operated its first package holiday to Tunisia since the 2015 Sousse attacks. However, in order to encourage holidaymakers to return, holiday prices to Tunisia were very low; a one-week all-inclusive holiday to Les Orangers Beach

Resort in Hammamet in March 2018 was £276. This was a significantly cheaper pricing structure than other Mediterranean resorts; for example, a similar package holiday to Malta at around the same time was 80 per cent more expensive at £498.

Hedging

Another way that organisations can try to shield themselves from a range of volatile factors, such as changes in fuel prices and currency exchange rates is to practise 'hedging'. Basically 'hedging' is when tour operators insure themselves against a negative event. For example, Thomas Cook's policy is to 'hedge' up to 80 per cent of the fuel needed for its flight schedule over the following two years by using approaches like fixed-price contracts. This means that a fixed or capped price for the fuel is agreed between Thomas Cook and the fuel supplier, which shields Thomas Cook from rises in fuel prices. However, if fuel prices fall, this may mean that Thomas Cook pays more to its supplier for fuel than the market rate.

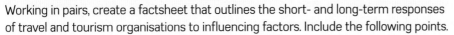

ACTIVITY

Working in pairs, create a factsheet that outlines the short- and long-term responses of travel and tourism organisations to influencing factors. Include the following points.
- How travel and tourism organisations respond to natural disasters in the short term.
- How travel and tourism organisations respond to natural disasters in the long term.
- How travel and tourism organisations might review or adapt what they offer to try to encourage visitors to return; for example, lowering the price of package holidays to the destination.

◻ Would a low price lure you to a destination that is considered 'risky'?

Managing public relations

Managing public relations effectively is essential when dealing with difficult situations, particularly if someone has been harmed. Thomas Cook was criticised for its handling of a case where two children were killed by carbon monoxide poisoning when staying in a holiday cottage in Corfu in 2006. Thomas Cook issued a 'sincere and heartfelt apology' to the parents of the children in 2015. The situation has resulted in negative publicity for Thomas Cook, who was found to have 'breached its duty of care' by an inquest jury in 2015.

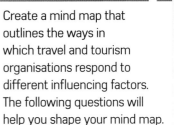

CHECK MY LEARNING

Create a mind map that outlines the ways in which travel and tourism organisations respond to different influencing factors. The following questions will help you shape your mind map.
- Why might a travel organisation review the destinations that it offers?
- How might a travel organisation encourage tourism after an event such as a violent political protest has occurred?
- How might extra staff training provided by travel organisations help visitors to feel safer?

Governmental responses to factors

GETTING STARTED

Working in pairs, think about an influencing factor that affects tourism such as: health issues, safety and security, natural disasters. Imagine that you represent one of the local, regional or national governments in an overseas destination and write down how you might react to a major event, such as a global disease pandemic. How would your level of government respond to this factor?

KEY TERMS

Local government refers to an administrative body for a small area such as a parish, town or county.

Regional government is responsible for the administration of larger geographical areas including collections of counties, in the UK, or states in larger countries such as Australia.

National government is responsible for the whole country and has the power to set laws.

Governments have a duty to protect people. Often in response to a situation, such as a natural disaster or terrorist threat, government agencies will issue travel advice to tourists. In fact, when you are going on holiday it is always advisable to check the current FCO travel guidance. If the FCO feels that a destination is unsafe to visit, it will issue travel advice against travelling there. Furthermore, insurance companies will not provide travel insurance to destinations that the FCO advises against visiting.

Providing the public with up-to-date information

Travel advice is often provided by **local, regional** and **national government** agencies. For example, local government agencies often provide travel advice relevant to the local area, such as traffic reports about possible delays on main routes through the local area, or weather warnings that could affect local travel. National governments may issue travel advice that affects a larger geographical area; for example, warnings about hurricane threats in the USA. The UK government issues advice through the www.gov.uk/foreign-travel-advice website.

Imposing travel restrictions

Governments have the power to impose travel restrictions in a number of ways. They can limit the ability of members of their own population to travel freely. This is most likely in countries where the majority of the population doesn't enjoy the freedom that we are used to in the West, for example in North Korea. Alternatively, they can restrict inbound tourist access to their country or a part of it, such as the 6-month closure of the tourist island of Boracay by the Philippines government.

Governments can also impose travel restrictions on people coming into their country by implementing visa restrictions. Research by the London School of Economics found that visa restrictions can reduce travel from between 52 and 63 per cent. This is significant in countries that are trying to promote tourism; for example, in China, where visa restrictions may be a barrier to tourism development. During the 2008 Summer Olympic Games in Beijing tourists complained about the tight travel restrictions and visa requirements.

Promoting a positive image

Tourism contributes significantly to the economy of many countries in the world, therefore it is in their interests to promote a positive image that encourages tourism. Many governments will have organisations that are responsible for tourism promotion; in the UK we have VisitBritain. You may have noticed advertisements for global destinations on TV, for example in 2017 an advert titled 'Living the Dream' was broadcast on UK TV networks by VisitCalifornia to promote the American state as a destination.

Promoting a positive image can be especially important in response to influencing factors such as health risks. In Brazil, after the main threat from the Zika virus had ended, politicians decided to invest more in tourism promotion, to try to encourage more people from abroad to visit Brazil. The government strategy includes plans to promote Brazil abroad through online advertising to reach global travellers who research trips and make reservations online.

ACTIVITY

Working in small groups, select one destination to research, provided by your teacher. Use www.gov.uk to source any FCO advice and any government-produced promotional information from the destination itself. Compare the FCO advice with any information produced to promote the destination. Is there any conflicting information about the destination? For example, the destination promotional material may state that the destination is safe whereas FCO advice might highlight risks that aren't mentioned in promotional materials.

Encouraging employment

According to UK government publications available via www.gov.uk, in 2015 the UK government pledged to help tourism grow by making £1.7 million of funding available to People 1st to provide 500 new apprenticeship places in tourism and help to create 1500 jobs.

The loss of visitors following the 2007–2011 recession impacted on overseas destinations and in turn contributed to unemployment in tourist-receiving countries such as Greece, which was especially badly hit by the recession. However, tourism in Greece since the recession has seen a resurgence in visitor numbers; in 2018 an estimated 32 million foreign visitors arrived in Greece, with tourism estimated to contribute one in four jobs to the Greek economy.

On the other hand, in response to the economic recession, more people in the UK opted for staycations. This sector experienced growth of 5.6 per cent during the recession, which would have resulted in jobs either being maintained or created in the UK. City breaks were found to be especially popular as 'staycation' destinations.

Improving infrastructure

In 2014 and 2016, the city of Rio de Janeiro in Brazil hosted the FIFA World Cup and Summer Olympic games, respectively. In response to the political need to show Brazil at its best on a world stage; one of the major impacts was that infrastructure within the city was greatly improved in order to accommodate visitors. In particular, transport routes between the airport and sporting venues were improved. A legacy of this is that improved transport now benefits the local population and tourists that visit areas of Rio, such as Copacabana Beach.

Introducing security measures

Governments constantly review their security measures due to the ongoing threat of terrorism. After the bombing of the Manchester Arena in 2017, the government issued advice to security managers that venues should now conduct bag checks before members of the public are allowed to enter.

LINK IT UP

Look back at Component 1 for an explanation and examples of direct and indirect employment, particularly Table 1.7. Can you think of one example of each?

CHECK MY LEARNING

Working individually, write a short summary about why governments might want to introduce travel restrictions or security measures in a destination. Think about the following questions.
- How important is it for governments to keep visitors safe?
- How important is it for governments to keep their own population safe?
- What are the consequences of not keeping visitors safe for governments and destinations?

Voluntary organisations' responses to factors

GETTING STARTED

Working in pairs, recap some of your learning from Component 1 by defining what the voluntary sector is. Give some examples of voluntary organisations that work within the travel and tourism sector. What are the main aims of voluntary sector organisations?

Voluntary organisations can play a really important role in global travel and tourism in a number of ways; some are concerned with the preservation of historic buildings, some want to promote sustainable tourism, some provide emergency support to destinations affected by major events.

Promoting sustainability, conservation and protection

The Travel Foundation is a UK-based tourism charity that works in partnership with businesses and governments to help tourism bring greater benefits to people and the environment. One of its main areas of focus is to work with stakeholders to encourage sustainability, conservation and protection.

In Saint Lucia, the Travel Foundation is working with a range of stakeholders to try to encourage the catching and eating of lionfish. The lionfish is a non-native species that has invaded the Caribbean Sea and is damaging local ecosystems by eating local reef fish. This initiative will bring about both environmental and economic benefits to the area, as lionfish numbers will be controlled, and local fishermen and restaurants will benefit economically from selling and serving the fish to visitors.

How can controlling numbers of edible but invasive species bring about environmental and economic benefits?

Campaigning for governments to affect change

One of the main objectives of some tourism voluntary organisations is to campaign for change and work with governments constructively to encourage sustainable tourism. How governments plan for sustainable tourism is an important political issue. The Travel Foundation has worked in partnership with a range of Caribbean governments to launch the 'Roadmap to Destination Success' course for ministries, government departments, tourism authorities and tourist boards. This course is designed to help plan the sustainable development of Caribbean tourist destinations.

ACTIVITY

Working in small groups, explore the Travel Foundation website (www. thetravelfoundation.org.uk) and the National Trust website (www.nationaltrust.org.uk). Make notes about their main roles in tourism.

Explore some of the campaigns that they are currently involved in. Make notes on the following:
- the name of the campaign
- the main aims of the campaign
- the destinations that are affected by the campaign.

Raising awareness of issues

The Travel Foundation also works with businesses and governments to raise the negative issues sometimes associated with global tourism. It believes that if tourism is not managed well then this can have negative impacts on local communities and environments and can cause long-term problems for residents, including the overall decline of tourism. However, it is involved in projects in different destinations that demonstrate the benefits of sustainable tourism in practice.

In Mexico, the Travel Foundation is raising the issue of poorly paid work in the Quintana Roo region. Despite local people generally being offered low-paid employment, tourism is vitally important to the economy of the area and contributes around 75 per cent of the region's GDP. The Travel Foundation has responded to this issue by promoting sustainable excursions that enable local people to make more money from tourism by offering tours of the region's unique natural environments.

Raising funds

Securing funding is a critical issue for tourism charities operating in the voluntary sector that want to promote sustainable tourism. One of the main voluntary tourism organisations in the UK that promoted sustainability, conservation and protection, called Tourism Concern, was forced to close in 2018 due to a lack of financial support.

Providing funds

Voluntary organisations can play an important role by providing support in response to a major incident, such as a natural disaster or terrorist attack. In 2018, a number of voluntary organisations, including Unicef, ActionAid and the Red Cross, raised funds for victims of the earthquake and tsunami that struck Indonesia on 28 September.

By early October 2018, it was reported that £8 million had been raised by the British public alone in the first few days after the disaster. The British Government also contributed a further £2 million to the disaster relief effort. Part of the appeal included an advert broadcast on British TV that encouraged people to make a donation to help the people of Indonesia who were affected by the disaster.

LINK IT UP

In Component 1, you learned about the ownership of voluntary organisations, including how they raise funds. Are you or any members of your family members of a voluntary organisation?

ACTIVITY

Working in small groups, visit www.responsibletravel.com. Search 'should I travel after a disaster?' Respond to this question by writing a short essay. Think about:
- the dangers of travelling to a place that has been affected by a disaster
- how tourists and visitors could help with the clean-up operation
- how tourist and visitor spending could provide much needed income to the local economy.

CHECK MY LEARNING

Working in pairs, prepare for the external assessment by reviewing your notes to create a series of revision questions. Test your partner using your revision questions.

Learning aim A: assessment practice

How you will be assessed

In this component, you will be assessed by a written assessment that will be set and marked by Pearson, the exam provider.

The exam board will provide your teacher with Sample Assessment Material (SAM) that will help you to practise for the real exam.

The assessment will assess your understanding of Section A: factors that influence global travel and tourism. This will include:

- explaining how different factors affect travel and tourism organisations, destinations and visitors
- assessing the potential impacts of tourism on destinations.

CHECKPOINT

Review your learning of this section by answering the following questions, this will help you to prepare for the external assessment.

Strengthen

- Identify three different factors that influence global travel and tourism.
- Describe how natural disasters can impact on travel and tourism destinations.
- Explain how tourists can protect themselves against infectious diseases, such as malaria, tetanus and typhoid.
- Explain three different safety measures that are used by airports to keep travellers safe.

Challenge

- Discuss the effects that economic factors can have on a destination.
- Assess the extent to which media coverage can have a positive impact on visitor numbers to a destination.

ASSESSMENT ACTIVITY 1 | LEARNING AIM | A

Read the following article about the impacts of different factors on travel and tourism.

Tourist destinations recover from terrorist attacks quicker than they would a natural disaster, according to travel analysts.

According to travel industry experts, terrorist attacks, such as the Brussels attack in 2016, lead to a short-term decline in bookings of 10-20 per cent, due to fears of future terrorist attacks. Destinations affected by terrorist attacks recover their visitor numbers, on average, after 13 months.

However, damage caused to infrastructure by natural disasters can have a much longer-term impact on visitor numbers. After the 2011 earthquake in Japan, it took the tourism industry 21 months to recover.

Now answer the following questions.

- Earthquakes are one type of natural disaster. State **one** other type of natural disaster.
- One economic factor that affects tourism is changing costs of fuel. State **one** other economic factor that affects tourism.
- Media coverage includes newspaper reports, online reviews and travel blogs. Describe **one** advantage of positive media coverage.
- In response to security threats such as terrorism, airports have a number of safety measures in place, such as luggage being screened by a security scanner. Describe **one** disadvantage of such safety measures for travellers.
- Give **two** negative impacts of terrorist attacks for travel and tourism destinations.
- Explain how political instability can result in cancelled holidays.
- Assess why natural disasters may have a greater impact on travel and tourism destinations than terrorist attacks.

ASSESSMENT ACTIVITY 2 · LEARNING AIM · A

For this assessment activity you will need to be able to interpret and use visitor data, such as that in Table 2.7.

◘ **Table 2.7: Visitors to the UK in 2017 by areas of residence in thousands**

	North America	Europe	Other countries
May	514	2524	521
June	674	2307	582
July	645	2535	863
Aug	473	2696	789

- Using Table 2.7, can you identify in which month most inbound visits from North America were made?
- Using Table 2.7, can you identify the number of inbound visitors to the UK in June from Europe?
- To what extent do you agree that inbound tourism from Europe is more important for the UK travel and tourism sector than inbound tourism from North America? Refer to Table 2.7 in your answer.
- VisitBritain needs to make a decision about where in the world its next marketing activities will focus on. Using data from Table 2.7, evaluate whether VisitBritain should focus on promoting tourism in North America or Europe.

CHECKPOINT

Review your learning of this component by answering the following questions; this will help you to prepare for the external assessment.

Strengthen
- Identify three ways that travel and tourism organisations respond to influencing factors.

Challenge
- Compare how government responses (public sector) to influencing factors might be different from responses from private sector organisations.

TIP

In preparation for the external assessment, make sure that you are familiar with graphical information and have practised some data interpretation. In the external assessment you may be asked to interpret data that is presented using a:
- bar chart
- pie chart
- scatter graph.

TAKE IT FURTHER

Have you checked that you are familiar with all of the different factors that can influence global travel and tourism? Are you aware of how different organisations respond to different factors? Make sure that you are aware of different case study examples and how real organisations deal with real situations. There are many examples online that you can research.

Impacts of tourism

GETTING STARTED

Working in a small group, list all of the social impacts of tourism that you can think of and decide if they would be classed as:

- positive social impacts that bring benefits to the people that live in a destination
- negative social impacts that bring problems to the people that live in a destination.

KEY TERM

Social impacts are the effects on the surrounding society, in the case of tourism the people and social structures in host destinations.

Impacts are the effects of tourism experienced by destinations and the people who live there. Tourism brings both positive and negative social, economic and environmental impacts. The way that tourism is both offered and managed is key to maximising the positive impacts of tourism.

Social impacts

People living in destinations that are more reliant on tourism income for their livelihoods are generally more at risk of exploitation. Remember **social impacts** affect people and their lives.

Negative social impacts of tourism on local communities

Tourism can bring many negative social impacts to destinations. Table 2.8 provides some examples.

Table 2.8: Tourism's negative social impacts

Impact	Example
Disruption to everyday life	Dealing with tourists can bring about disruptions to people's everyday lives. Such as opening shops and having to run facilities for longer hours.
Loss of culture	Destinations adapt to meet the needs of tourists; this results in the loss of traditional culture. Benidorm, Spain has become unrecognisable from the small fishing settlement it once was. In response to a demand for British culture abroad, British-themed pubs feature at the expense of traditional Spanish eateries and bars.
Resentment towards visitors	In 2017, it was reported that an increasing amount of anti-tourist protests, including graffiti, were being seen in Barcelona, Spain, with 'tourists go home' spray-painted in a number of locations.
Increased crime	Either an increase in crimes being committed by tourists, or tourists being the victims of crime. For example, in Prague, Czech Republic, tourists are often targeted by pickpockets. Tourism can encourage criminal provision of 'black market' services, such as drug dealing and prostitution.
Staged authenticity	Heritage destinations may 'stage' traditions and rituals for the benefit of tourists. While this may be educational, this can also sometimes be considered exploitative of local people, who may be recreating such traditions and rituals just for the sake of tourists.
Exploitation of locals	'Exploitation' means treating someone unfairly to gain benefit. There are particular types of tourism that are seen as particularly exploitative of local people. 'Slum tourism' involves visiting an extremely impoverished area that a tourist would not normally visit. This includes tours of the homeless areas of Amsterdam, favelas in Rio de Janeiro and the slums of Mumbai. One of the main criticisms is that the local people, who could potentially benefit the most financially from tourism, do not get to share in the wealth that 'slum tours' generate.
Loss of traditional lifestyles	The demonstration effect in tourism is when members of the host community copy visitor's behaviours, dress codes and preferences at the expense of their own traditional lifestyles. For example, younger members of the host community begin to adopt the clothing types of visitors in place of traditional forms of clothing.

Positive social impacts of tourism on local communities

Improved quality of life

Many tourists spend generously when on holiday. Depending on what products and services they buy, tourist spending can benefit the host community greatly. Tourism creates jobs for the local community, which in turn provides an income for families to support themselves.

Access to facilities

Tourism income is often invested in improving local facilities, such as hospitals and schools. This spending is especially important in less wealthy countries, such as Jamaica, as investment in facilities can help a country to become more developed. New or improved hospitals benefit tourists and locals alike, because both groups have access to better healthcare.

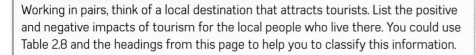

ACTIVITY

Working in pairs, think of a local destination that attracts tourists. List the positive and negative impacts of tourism for the local people who live there. You could use Table 2.8 and the headings from this page to help you to classify this information.

Improved transport and infrastructure

Governments often recognise the importance of infrastructure in facilitating tourism. As a result, a country wanting to develop tourism will invest in improved transport links and infrastructure. One benefit of this for local communities is that they can also make use of improved transport links and infrastructure. For example, in Bulgaria, government authorities have invested in motorway improvements that have significantly cut travel time from the capital city, Sofia, to Bulgaria's main tourist-receiving areas on the southern Black Sea coast.

LINK IT UP

Refer back to the definition and discussion of infrastructure in Section A of this component. Can you think of an example of new infrastructure benefitting tourism, either in your local area or in a destination you have recently been to?

Improved cultural awareness

Tourists are often keen to learn the traditions and cultures of the areas that they are visiting. This provides opportunities for the host community to share their cultural practices with others and also to benefit economically. For example, in Kenya and Tanzania, tourists are transported to areas inhabited by the Maasai people. Once there, tourists are given the chance to witness traditional dancing and purchase hand-made goods from the host community, such as bead necklaces.

DID YOU KNOW?

In Tanzania, US$1.5 million per year is allocated to the Maasai community pastoral council to encourage income-generating tourism projects for the Maasai community.

CHECK MY LEARNING

Working as a class, look at some Google images of tourism. Decide if tourism has an overall positive or negative social impact.

Economic impact of tourism

GETTING STARTED

Working in pairs, create a mind map of the economic benefits of tourism. For each benefit that you have thought of try to offer a criticism. For example: Tourism creates jobs in host destinations (economic benefit). However, many of these jobs are low paid and, in some cases, only last for the tourist season (criticism).

KEY TERM

A **trade union** is an organisation of workers from a particular profession that protects and furthers their rights and interests.

LINK IT UP

Further on in this component, you will learn that in some types of destination the local economy is over-reliant on tourism. Why do you think this could be an issue for some destinations?

Tourism can bring economic benefits to host areas. However, often local communities do not receive a fair share of the overall income generated by tourism. Too much of this can go to the multinational organisations that provide the holidays and not to the people and local organisations who are in direct contact with the tourists.

Negative impacts of tourism on the economy

Low-paid jobs

Many jobs in the travel and tourism sector are low paid and involve working unsociable hours. In 2018, the *Guardian* reported that hotel workers on the Isle of Skye in Scotland were unhappy about low wages and had contacted **trade unions** about their low pay and poor conditions.

In many poorer countries, employees do not enjoy the same rights as those in more developed countries, such as the UK, and do not have access to trade unions; they may not be entitled to the things that others take for granted such as paid sick leave, maternity pay and paid holidays.

Seasonal unemployment

In many destinations, tourists follow the weather; summer sun destinations rely on warm weather, whereas winter sport destinations rely on the snow. A downside of this seasonal demand for tourism is that people employed in the tourism industry may experience unemployment at times of low demand.

Leakage

Leakage is the way that money generated through tourism in one country is then lost to another country's economy. This is a particular problem with all-inclusive holidays where much of the profit is returned to the resort operator and not to the local community. As most resorts are owned by overseas organisations tourism spend 'leaks' out of the country.

Increased cost of living

Increased demand from tourists usually leads to an increase in prices. These increases in prices range from an increase in the cost of food and drink in local shops and restaurants, to house price increases. This can sometimes force the host community out of their local area because they can't afford to buy a house. This has happened in the village of Chapel Stile in the Lake District; demand for 'second homes' from tourists has pushed out local people. Up to 70 per cent of local housing was not regularly occupied due to tourist ownership.

Positive impacts of tourism on the economy

Economic multiplier effect

Possibly the greatest positive economic effect is the multiplier effect, which happens when tourists spend money on direct goods and services that in turn benefits other organisations, the opposite of 'leakage' (Figure 2.2). Table 2.9 details other positive effects which help to build and expand the multiplier.

◼ Table 2.9: Tourism's positive economic impacts

Impact	Example
Employment opportunities	Tourism can lead to an increase in both direct and indirect employment opportunities for people. Hotels, airports and local attractions all require staff to function effectively; therefore tourism creates employment opportunities within the host community.
Training and education	Many jobs in the travel and tourism industry require specific training. This can be provided to the local community so that they have the ability to manage tourism effectively and sustainably themselves.
Foreign currency earnings	Foreign currency earnings are the amount of income a country generates through the arrival and spending of inbound tourists. Foreign currency earnings are especially important in countries where a large proportion of their GDP is linked to tourism: inbound tourism earnings contribute 39.6 per cent to the GDP of the Maldives, compared with just 3.7 per cent of the UK's economy.
Contribution to taxes and GDP	In 2017, tourism tax generated €64.3 million towards Majorca's GDP. Tax revenue generated in 2017 and the previous year was invested in 108 projects related to improving the environment and infrastructure for the benefit of both the host community and tourists.

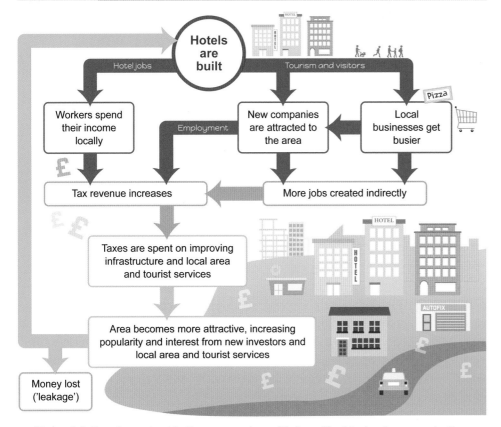

◼ Figure 2.2: How important is the economic multiplier effect to host economies?

LINK IT UP

Look back at Component 1 to remind yourself about tourism's contribution to GDP. Can you name two ways tourism contributes to UK GDP?

CHECK MY LEARNING

Working in pairs, research one job linked to tourism in the UK; for example, https://www.merlincareers.com/en/brands-and-attractions/alton-towers-resort or from your local area. Describe the characteristics of the job.

• Is the job low paid?
• Is the job seasonal?
• Does the job involve working unsociable hours?

ACTIVITY

Working in small groups, research the economic impacts of tourism in a foreign destination. Use national tourism and government websites to support your research. Refer to both positive and negative economic impacts.

Negative environmental impacts of tourism

GETTING STARTED

Working in pairs, make a list of environmental problems that tourists might bring to a beach resort. Think of any beaches that you have visited and the problems that you might have witnessed while you were there.

One of the biggest global issues right now is how we care for the environment. People are worried that tourism currently places too much burden on the environment and that irreversible harm is being done, such as the effects on wildlife (Figure 2.3). However, many people and organisations are making huge efforts to make tourism more ethical and sustainable.

Habitats	• Tourism unintentionally affects wildlife in the shared environment • Zakynthos, Greece; loggerhead sea turtles pushed off beaches
Wildlife	• Wildlife tourism is growing at 3 per cent each year; currently it is 7 per cent of all world tourism • Wildlife itself is at risk from illegal trade, overdevelopment and overexploitation • If wildlife goes so will wildlife-based tourism
Threatened species	• WWF warns that the world is facing the biggest extinction since the dinosaurs • Threatened species include elephants, mountain gorillas, turtles, tigers, giant pandas, rhinos, polar bears, Amur leopards and the Yangtze finless porpoise

◻ Figure 2.3: Loss of habitats, wildlife and threatened species

Increased pollution

Recent research published in 2018 has highlighted that tourism is responsible for nearly one-tenth of the world's carbon emissions. Air travel is the most significant sector of tourism that causes pollution. Some people are worried that as countries get richer and demand for air travel increases, the problem may get worse. The countries that contribute most to air travel pollution currently are the USA, China and Germany.

Along with air pollution, noise and water pollution are significant environmental impacts of tourism. Research into noise pollution in south-western Spain highlighted that this was a particular problem in the summer, during the height of the tourist season. The main sources of noise were identified as traffic and recreational activities. Cruise ships have been identified as a significant source of water pollution, often due to the huge amounts of waste that they dump into the ocean, such as untreated sewage.

Overcrowding

Overcrowding is a problem that affects some destinations more than others. Overcrowding can alienate locals, push infrastructure to its limits and impact negatively on the visitor's experience. Some destinations go to extreme lengths to avoid overcrowding. For example, in the Galápagos Islands tourist numbers are strictly limited.

In other areas of the world, action has been taken to tackle overcrowding. In the past the Thai government has temporarily closed Maya Bay; a destination made famous in the movie *The Beach*, released in 2000. It is believed that Maya Bay's coral is being severely damaged by the anchors of mooring boats.

Traffic congestion

Many of the most popular places that people visit suffer from traffic congestion during times of 'peak' demand. Traffic congestion can be negative for the environment and result in visitor dissatisfaction. Many destinations and attractions use approaches to traffic congestion management such as the introduction of 'park and ride' schemes that keep car traffic out of busy areas, as visitors leave their car in a car park on the outskirts of the destination and take public transport into the centre.

Reduced biodiversity

Reduced biodiversity is the loss or extinction of species of plants and animals. Unfortunately, tourism contributes both directly and indirectly to reduced biodiversity. Directly: visitors to new environments can sometimes introduce new species which can lead to a biological invasion and loss of local species. Indirectly: tourism contributes to climate change, which is seen as one of the biggest threats to global biodiversity. In parts of Africa it is believed that droughts caused by climate change could lead to the mass extinction of species such as the African elephant.

Environmental degradation

Environmental degradation caused by tourism is a serious issue. Often environmental degradation can be caused when tourism is not properly planned for. Sometimes tourists are not aware of the harm that they can cause to the environment. For example, the introduction of golf courses to resorts places huge demands on resources, such as water, and alters the natural landscape into something more artificial.

In extreme cases, some areas popular with visitors are closed to tourism due to concerns about sustainability. In 2016, Thai officials banned tourists from three islands so that they could review the impacts of tourism there. The islands of Koh Khai Nok, Koh Khai Nui and Koh Khai Nai were very popular with day trippers from Phuket; however, damage to ecosystems valued by local communities has been blamed on unsustainable numbers of tourists visiting them.

Erosion

Erosion by humans is the gradual wearing away of the natural landscape by constantly walking or driving over it; this is a very common problem that affects destinations all over the world. In the Grand Canyon, USA, footpath erosion is a current issue. It may cause problems for visitors in the future, making certain parts of this landmark inaccessible, not to mention the effect on wildlife living there. The impact of footpath erosion is most visible in areas of heavy use by both people and mules that carry both tourists and supplies into the area.

Riverbank and lakeshore erosion are also environmental impacts of tourism. Along the Kilim River in Malaysia, hire boats are popular with tourists, who are attracted to the wildlife in the area. However, the volumes of boats used, number of trips and uncontrolled speed boats have contributed to riverbank erosion. In the UK, lakeshore erosion is a problem around Lake Windermere in the Lake District, due to the number of tourists who walk along the lakeshore and unwittingly damage plant life and contribute to the erosion of the shoreline.

What long-term impacts could footpath erosion have?

ACTIVITY

Working in small groups, you will be allocated a global destination to research. Use national tourism websites and government websites to support your research. Identify at least four negative impacts of tourism on the environment.

Next, create a wall display that highlights your findings.

CHECK MY LEARNING

Working individually, create a list of ideas about how organisations and/or tourists could help to reduce the negative impacts of tourism in a destination. Think about the ways that land, air and water pollution could be reduced.

Positive environmental impacts of tourism

GETTING STARTED

Working individually, firstly, think about how tourists going on safari to Africa could benefit the local environment. List some positive environmental impacts that tourists could bring to the area.

Secondly, list how tourism could benefit the environment of an area in a town or city that you have visited. Include examples that already exist, such as the conversion of a unit and derelict dockland area into smart-looking hotels and restaurants.

Publicity surrounding the negative environmental impacts of tourism is widespread, however, tourism can in fact benefit the environment. For example, by helping to raise awareness about the fragility of the environment, people are likely to become more considerate when visiting delicate ecosystems. In fact, some tourists may be motivated to travel for reasons of conservation and environmental protection.

Conservation

Tourists can help to encourage conservation through ecotourism. Ecotourism involves travel to spectacular, relatively undeveloped destinations such as Antarctica, the Galápagos Islands, the Amazon rainforest and the Great Plains of Africa. Ecotourism tries to ensure that part of the money raised through tourism goes towards the conservation of the host area. For example, tourism revenue contributes to wildlife-protecting, anti-poaching patrols across Africa.

Another aspect of conservation is the creation of special protected areas to promote the natural beauty of a location and prevent uncontrolled development. Here in the UK we have National Parks, areas of natural beauty that are protected from overdevelopment by government legislation. Similarly, many global destinations have designated national parks including the USA, Canada, France, Spain and South Africa.

Environmental education

An increasing number of organisations are encouraging tourism through environmental education and conservation initiatives. Camps International Ltd is a UK-based organisation that collaborates with schools to offer visits to a vast range of global locations including Ecuador, Kenya and Cambodia.

In East Africa, Camps International Ltd encourages its volunteers to work with local communities to educate them about the benefits of living peacefully alongside wildlife and the benefits of reducing human and wildlife conflict. Furthermore, the trips offer young people the chance to learn about different cultures, help local people by contributing to the building of facilities and to take part in leisure activities, such as scuba diving.

ACTIVITY

Working in small groups, carry out some research into the positive environmental impacts of tourism in the same destination or a similar destination that you looked at last lesson. Identify at least four environmental benefits of tourism.

Next, add to your wall display from last lesson by including the environmental benefits of tourism that you have identified. Remember to use some of the headings from this page to help you:
- benefits of regeneration
- creation of open spaces
- benefits of environmental education.

Open spaces and improved street furniture

Open spaces or 'greenspaces' can be important in improving the appeal of urban areas for both local residents and visitors. A study by Forest Research suggests that high-quality open spaces or greenspaces in urban areas support tourism by providing an area where activities such as wildlife watching and walking can take place. An example of a successful greenspace is Central Park, one of New York's most visited attractions.

In Greenwich, London, a design studio called Raw Edges created a range of concrete street furniture in Greenwich Peninsula designed to look like 'scaled up' armchairs. One of the aims of the project was to create a small urban landscape that could be used as a relaxing spot for people to enjoy together.

Regeneration

The term 'regeneration', or 'urban renewal', means to improve a building or area to make it more attractive. This could include regenerating an old or run-down building for the purpose of tourism. You may be familiar with some examples of regeneration in the UK. For example, the regeneration of the Albert Docks in Liverpool began in the 1980s and involved converting an area of old disused docks into a popular tourist attraction that includes a range of shops, museums and restaurants.

Similarly, New York has seen the reuse of traditional buildings for new activities. For example, Trinity Place Restaurant and Bar was built inside an old bank vault located on Broadway. Other forms of regeneration in the city include the conversion of a disused railway line in Manhattan into a popular park. The High Line is a 'greenspace' that has been created for both visitors and residents of New York to enjoy.

DID YOU KNOW?

New York's most famous open space, Central Park, was modelled on Merseyside's Birkenhead Park.

LINK IT UP

Further on in this component, you will learn more about destination management and how different types of organisation work together to try to maximise the positive impacts of tourism on destinations.

CHECK MY LEARNING

Working individually, participate in whole group feedback and write down the positive environmental impacts that tourism has in different destinations. Think about the following questions.
- How can tourism benefit the environment?
- How does education encourage visitors to act responsibly towards the environment?
- How can tourists get involved in environmental protection?

Sustainability and managing social impacts

GETTING STARTED

Working in pairs, define what you think sustainability means. Next, use tour operator websites such as www.thomascook.com/travel-advice-and-safety and other tourism advice websites such as www.gov.uk/foreign-travel-advice/united-arab-emirates to find out what sort of advice is given to tourists visiting Dubai, including how to behave appropriately and how to keep themselves safe. For example, are there any local dress codes that visitors need to be aware of?

◘ Do you think having British police patrol European destinations reduces negative behaviour?

The social impacts of tourism can be managed in a sustainable way through education, infrastructure development, the inclusion of local communities in decision making and partnership projects, and taxation and reinvestment of the money raised in the community.

Educating visitors

Education is key to bringing about improvements and development; education can enlighten people about the impacts of their behaviour and show them how things can be done differently. When it comes to destinations, educating visitors can encourage them to behave sustainably and contribute positively to how the destination functions.

Reducing negative impacts of behaviour

When on holiday, most tourists like to 'let their hair down'; however, this sometimes involves 'excessive' behaviour, such as drinking too much alcohol. You may be aware that some British tourists have a poor reputation abroad, especially young adults when visiting party destinations such as Magaluf and Benidorm. Unfortunately, actions, such as drinking too much alcohol, can have a negative impact on the host destination. This includes rowdy behaviour and noise pollution, indecency by not respecting local dress codes and the diversion of local services like ambulances, which have to spend a significant amount of time dealing with drunk tourists.

One solution that has been trialled has been to have British police walking the streets of Magaluf and Ibiza to act as a visible deterrent to those who wish to break the law or engage in antisocial behaviour.

ACTIVITY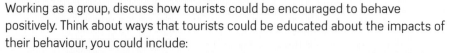

Working as a group, discuss how tourists could be encouraged to behave positively. Think about ways that tourists could be educated about the impacts of their behaviour, you could include:
- FCO advice about the expectations of visitors to the destination
- any advertising or promotion linked to tourist behaviour such as posters warning of fines for antisocial behaviour
- any news bulletins that were issued to create awareness of initiatives that discourage antisocial behaviour, such as British police patrols in Magaluf.

How to behave and dress appropriately

Many destinations have cultural practices that are different from our own; often these relate to religious guidelines. These include how to behave and dress appropriately in public, especially in non-western destinations. Many Muslim destinations have strict rules about how to behave in public; for example, not openly kissing. In India, a mainly Hindu country, tourists are advised to dress modestly; for example, by wearing light-coloured, tunic-style tops that cover much of the upper body and legs and keep the body cool.

ACTIVITY

Working in pairs, discuss the following scenario about a tourist's conduct abroad.

A male visitor from the UK to Dubai visits Dubai Mall. He is wearing a cap, sunglasses, a pair of shorts and a vest. A number of tattoos on the visitor's arm and legs are exposed and visible.

1 Decide how the way the tourist is dressed in the scenario might be considered to be offensive to local people.

2 Design a leaflet guide for tourists that encourages them to behave appropriately in order to reduce the negative impacts of their behaviour on the local community.

How to show respect to traditions and religions

Tourists are generally welcomed to participate in local traditions and religions; in many places, embracing such events is a sign of great respect. In fact, taking part in such events can enhance the experience of the holiday for tourists and educate them about different cultural practices. For example, www.goturkeytourism.com advises tourists visiting Turkey to take part in their two main religious festivals; Ramadan Festival and the Festival of Sacrifice.

DID YOU KNOW?

The most visited site on earth is the Kaaba in Mecca. It is estimated that 2–3 million Muslims make the Hajj pilgrimage each year.

How to avoid conflict

The most common source of conflict for tourists is offending the local population by behaving in a manner that is inconsiderate or offensive; www.theabroadguide.com has issued some guidance about how to be respectful while travelling abroad (Figure 2.4).

◧ Figure 2.4: Considerate behaviour goes a long way to avoiding conflict.

CHECK MY LEARNING

Working individually, create a mind map of the social impacts of tourism. The following questions will help you to plan your mind map.

- Why is educating visitors about the social impacts of their behaviour important?
- How can tourism promote social benefits for the host community?
- Why is it important for visitors to avoid conflict with the local community?

How infrastructure development can benefit local people

GETTING STARTED

Working in pairs, find out the meaning of the term 'infrastructure' using the internet or from your teacher. List the different types of infrastructure that tourism relies on.

A destination cannot function effectively without good infrastructure. Infrastructure includes transport links such as roads and railways, telecommunication networks, buildings, power supplies, and water and sewerage systems. Tourism can help to encourage the development of infrastructure as visitors from relatively wealthy parts of the world demand a decent level of service provision. This includes comfortable access to their destination, hygienic sanitation facilities and the ability to remain in contact with home.

Transport infrastructure

Transport infrastructure includes roads, railways, airports and other types of transport links such as tramlines. One of the main benefits of transport infrastructure for the local community is that it can benefit both residents and tourists. For example, in Nepal there have been improvements to roads that lead to towns such as Jomsom. These roads are used by tourists who visit Nepal to go trekking, along with local people who rely on the roads to access other towns and villages. This could be considered a sustainable development because the road has relatively low volumes of traffic, yet brings significant benefits for local people.

Telecommunications networks

When people go on holiday, they often like to instantly share images and videos of their experiences; to do this they would normally require access to Wi-Fi. Although many destinations now offer full Wi-Fi, there are many parts of the world that lack coverage. For example, in Africa, there are large parts of the continent that do not have Wi-Fi coverage. Having greater Wi-Fi coverage could help to boost sustainable economic growth in Africa, including within the travel and tourism sector.

ACTIVITY

Working in pairs, create a table from the list of types of infrastructure you identified in the starting activity. Add a column to indicate how each type of infrastructure benefits local people.

Buildings

DID YOU KNOW?

Over 1 million people visited Rio de Janeiro during the Olympic Games in 2016.

Local facilities in a destination, such as police stations, doctor's surgeries and hospitals, serve both tourists and the local community. Often if a location becomes a popular tourist destination, this can encourage the construction of new facilities that can be used by the local community and tourists alike. In preparation for the 2016 Summer Olympics in Rio de Janeiro, a new museum called the Museum of Tomorrow, which opened in December 2015, was constructed in the port area, along with a new tram service, waterfront walkway and pedestrianised square.

Power supply

Similar to other forms of infrastructure, most tourists expect access to electrical power. In August 2018, on the Greek island of Hydra, many tourists were left without electricity for over 24 hours. One major concern for the mayor of the island was that the island was full of visitors at the time and the electricity blackout gave a very bad impression.

The lack of power supply left many tourists without access to working cash machines. Furthermore, local businesses suffered when large amounts of refrigerated and frozen stock were ruined. This situation was caused by damage to an undersea power cable that supplied the island with electricity. To become more sustainable, such destinations could seek to make greater use of renewable energy; for example, solar power, given that places like Hydra experience long periods of sunshine.

ACTIVITY

Working in small groups, you will be allocated a National Park to study. Use its website to find out about tourism infrastructure within the park; discuss how this infrastructure benefits local people.

◨ Figure 2.5: How does tourism infrastructure in National Parks contribute to economic development?

Water and sewerage systems

Many parts of the world do not enjoy access to sustainable supplies of clean water or adequate sewerage systems. You may have experienced this yourself on holiday; for example, some hotels in Southern Europe do not allow you to flush toilet paper away. In fact, the issue of water and sewerage is quite controversial for the tourism industry. For example, there are parts of Kenya that serve the tourist industry, yet local residents don't have easy access to clean running water.

In order to be more sustainable, the tourism industry, and hotels in particular, needs to work with local residents to ensure fair access to water for the people that live there. For example, the hotel chain Marriott has a 'Nobility of Nature' programme through which the chain works in partnership with Conservation International to protect sources of fresh water in Asia for more than 2 billion people.

LINK IT UP

In Component 1, you will have learned about how growth or decline in tourism can affect infrastructure development.

CHECK MY LEARNING

Individually, review your notes and create a mind map of the impacts of tourism for revision. The following questions will help you to plan your mind map.
- What is infrastructure?
- How does having good infrastructure benefit tourism?
- How does having good infrastructure benefit the host community?

Engaging local communities and partnership projects

GETTING STARTED

Working in pairs, discuss the meaning of public, private and voluntary sector; list the main interests of each sector.

Now working as a whole group, discuss the question: 'Should the private sector have full control of tourism development in a destination?'

Having the support of the local community is essential for any project to succeed; this includes new businesses, housing, infrastructure and, of course, tourism development. Without the engagement of local communities, conflict can quickly arise.

Including local communities in decision making

It is recognised that including local communities in tourism decision making can be mutually beneficial for all stakeholders in an area. Research carried out in places as diverse as Tanzania and Hong Kong agrees that involving local communities can bring about long-lasting and sustainable benefits for tourism.

Our own government recognises this and has published guidelines for 'engaging communities in tourism services'. Table 2.10 details some suggested success factors for ensuring local communities are included in decision making.

◻ Table 2.10: Success factors for local community inclusion

Success factor	Detail
The tourism strategy for the area has residents at its heart.	The strategy recognises residents as users of tourism and beneficiaries of the economic development of tourism.
There is involvement of residents in the development of tourism vision and strategy.	Councils and other stakeholders consult and involve communities in the development of their vision.
There is involvement of residents in the delivery of that strategy and development of the tourism offer.	This could involve consulting with local residents to make an attraction out of an area or activity of which they are proud.
Capital developments for the benefit of tourists also involve and benefit local residents.	Ensuring the development of facilities that will benefit from community usage outside of the tourism season.
There is a balance between the development of tourism and the needs of residents.	Where there are conflicts of interest, local residents are able to voice their concerns and be listened to.
There is effective support for local businesses that depend on tourism.	Local businesses have a say in delivery; for example, scrapping parking charges.

Partnership projects

LINK IT UP

In Component 1, you will have learned about different types of partnership and how organisations work together.

Partnership projects can involve a range of stakeholders working together; this could include a public–private sector partnership, private–voluntary sector partnership, or a combination of the three.

An overseas example of a partnership project is the Chalalan Ecolodge in Bolivia; this is a facility that is owned in partnership with the indigenous population. The Chalalan Ecolodge was constructed to provide income and employment to the indigenous community in an area that was previously suffering from excess logging, the idea being that visitors to the area would appreciate the standing forest and provide an alternative income to local communities.

The Chalalan host community has benefitted directly from employment and income generated by the ecolodge and also from investment in health and education funded by profits made by the ecolodge. Employment created by the lodge has also given young people a reason to stay in the region rather than moving to the cities. Employees at the lodge have gained skills in business management, tourism services, biodiversity monitoring and marketing.

ACTIVITY

Working in pairs, visit the following website: www.responsibletravel.com. Find the example of the Chalalan Ecolodge and research how the local community has a share of ownership and employment opportunities.

Next, still working in pairs, discuss how such partnerships work and benefit different groups, including:
- members of the local community
- visitors to the area
- the local environment.

Overseas, public–private partnerships, known as PPPs, have helped tourism developments in Goa, India. Public–private investments have been essential for tourism infrastructure projects, including the construction of airports, ports and railways.

The benefits of partnership projects

Successful public–private partnerships are essential for sustainable tourism because by combining their resources they can increase the amount of investment in an area; furthermore, organisations can share costs and their expertise. Figure 2.6 summarises some of the specific benefits of successful public–private partnership projects.

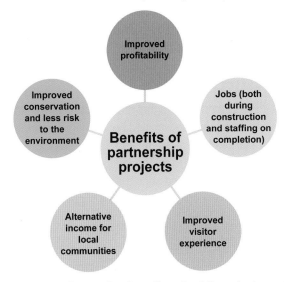

◼ Figure 2.6: Can you think of any other benefits of public–private partnerships?

ACTIVITY

Working in a small group, you will be allocated a role: a member of the local community, private company owner or local government. Firstly, consider what your character's main tourism interests are. Next, role play a meeting regarding the opening of a new tourist attraction. Discuss who should be involved, how and why.

CHECK MY LEARNING

Working individually, create a mind map that outlines ways in which the travel and tourism industry can involve local communities in decision making. For example, asking the local community about facilities that could benefit both local people and visitors.

Next, conclude this activity by stating three benefits of involving local communities in decision making.

Tourist taxes and funding community projects

GETTING STARTED

Working as a group and using the examples on this page, discuss types of tourist tax. Discuss the questions below.
- Should tourists pay taxes to arrive in a destination or stay in a hotel?
- Should tax income go towards funding community projects?

Tourism taxes can be very important for a host area; these can bring in much needed income that can be invested in improving infrastructure and funding community projects. However, in most destinations it is important that a sustainable 'tax balance', as shown in Figure 2.7, is achieved where tourist taxes are fair and proportionate.

Tourist taxes

There are many ways that tourists pay tax either directly or indirectly. Some taxes are specifically levied on tourists, while others are common to both residents and visitors. Some examples include the following.
- Air Passenger Duty (APD) – a charge levied on larger aircraft carrying more than 20 passengers out of the UK.
- Departure tax – similar to APD, many countries charge tourists to use one of their airports to leave the country.
- Value Added Tax (VAT) – a tax common in the EU and many other countries that is applied to the purchase of good and services.
- Fuel duty – a tax that is applied to the purchase of fuel for cars and other motorised vehicles.
- Sustainable Tourist Tax – applied to holiday accommodation on Spain's Balearic Islands.
- Hotel/city taxes – common across Europe (except in the UK) and the USA, usually a per person per night charge; use of the revenue raised varies widely between destinations, in some it is used to fund local and tourist initiatives, while in others it is taken by central government.
- New Zealand Tourist Tax – to be introduced in 2019; the tax on international visitors of NZ$24.40 per person is intended to help fund infrastructure projects.

Other charges

Other charges applied to visitors to an area may also be considered a form of tax. For example, car parking charges tend to be higher in areas popular with tourists. Some places have also been known to target tourists with additional charges referred to as a 'tax'. In the Belgium city of Bruges, chip vendors have admitted to charging tourists 10 per cent more for a portion of chips compared with locals. The *Independent* referred to this as the 'Bruges Chip Tax', however in reality the increased price charges were made at the discretion of the local businesses concerned and not linked to any form of government legislation.

▣ **Figure 2.7: Why is it important that destinations get the tax balance right?**

ACTIVITY

Working in the same group as last lesson, maintain the same roles and hold a meeting to discuss the positive and negative effects of tourist taxes. In your meeting consider:

- how tax income could help the local community
- how tax income could help other stakeholders involved in tourism.

Next, talk about the outcomes from your discussion. Make individual notes about your answers from the meeting and share your findings with the other groups.

Using tax income to fund community projects

One of the benefits tourism brings to host destinations is the tax income generated, which can be reinvested in local areas and be used to fund projects that benefit local communities.

The sustainable tourism tax

An example of a tax that is intended to benefit the local area is the sustainable tourism tax; a charge introduced in 2016 that applies to visitors to Spain's Balearic Islands, including Ibiza and Majorca. One of the main purposes of this tax is to raise funds that can be invested in the host destination. This includes funding community projects related to tourism, maintaining landscapes and reversing damage caused by tourism.

However, a similar tax introduced in 2002 was scrapped in 2003 because holidaymakers chose lower-cost destinations in Egypt, Tunisia and Turkey. According to CABI, the 2002 tax added around £60 extra to the price of a two-week holiday for four and contributed to a dramatic decline in visitors from countries such as Germany, where arrivals from Germany to Majorca fell by 25 per cent.

 What benefits might a sustainable tourism tax bring to local communities living in Ibiza?

Taxes and fees in the Galápagos Islands

Charging high fees and taxes can benefit a destination like the Galápagos Islands in two ways; raising income for the local area for community projects and discouraging mass tourism. The Galápagos National Park fee is US$100 and must be paid on arrival to the airport; 40 per cent of this fee is then reinvested into conservation initiatives with the National Park.

This income has facilitated the development of a management plan for the Galápagos National Park which includes objectives such as: conservation of ecosystems, promoting participation, using scientific knowledge to manage the ecosystem and promoting international cooperation for the conservation of the Galápagos Islands.

CHECK MY LEARNING

Working individually, review your notes about the environmental impacts of tourism and make notes for revision.

Sustainability and managing economic impacts

GETTING STARTED

Working in small groups, list how tourism benefits local communities. This could include:

- economic benefits
- social benefits
- environmental benefits.

The economic impacts of tourism can be sustainably managed through the employment and training it brings, encouraging visitors to support the communities they stay in, governmental restrictions on foreign ownership of facilities and the retention of a greater proportion of visitor spend.

How tourism can provide employment and training opportunities

There is a diverse range of jobs within the travel and tourism sector. Different jobs requiring different skills and attributes makes travel and tourism an appealing sector to work in. Furthermore, tourism can aid development in poorer parts of the world by providing local people with jobs.

Opportunities for local people

Tourism employs lots of people globally. In the EU alone, 12 million people are employed in tourism-related jobs. Many tourism jobs involve local people providing tourism products and services in the local area.

Responsible Travel, an organisation that works in partnership with specialist holiday companies, believes that for a destination or organisation to be considered responsible or sustainable, it must employ local staff and local guides. It believes that tourism should benefit the host community, especially by providing employment to local people, as this brings about economic benefits for people living in the area.

One such example is the employment of porters and Sherpas for trekking adventures in mountain locations such as the Himalayas. Tourists should ensure that they do not ask them to carry an unreasonable amount and should pay local staff that they employ fairly and in accordance with any pay guidelines that exist.

ACTIVITY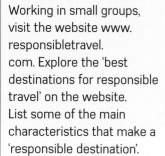

Working in small groups, visit the website www.responsibletravel.com. Explore the 'best destinations for responsible travel' on the website. List some of the main characteristics that make a 'responsible destination'.

Access to higher-paid jobs

A lot of the jobs created by tourism are low paid, and this is a criticism often made. However, tourism can provide training and employment opportunities for local people and give them access to education and higher-paid jobs (Figure 2.8). This is especially important in many poorer countries that rely on tourism to provide employment for a significant proportion of the population. For example, in the Bahamas, just under 50 per cent of the population are directly employed in tourism.

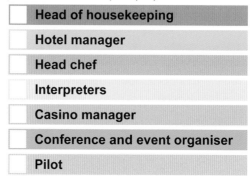

	Head of housekeeping
	Hotel manager
	Head chef
	Interpreters
	Casino manager
	Conference and event organiser
	Pilot

Figure 2.8: Better-paid jobs in tourism (you could rank them 1 (best) to 7 (worst) in a spare moment)

Employment in tourism can provide a pathway into the workforce for young adults and persons without higher education. Furthermore, employment in tourism can provide entry-level workers without many qualifications with essential skills, such as communicating verbally, working as part of a team and problem solving. From this, employees who develop their tourism skills and show that they are proficient at their job are often presented with the opportunity to advance their careers and access higher-paid jobs (Figure 2.9).

Figure 2.9: How do people get access to higher-paid jobs in the travel and tourism sector?

There are a number of routes to accessing higher-paid jobs in tourism. One route is to start in an organisation at a lower level and work your way up. For example, starting as a bar person, then being promoted to bar manager and so on. Another route to accessing a higher-paid job in tourism is to obtain a higher-level qualification such as a degree; this would usually enable someone to join an organisation at a higher level, such as at the managerial level.

Opportunities for education and training

Many organisations see the benefits of investing in education and training for staff. Better-trained staff can help make an organisation more profitable by offering a higher level of service and coming up with ideas and initiatives that could benefit the company financially. For example, in 2017, British Airways announced that it was going to invest £4.5 billion to 'bring back the glory days', with training staff one of the priorities for the organisation. However, in poorer countries that rely on tourism for income, persuading organisations and governments to invest in education and training for tourism can be a challenge.

ACTIVITY

Working in pairs, discuss how local people will benefit if tourists are encouraged to use local services and buy local products.

Share your opinions and create a mind map to express your thoughts.

CHECK MY LEARNING

Your teacher will provide you with some sample questions about impacts of tourism and sustainability. Add some of your own revision questions that you have been creating throughout this section. Some example questions that could be used are below.

- Can you identify three positive environmental impacts of tourism?
- Can you explain how educating visitors can encourage more sustainable behaviour?
- Can you explain how tourism creates job and training opportunities?

How can visitors support local communities?

GETTING STARTED

As a class, discuss the negatives of all-inclusive resorts for local communities. In particular, think about how all-inclusive resorts can impact on the economy of an area. Try to use the key phrase: 'economic multiplier effect'.

DID YOU KNOW?

According to the ABTA Holiday Habits Report 2017, 17 per cent of holidays taken by UK tourists in the previous 12 months were classed as visits to all-inclusive resorts.

KEY TERM

A **rickshaw** is a light, usually two-wheeled, passenger vehicle that is usually pulled by a person either on foot or a bicycle.

Many locations rely on the economic benefits that tourism brings, including employment and income for the host area. However, it is common for destinations not to gain as much income from tourism as they should. One of the key principles of sustainable tourism is the idea of financial fairness; that local communities receive an appropriate income for the products and services that they provide.

Buying local products

If you have ever been on a holiday, you may have found that one of the most enjoyable activities is to sample and purchase local produce, such as food, gifts and crafts offered by the local community.

Unfortunately, many all-inclusive resorts do little to encourage tourists to leave the hotel complex, where they are provided with an unlimited supply of food, drink and entertainment included in the price of the holiday. In destinations with a high density of all-inclusive resorts, such as Diani Beach in Kenya, local businesses often miss out on the financial benefits that tourism can bring.

Many larger destinations have multinational brands such as McDonald's, KFC and Burger King. While some tourists enjoy the familiarity of such brands, others with more adventurous tastes are keen to try local cuisine. Trying local cuisine in small, family-run establishments is a much more sustainable way to enjoy the destination. The profits made from such businesses stay with the local community rather than leaking out of the country back to the home bases of multinational organisations. Furthermore, this creates jobs for local people and helps a destination to retain its cultural identity.

Using local transport

Some destinations are famous for the local transport that has become a part of their cultural identity; for example, yellow taxis in New York, cable cars in San Francisco, Zulu **rickshaw** pullers in Durban, South Africa. A benefit of using local transport rather than tour operator-organised excursions is that the profits generated go to the local community and local services rather than to the tour operator. Also, it leads to a more authentic experience for the visitor.

Although some local people may work on behalf of large transport organisations, many are self-employed and own the form of transport that they offer to tourists; in Durban, there is a policy that rickshaw pullers must own their own rickshaw. A benefit of this set-up is that the rickshaw pullers are self-sufficient; they do not have fuel costs and all of the money that they make is their own.

However, there have been some well-publicised examples of rickshaw pullers trying to overcharge tourists. For example, in 2015 it was claimed that a London rickshaw driver tried to charge a Dutch tourist £600, for a 30-minute tour of the city.

Government restrictions

Some destinations have government restrictions in place to prevent multinational brands from setting up there. Some examples of this are shown in Table 2.11.

◻ **Table 2.11: Government restrictions that affect global travel and tourism**

Restriction	Action taken
Foreign-owned companies	Some destinations have government restrictions in place to prevent multinational brands from setting up there. For example, McDonald's was prevented from setting up a restaurant in Florence, Italy.
All-inclusive resorts	In 2018, the Balearic government announced plans to ban free unlimited alcohol being served at resorts as part of all-inclusive package deals.
Foreign workers	In Egypt, the government has forbidden foreigners from working in certain professions, such as tour guiding, in order to preserve jobs for Egyptian nationals.

Increasing and retaining visitor spending

There are many techniques that travel and tourism organisations can employ to try to increase visitor spending. At many visitor attractions, ranging from purpose-built attractions to heritage attractions, clever positioning of gift shops can help to increase visitor spending. For example, at many National Trust properties, the gift shop is positioned within the entrance and/or exit areas, so that visitors are forced to go through the gift shop before they enter or exit a property. This strategy can increase sales by confronting visitors with a range of products that may tempt them into making a purchase.

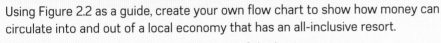

ACTIVITY

Using Figure 2.2 as a guide, create your own flow chart to show how money can circulate into and out of a local economy that has an all-inclusive resort.

Identify the points where money leaks out of the host country.

Add notes or additional points to the flow chart to show where and how income could be retained in the destination by visitors spending locally.

LINK IT UP

Refer back to Figure 2.2, the economic multiplier effect.

Some organisations are able to retain a greater proportion of visitor spending by adapting the products and services that they offer. For example, Alton Towers Resort previously worked with Burger King and KFC to provide fast-food catering within the theme park. However, in 2012, Alton Towers Resort began to operate their own 'in house' versions of these chains in the form of Burger Kitchen and Fried Chicken Co. As these brands are managed by Alton Towers Resort and their owner, Merlin Entertainments, the organisation is able to retain more of the profits made through its fast-food catering. Furthermore, these brands can be found at other Merlin-owned, purpose-built attractions, such as Chessington World of Adventures.

CHECK MY LEARNING

Working individually, you should create a mind map about sustainability and managing social and economic impacts.

Sustainability and managing environmental impacts

GETTING STARTED

Working in pairs, think about the ways in which a destination that you have visited is managed. Write down between three and five things that you think that effective destination management should include. For example, a strategy to reduce the amount of traffic in the central and busiest parts of the destination. This could include the use of public transport or pedestrianised areas of the destination.

The environmental impacts of tourism can be sustainably managed through careful control of visitor numbers, traffic and transport options, proactive planning of new buildings, and education, legislation and regulations to control resource use, waste management and to protect the environment.

Visitor management

Visitor management is a key part of sustainable tourism. Many destinations are popular for their natural beauty; however, such environments are often fragile and therefore need protecting. Visitor management done properly can restrict damage to the natural environment and in some cases, positively contribute to conservation.

Restricting the number of visitors

Until relatively recently the number of tourists visiting Antarctica was unrestricted. In 2009, new legislation was imposed to restrict the size of cruise ships that are able to land around the coast of Antarctica. Specifically, Antarctic tour operators are only allowed to navigate ships with a capacity of less than 500 passengers to landing sites around Antarctica. Furthermore, the number of passengers allowed on shore at a time is limited to 100, with a ratio of one guide per 20 visitors.

Controlling movement of people

Controlling the movement of people can be an effective way of ensuring their safety and protecting the environment, be it built or natural. An example of controlling the movement of people that you may be familiar with is queuing systems at theme parks like Disneyland in the USA and Paris, France. Here, fencing is used to fit a maximum number of people into a relatively small area safely.

Historic buildings owned by the National Trust and English Heritage that are open to visitors also carefully control the movement of people. This may include having areas of significant historical interest behind a 'velvet rope' that visitors can view, but not walk around.

Stampede in Mina, Mecca

One terrible impact of failing to control the movement of people effectively is 'crush and stampede'. On September 24th 2015, hundreds of Muslim pilgrims were killed when overcrowding led to a fatal crush; the victims were making the annual Hajj pilgrimage to Mecca in Saudi Arabia.

DID YOU KNOW?

Since 1969, the average number of tourists who visit Antarctica has risen annually from a few hundred to over 34,000.

ACTIVITY

Working as a class, refer back to the examples in Component 1 and look at the examples of World Heritage Sites from www.nationaltrust.org.uk. You will be given one of the following strategies to manage visitors:

- restricting number of visitors
- controlling movement
- direction of flow.

Now think about how your strategy could help to manage visitors in either an island destination, countryside area, Area of Outstanding Natural Beauty or World Heritage Site.

Direction of flow

Similar to controlling the movement of people, many places like museums and historic buildings have a preferred direction for people to walk in to maintain safety and order. The Great Pyramid of Giza, Egypt employs a direction of flow system for tourists visiting this World Heritage Site. The internal corridors leading to the main chamber of the Great Pyramid are very narrow; therefore, a one-way system is operated in order to ensure that visitors can access the main areas of interest safely.

Maximum visa time limits

One way of restricting the number of visitors to a destination is to issue a limit on the length of stay permitted. Different destinations outside of the EU have different rules that apply to visitor time limits. Figure 2.10 details the limits for UK nationals in several popular destinations.

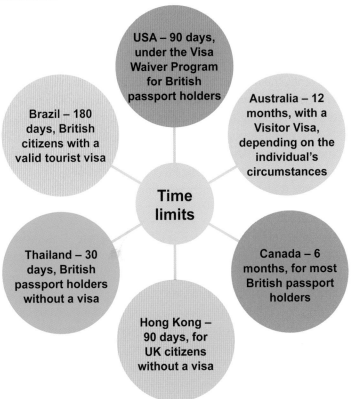

- Figure 2.10: Did you know how long you could stay in these places?

LINK IT UP

Further on in this component, you will learn more about the organisations that specialise in destination management.

CHECK MY LEARNING

Working individually, recap your learning from this lesson by writing down five things that you have learned about destination management. Next, create revision questions about this topic.

ACTIVITY

Based on the destination that you chose earlier in the lesson, find out: the population of the destination, the number of visitors each year and any visa restrictions that exist.

In your notes, discuss how restricting or not restricting tourist numbers might affect the destination over the next five years.

Traffic management

GETTING STARTED

Working in pairs, make a list of transport types. Arrange them in order of best to worst, considering their impact on the environment.

One of the biggest sustainability issues that faces many destinations, in particular major cities, is traffic congestion. There are a number of traffic management strategies that different places use that aim to restrict the amount of traffic on the roads. One benefit of this would be improving the quality of air in major global cities like London, Paris and New York.

Restricting traffic

London

London has a number of traffic management systems in place, such as the congestion charge, that aim to reduce congestion. In 2018, the cost to drive a private car in London city centre was £11.50. All of the money raised through the congestion charge is invested back into London's transport system; this includes spending on London's public bus service operated by Transport for London.

DID YOU KNOW?

A study conducted by the traffic information company, Inrix, found that London is the seventh-worst city in the world for traffic congestion.

Paris

In 2017, the mayor of Paris, Anne Hidalgo, announced plans to restrict traffic in the city and to pedestrianise the city centre. She wants to halve the number of private cars that drive around the city and introduce a new electric tramway, along with encouraging the use of more bicycles, electric cars and scooters. Part of this strategy has seen the closure of stretches of road that run alongside the River Seine. However, drivers' organisations have pointed out that road closures increase congestion and traffic pollution.

New York

New York is one of the most congested cities in the world. It is estimated that traffic congestion costs the city's economy US$20 billion a year. Unlike other major cities, such as London, New York does not currently have a congestion charge to restrict traffic flow in the city centre. In 2007 the then mayor, Michael Bloomberg, wanted to introduce a congestion charge for drivers wanting to enter the Manhattan central business district, however, this proposal was overruled by the New York State Assembly. Similar proposals have included introducing tolls for all East River bridges.

ACTIVITY

Working in the same groups as last lesson, select a destination and explore what type of traffic management strategies could work at your chosen destination.

Affordable and frequent public transport

Most major global cities operate an affordable and frequent public transport service; predominantly this includes bus and rail services. Cities such as New York and London operate an underground rail network; such destinations lack useable space above ground, therefore having an underground system is an effective way of moving the issue of city transport below ground.

In Hong Kong, public transport is so well developed in terms of frequency, efficiency and affordability that few people own cars or even have driving licences. Public transport makes up 90 per cent of all daily journeys in Hong Kong; this is the highest usage of public transport anywhere in the world. All public transport in Hong Kong is bilingual in English and Chinese; this also helps to make public transport extremely accessible to tourists.

Reinvesting charges in public transport

One of the key principles behind congestion charge schemes is that a significant proportion of revenue generated should be reinvested into public transport. One of the main reasons that public transport is seen as a sustainable solution to traffic management in destinations is that one public bus service, with a capacity for 50 passengers, could replace 50 individuals with cars driving on the road.

Adequate parking facilities

Finding adequate parking in destinations can depend on the size and popularity of the destination. Generally speaking, it is easier to find adequate parking in destinations that are smaller and less popular with visitors. Some car parks are privately owned and some are owned by local authorities; one benefit of using local authority-owned car parks is that the income raised through parking charges is often reinvested into the local community.

As many major cities want to deter cars from using city centres; parking charges in the central area are often very high. This is also because land in the city centre is very valuable; therefore, higher car parking charges reflect this.

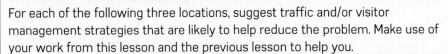

ACTIVITY

For each of the following three locations, suggest traffic and/or visitor management strategies that are likely to help reduce the problem. Make use of your work from this lesson and the previous lesson to help you.

Location	Problem
1. London	London has suffered from illegal levels of air pollution since 2010.
2. Amsterdam	Amsterdam is a city destination that suffers from overcrowding with an overburdened infrastructure network.
3. Dubrovnik	UNESCO has warned that Dubrovnik's World Heritage Status is at risk due to an unsustainable number of tourists visiting the city.

Park and ride schemes

Park and ride schemes are an effective way of keeping car traffic out of city centres and encouraging the use of public transport. A park and ride scheme involves car users parking at an out-of-town location, then being transported to the destination or city centre via public transport, such as a bus. Currently, almost every major city in the UK operates a park and ride scheme. In 2018, park and ride feasibility trials began in Sydney, Australia; the Opal Park and Ride trial offers free parking for people that use public transport to access the city.

Alternative types of transport

As a result of public transport investment, new low emission bus zones have been created by Transport for London, to try to improve the quality of air in the city. The first zone was introduced in March 2017 along Putney High Street. Furthermore, Transport for London plans to introduce around 3000 electric and diesel hybrid ultra-low emission double-decker buses into central London by 2019 and over 250 electric zero emission single-decker buses into central London by 2020.

Another transport innovation has been the introduction of car-pooling or car-sharing organisations. Liftshare is a UK company that organises car sharing between people travelling in the same direction. This enables people to journey together and share travel costs, while reducing congestion and pollution created by traffic.

CHECK MY LEARNING

Working individually, choose one type of alternative transport that you feel would have a positive impact on travel management and the environmental impacts of tourism. Write a short summary justifying your choice.

Planning and legislation

GETTING STARTED

Working in pairs, create a mind map to show how effective planning control and legislation can:

- encourage more sustainable tourism practice
- reduce the negative environmental impacts of tourism.

Planning and legislation play a hugely important role in the sustainable development of destinations. If planned carefully, new developments can be sustainable; they can bring about many benefits for organisations, tourists and, most importantly, host communities and the local environment.

Building regulations

Building regulations are a set of building quality standards that are decided by governments. They relate to the design and construction of new buildings and alterations to existing buildings.

On a global scale, different countries adopt different building regulation standards; in general, the more developed the country, the tighter and more stringent building regulations will be. You may have seen video footage of natural disasters such as earthquakes; usually the impacts of such disasters are worse in poorer countries where less robust building materials and regulations may have been used in construction. Building regulations in cities such as Tokyo, which is at constant risk of earthquakes, ensure that buildings are constructed to an exceptionally high standard and are almost 'earthquake proof'.

Planning permission

Planning permission is the formal approval to construct a building (house, hotel or business), facility (e.g. car park) or change the use of land (e.g. from farm land to commercial) and is usually obtained from the government. Similar to building regulation, different countries adopt different planning permission rules.

Gaining planning permission can be a challenging and often lengthy process. Many factors can determine whether or not planning permission will be granted. Furthermore, in many places, stakeholders such as local residents and other organisations are given the opportunity to have a say about planned developments.

ACTIVITY

Working in pairs, visit www.papuanewguinea.travel to explore the destination. Discuss how planning control legislation may be used by the government to encourage sustainable development. Write down five ways planning legislation can be used to encourage sustainability.

Heritage protection

At the international level is UNESCO, the agency of the United Nations that designates global locations as World Heritage Sites. If it feels that a proposed development compromises the integrity of a World Heritage Site, then it will voice its opposition and threaten to remove the site from its list, which would be damaging to the reputation of the destination.

There is also protection at the national level in some countries. In the UK, there are designated conservation areas, where new developments are restricted, and listed historic buildings and scheduled monuments are protected by law. Special permission is needed to alter them or develop close by.

Size and location of developments

KEY TERM

A **brownfield site** is an area of land that has previously been built on.

Size and location of developments is an important factor in sustainability. Developments that improve **brownfield sites** are more likely to get planning permission because this can often aid the regeneration of a run-down area and improve the quality of the built environment.

However, in some previously undeveloped destinations such as Dubai, brownfield sites do not exist and therefore new construction projects take place in the desert ecosystem that surrounds the city. An even more extreme example in Dubai is the Palm Islands development, which involved the creation of three artificial islands along the coast of Dubai.

Maintaining local styles

When approving new developments, planners need to balance maintaining the historical integrity of a location with the desire to modernise. Often in cities, where land values are high and space limited, the solution is to build skyscrapers, however, these alter historic skylines and can compromise the identity of places. Furthermore, in some destinations such as Lanzarote, local authority regulations mean that there are no high-rise buildings, with the exception of the Gran Hotel and Spa in Arreciffe.

A more sustainable approach is to avoid modern buildings, such as skyscrapers, and have new buildings constructed in a manner that reflects local styles, sometimes using old-fashioned techniques such as roof thatching. For example, in Copenhagen, Denmark, there are no skyscrapers and most buildings found in the centre of the city reflect a traditional Danish-style of building, although there are some modern buildings, such as the Copenhagen Opera House. In 2008, a law was passed that prohibits the construction of new skyscrapers in central Copenhagen, where most buildings are between three and six stories high.

Encouraging sustainability

Many new developments incorporate sustainable design for a number of reasons. In the UK, there is environmental legislation and incentives for the construction industry that encourage sustainable building developments. There are also a number of legally binding EU directives that the UK government has agreed to, such as the 2010 Energy Performance of Buildings Directive which legislates for the construction of energy-efficient buildings.

From a marketing perspective, consumers are becoming more and more aware of the fragility of the planet and are keen to make sustainable choices. Therefore, developing and marketing a facility or location as sustainable can help to increase sales alongside meeting legislative requirements.

Incentives to build green

Adopting sustainable practices can actually save organisations money and so make them more profitable. For example, using energy saving, automated lighting and recycling rainwater for use in toilet facilities uses less resources and can therefore reduce overheads for organisations (Figure 2.11). Furthermore, government schemes in the UK encourage businesses to apply for schemes to help them become more energy efficient by offering tax reductions.

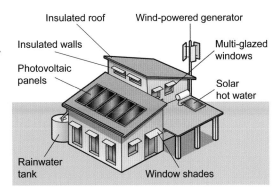

■ Figure 2.11: How can buildings used by tourists be constructed in a sustainable manner?

LINK IT UP

Further on in this component, you will learn more about the role of local and national government in supporting, approving and controlling the development of infrastructure and facility projects. Why do you think local and national government are involved in controlling major tourism infrastructure projects?

CHECK MY LEARNING

Working in the same pairs, answer the following revision questions.

1 How can planning permission impact on tourism building developments?

2 How might the size and scale of a development, such as a new hotel complex, impact on the local area?

3 Why might local authorities ban certain types of building that don't match the style of the area?

4 How can planning legislation help to encourage sustainable tourism developments?

Visitor education

GETTING STARTED

Working in pairs, discuss the benefits of visitor education and how this can help to reduce negative environmental impacts on the destination. Create a list of ways that education can encourage visitors to look after the environment in different types of destination.

Visitor education can be crucial to the sustainable management of a destination. Through education, visitors can be informed about the ways in which they could help the destination; for example, through helping with a conservation project or donating to a particular scheme.

Reducing the impact of visitors on the local environment

There are many ways that visitors can be educated about the impacts of tourism on destinations. UNESCO has issued a 'World Heritage Sustainable Tourism Toolkit' that contains specific guidance about how to communicate with and educate visitors to destinations with World Heritage Status. The seven key steps to success are outlined in Table 2.12.

▣ Table 2.12: Steps to success for sustainable tourism

Steps to success	Details
Have a clear script for the destination to follow and key messages that everyone will understand.	This means finding out what a range of key stakeholders, such as the host community, want and need visitors to know about the destination.
Ensure that tourism marketing of the destination highlights the potential added value of World Heritage Status.	This involves making sure that visitors know that the destination has World Heritage Status as this is a powerful brand for attracting cultural tourists.
Make understanding the site easy.	This involves bringing all of the information about the site or destination into one place that is easy to access; for example, on a website.
Be creative – communicate through everything, throughout the whole life cycle of the visitor experience.	This involves providing visitors with key information about the site or destination before they visit, so that visitors are clear about what they can and cannot do. This includes providing information via brochures, booking websites and other forms of media.
Explore the importance of the site and its outstanding universal appeal (OUV) in the most appropriate areas.	This involves using storytelling and interpretation to encourage people to visit areas where they are less likely to damage a site.
Outsource communication of key sustainable tourism messages.	This involves training and helping tourism professionals to deliver key messages about the site or destination.
Use communication to build lasting relationships with visitors.	This involves keeping in communication with visitors after their visit. This includes keeping the contact details of visitors as they may be willing to donate to projects in the future.

ACTIVITY

Case Study: Responsible Tourism in West Africa

Visitor education has been a key focus of the 'responsible tourism in West Africa scheme', which aims to encourage cultural interaction between visitors and the local community. Western visitors are given opportunities to engage with the culture and history of rural communities and experience traditional practices, such as music and dancing. In one example, the village chief's son educated visitors by explaining the structure and formation of the village.

Using the example above, work in a small group to explain how visitor education can be used to encourage more sustainable forms of tourism.

For further examples of visitor education visit the website sustainabletourism.net. Explore another of the case studies from the website, then write down examples of how visitor education can reduce the negative environmental impacts of tourism and help to make the destination more sustainable.

◼ How does visitor education reduce the negative environmental impacts of tourism?

How visitors can contribute to looking after the local environment

There are many reasons why visitors travel to destinations; some visit for sun, sea and relaxation, while others are educated to know that their visit can make a positive contribution to the host area. At the very least, sustainable tourists should have no negative impact on the local area. This includes being educated about basic principles such as behaving and dressing appropriately, using local produce, supporting local businesses and using the provided waste disposal and recycling available where possible.

Some visitors travel because they have been educated about how they can make a positive contribution to the host community and local environment. Holidays that give tourists the chance to help preserve the environment have been growing in popularity for many years. This includes volunteering holidays that provide people with the chance to work on conservation projects in places as diverse as Thailand, the Amazon, Sumatra and Ecuador.

DID YOU KNOW?

A study conducted by Tourism and Research Marketing found that as many as 1.6 million people volunteer abroad each year.

LINK IT UP

In Component 3, you will learn more about the needs of customers, including those that express a preference for holidays that involve conservation volunteering and green tourism. How can this type of tourism contribute to the management of the local environment?

CHECK MY LEARNING

Working individually, come up with a list of ways in which visitors could be educated about the benefits for the environment of using less plastic, such as carrying a reusable water bottle.

Controlling resources and protecting natural areas

GETTING STARTED

Working in pairs, make a list of the different resources that tourists may use on a holiday. This can include:
- resources that tourists take with them such as mobile devices
- resources at the destination, such as drinking water.

KEY TERMS

A **resource** is a consumable item or supply, such as water, metal or fish. Can also be applied to people; for example, staff and labour.

Biodegrade means the breakdown of an object by bacteria and other living organisms.

Water stress is when an area does not have enough water to meet the needs of the population.

Controlling the use of resources is an essential part of sustainable destination management. Tourism is a **resource**-hungry industry, where consumers have high expectations of their holiday product, which in turn places demands on resources such as energy, food and water.

Waste management

Waste is managed by tourism organisations in a number of ways, often depending on the location of the organisation and the type of waste. Recycling is the preferred and most sustainable way for most places to deal with waste. Almost every item that is thrown away can be recycled in some way. However, non-recycled waste is often sent to landfill sites where it is either buried or burned, which is very bad for the environment.

Plastic pollution is a global issue; mainly because plastic is very, very slow to **biodegrade** and therefore pollutes many fragile ecosystems. However, plastic can be recycled; in India, many roads are now built using plastic. Furthermore, in the UK a few councils, such as Enfield council, are trialling building roads out of plastic. This is an important development for the travel and tourism sector as future infrastructure projects could include the widespread use of recycled plastic.

Toilet waste from hotels is commonly disposed of via a sewerage system. However, if the hotel is not in a built-up area, or isolated and difficult to access, then quite often a septic tank system will be used to store toilet waste hygienically.

Energy

Many tourism organisations, such as hotels, use lots of energy. In the past, the energy needs of such organisations have been met via energy supplied through a national grid system powered by the burning of fossil fuels. However, climate change fears have prompted national governments, organisations and private individuals to make use of greener sources of energy, such as solar, wind, geothermal and tidal power.

Water supplies

Water supplies are plentiful in certain parts of the world and under real **water stress** in others. Generally speaking, the hotter the country, the more it will experience water stress. Climate change is a factor that could lead to increased water stress in certain parts of the world in the future, particularly around Sub-Saharan Africa.

One response from the travel and tourism industry has been to encourage hotels to limit the number of swimming pools that they have in order to preserve water. This also includes restricting the use of fountains and water features that do not recycle water. Many organisations also now have rainwater-collecting equipment that make use of rainwater in toilet-flushing facilities. Also, many hotels try to reduce water and energy usage by asking customers not to leave used towels to be washed every day.

How can visitors help to reduce demand on resources?

ACTIVITY

Case study: Vamizi Island, Mozambique

The Vamizi Island scheme offers ten low-impact beach houses. The design of the properties has aimed to be self-sufficient in the way that they use resources and the construction of each beach house has used almost entirely local materials, including the timber and thatch. The scheme also provides islanders with a boat to patrol for illegal fishing.

Using the example above, work in pairs to explain how the Vamizi Island scheme is trying to use and manage resources sustainably.

Next, select a different destination such as Papua New Guinea. Research the destination and note down how it is vulnerable. As a pair, decide how the destination could be protected and note your ideas down.

Managing demand in fragile natural areas

Many natural areas are vulnerable to the high volume of tourists that visit. In response, many places have designated nature and marine reserves that control where visitors can access and what they can do when there.

The Cerbère-Banyuls Natural Marine Reserve, off the Mediterranean coast of south-west France, limits visitor access. Divers must sign an agreement regulating their conduct when underwater and those visiting by boat are not permitted to land. Some areas are open only to research scientists.

Great Barrier Reef

The Great Barrier Reef Marine Park Authority has allocated zones to different areas of the Reef, located off the Queensland coast, Australia, which determine how that area can be used. The general use zone, which is used by a range of groups including tourists, encompasses 30 per cent of the reef. Other zones such as the Habitat Protection Zone and Conservation Park Zone ban access for activities such as fishing.

LINK IT UP

Refer back to the examples of visitor management at Boracay, Philippines, the Galápagos Islands, and the islands of Koh Khai Nok, Koh Khai Nui and Koh Khai Nai in Thailand earlier in this component.

CHECK MY LEARNING

Create a mind map about how resources are controlled and managed in tourism. Include information about how demand is managed in fragile natural areas.

Wildlife conservation and education

GETTING STARTED

Working in pairs, come up with a definition of 'wildlife conservation'. Can you give any examples of wildlife conservation organisations, other than the WWF, to support your definition?

KEY TERM

The **WWF** (The World Wide Fund for Nature) is an international organisation dedicated to wildlife conservation.

You may be familiar with wildlife conservation organisations such as the **WWF**. One of its aims is to educate people about the benefits of humans living in harmony with nature, this of course, includes tourists. Educating tourists can play a positive role in wildlife conservation, as there are many ways that tourists can contribute to the sustainability of destinations.

Wildlife

The chance to learn about diverse wildlife can be a real draw and an educational experience for tourists, especially if they are viewed in their natural setting. Many African countries, such as Kenya, make the most of their amazing natural wildlife by offering educational safari tours that promise views of creatures such as lions, giraffes, rhinoceros and hippopotamuses. Such activities could be considered 'sustainable' if they benefit local people, such as tour guides, and do not interfere with wildlife.

Hunting and animal interaction

However, some specialist tour operators, such as ASH Adventures, offer a 'big five' hunting experience across the Southern African countries of South Africa and Zimbabwe. The 'big five' refers to the elephant, Cape buffalo, lion, rhinoceros and leopard. While there may be a demand for hunting of this nature, such activities are at odds with the principles of sustainable tourism and educating visitors about the benefits that they can bring to an environment.

Although not as extreme as hunting, some people have issues with any tourist activity that involves humans interacting with animals outside of their natural habitat. One such activity that has proved popular with tourists, yet controversial, over the years is swimming with dolphins. Organisations such as Cancun.com promote swimming with dolphins as an activity that mixes fun with education.

ACTIVITY

Working individually, consider the question: 'Should tourists be allowed to swim with dolphins?' Provide a written answer to this question, including:
- an introduction to the issue
- any benefits of tourists swimming with dolphins
- any negative impacts of tourists swimming with dolphins
- a conclusion: do you agree or disagree that tourists should be allowed to swim with dolphins?

The natural world

KEY TERM

An **ecosystem** is a community of interactions between the living and non-living environment.

Many of the world's most beautiful locations are difficult to access and relatively unpopulated. A particular threat to these locations is that they have a delicately balanced **ecosystem** that could be disrupted by mass tourism; Figure 2.12 shows the world's main ecosystems. One of the issues that large numbers of visitors can unwittingly bring with them is the introduction of foreign species to already finely balanced ecosystems.

For example, as Antarctica is now warming up, the continent is at risk of invasion from plants and insects, such as the common fly, which may be able to adapt to the warmer Antarctic climate.

Visitor education is critical in ensuring that people do not unwittingly introduce new species to such places. Measures as simple as buying brand new clothes or ensuring that all footwear is exceptionally clean can prevent things like seeds and bugs being transported to new locations.

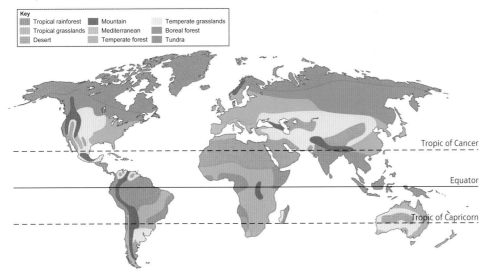

□ Figure 2.12: What do you know about the world's main ecosystems?

ACTIVITY

Working in pairs, you should select and research a destination where wildlife is the main attraction. Create a PowerPoint® presentation that includes:

- the name and location of the destination
- a description of the wildlife that attracts visitors
- an explanation of how wildlife is protected within the destination.

Special qualities of the environment

Depending on where you visit in the world, there are many fascinating ecosystems to discover, each with unique qualities that make it special. Some organisations seek to make the most of these special qualities and encourage visitors to get involved in the conservation of such places. The Mighty Roar is an international wildlife and community volunteer abroad programme. It offers participants the opportunity to volunteer in a range of schemes at a wide variety of destinations in different ecosystems around the world, in countries like Bali, Costa Rica, India, Namibia and South Africa.

Guides

Using local guides can be an effective way to educate visitors about the wildlife and special qualities of the environment in a host area. As local people often have the expertise and knowledge of an area, this can be beneficial for the visitor's experience. Using local guides fits in with the principles of sustainable tourism as this can provide employment and economic benefits for local people. Some destinations, such as Egypt, use legislation to ensure that all tour guides are residents of the host nation.

LINK IT UP

In Component 3, you will learn that some tourists desire a holiday experience that reflects responsible tourism. Why do you think some tourists want a holiday that is environmentally friendly and minimises their carbon footprint?

CHECK MY LEARNING

Create a mind map about the benefits of educating visitors about wildlife conservation. The following questions will help you to plan your mind map.

- Why are visitors attracted to wildlife?
- How can visitors assist with the conservation of wildlife?
- Should some areas of the world remain 'out of bounds' for tourists?

Learning aim B: assessment practice

Although the topics from the whole component could occur in any of the questions across the assessment, some examples of the types of question that may be asked in relation to topics in Section B are shown here. Before answering the following questions, refer to the command words found on page XXX.

Part of the assessment will assess your understanding of Section B: Impact of travel and tourism and sustainability. This may include:

- explaining the different types of impact that may affect local communities and environments in global destinations
- explaining how some global destinations aim to minimise the negative impacts of tourism and maximise the positive impacts to achieve sustainable tourism
- assessing how governments and travel and tourism organisations can achieve sustainable tourism.

TIP

When you are talking about the impacts of tourism on destinations, remember to classify each impact as:

- social – these are the impacts that affect people, their culture and way of life
- economic – these are the impacts that affect jobs, cost of living and the contribution of tourism to the wealth of a destination
- environmental – these are the impacts that affect the surroundings in a destination – both natural and built.

CHECKPOINT

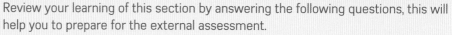

Review your learning of this section by answering the following questions, this will help you to prepare for the external assessment.

Strengthen

- Identify three positive economic impacts that tourism can have on a destination.
- Identify three negative social impacts that tourism can have on a destination.
- Explain how tourism can disrupt the everyday lives of the local community living in a destination.

Challenge

- Compare the positive and negative environmental impacts that tourism can have on a destination.
- Assess the possible negative impacts that tourism can have on the economy of a host destination.

ASSESSMENT ACTIVITY 1 | LEARNING AIM | B

Read the following article about the sustainable management of tourism at Uluru, Australia.

Uluru (also known as Ayers Rock) in Australia is one of the largest monoliths (large rock) in the world. The rock was suffering from erosion caused by tourists climbing the monolith using a rope and pole path fixed into the side of the rock.

In the 1980s, the Australian government gave the land on which Uluru stands back to the aboriginal inhabitants, called the Anangu. The Anangu ask that tourists do not climb the rock as it has special spiritual significance for them.

Today, Uluru is managed by the Anangu, working with park rangers and scientists to look after the land, plants and animals according to traditional law. The Anangu provide traditional land management training to non-aboriginal park rangers and scientists.

Now answer the following questions.
- Litter is a negative environmental impact of tourism in locations like Uluru. Give **one** other negative environmental impact of tourism
- Uluru has special spiritual significance to the Anangu, therefore tourists have been asked not to climb the rock. Give **one** social benefit of this request.
- Give **two** examples of the positive economic impacts of tourism in a location like Uluru.
- Explain the social impacts of tourists failing to respect local culture.
- Assess the importance of key stakeholders working together to manage tourism in locations such as Uluru.

ASSESSMENT ACTIVITY 2 | LEARNING AIM | B

Read the following article adapted from the *Guardian* about the economic impacts of tourism.

Tourism is often cited as the world's largest industry – and for good reason. One in every 11 people worldwide is employed in the sector, which contributes about 9.5 per cent of global GDP.

According to the World Bank Group, it is one of the few industries that can promote economic development in poorer countries. It is no wonder that 83 per cent of global southern countries recognise tourism as their main export.

However, of every US$100 spent by the average developed-world tourist, only US$5 remains in the destination's economy.

Now answer the following questions.
- How many people are employed in the tourism sector worldwide?
- GDP stands for Gross Domestic Product. What does this mean?
- Encouraging investment is an economic benefit of tourism. Explain **two** other economic benefits of tourism.
- Explain how tourism can promote economic development, especially in poorer countries.
- Assess why 'of every US$100 spent by the average developed-world tourist, only US$5 remains in the destination's economy.'

TIP

Don't forget the importance of learning real case studies and using them in your assessment practice. For example, if you are describing a partnership project, give a real example of a partnership project that is happening right now.

TAKE IT FURTHER

Have you checked that you know the different social, economic and environmental impacts of tourism on global destinations? Are you aware that these impacts can be managed in a sustainable way? Remember to give real examples of how destinations manage tourism in a sustainable manner.

Tourism development

GETTING STARTED

Tourism development, with the increased numbers of visitors and the building of visitor facilities, amenities and infrastructure it brings, can dramatically affect destinations. Can you think of both a negative and positive example?

KEY TERM

Destination management is the coordinated management of the different elements that make up a tourist destination, including visitor attractions, infrastructure, marketing and pricing.

Throughout their life cycle, tourist destinations will experience stages of growth, stagnation and decline or rejuvenation. This is true of destinations that you may be familiar with, such as Blackpool in the UK and Benidorm in Spain. Sometimes destinations need to reinvent themselves in order to remain relevant and popular with tourists; effective **destination management** is of vital importance to locations that may be experiencing decline.

Butler's Tourism Area Life Cycle (TALC) Model

Butler's TALC model shows how tourist destinations experience six distinct stages throughout their life cycle (Figure 2.13).

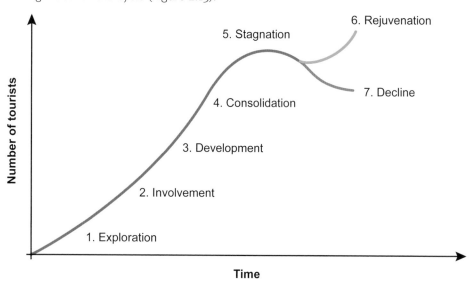

▣ Figure 2.13: Do you know any destinations that fit the TALC model?

Exploration

Exploration is when smaller numbers of people visit an area because of something unique like an amazing natural feature, such as a beach, or site of historical interest, such as a castle. At the exploration stage tourism is very small scale and low key.

Involvement

Involvement is when the local population begin to respond to the needs of visitors by introducing amenities including hotels, restaurants and transport facilities, such as new bus routes and car parks.

Development

Development is when larger organisations, such as tour operators, start to notice the potential of an area for tourism development. At this stage, hotels are built and locations are marketed as tourist destinations. Job opportunities for the host community to work in tourism increase as the number of visitors rises dramatically.

LINK IT UP

In Component 1, you will have learned about specific destinations in detail. Can you recognise where they would fit on the TALC model?

Consolidation

Consolidation is when tourism becomes embedded in the local area. Many local residents work in tourism-related occupations and visitor numbers still grow steadily. However, at this point some of the older amenities and facilities may be becoming dated and untidy. Towards the end of the consolidation stage, destinations risk becoming less attractive and unpopular with certain tourist groups, such as young professional families.

Stagnation

Stagnation is when the number of visitors begin to level off, often due to a negative image of the destination or competition from upcoming developing destinations. This then leads to a loss of business for local organisations which may experience difficulties, such as being forced to reduce prices, or even close. Some of the original features that attracted tourists may also experience issues, such as overcrowding and litter on beaches.

Decline or rejuvenation

Decline is caused by visitor numbers falling dramatically. The main type of tourist attracted to the destination is those on a budget seeking a cheap break. Many tourist facilities such as smaller hotels are forced to close. In some cases, accommodation is purchased by the local authority and used to house tenants.

Rejuvenation is the preferred option for destinations; this often involves new investment to 'smarten' up local features such as the seafront, or by reinventing the destination to try to find a **niche market**; for example, Brighton has reinvented itself as an 'alternative' destination.

KEY TERMS

A **niche market** is a small or specialised market for a particular tourism product.

Rejuvenation means restoring to a previous, better state or revitalising, improving the appearance of something.

ACTIVITY

Working in a small group, chose a destination to study. Discuss and agree what stage of the TALC model the destination is at and why. Create an information sheet to support your argument. Include information such as data about visitor numbers.

CHECK MY LEARNING

Working in the same small groups, present your findings to the rest of the class. The following questions will help you to recap the TALC model.
- What are the main characteristics of a destination during the exploration phase?
- What are the main characteristics of a destination during the stagnation phase?
- Why is it important for destinations to rejuvenate themselves?

Applying Butler's TALC model

GETTING STARTED

Working in a small group, recap the six stages of the TALC model.
- Exploration.
- Involvement.
- Development.
- Consolidation.
- Stagnation.
- Decline or rejuvenation.

Explain each stage.

As we saw in the previous lesson, Butler's TALC model has six distinct stages, which can be matched to many destinations that exist today. The model is an important tool for destinations to use because it may help them to identify when rejuvenation is required to increase tourism and prevent the overall decline of the destination.

Butler's TALC: case studies

The idea is that most destinations start out as small towns or villages, unaffected by tourism. However, over time visitors to the area discover the positive features of the location, revisit and tell other people about the place. At this point, the destination responds by providing visitor-friendly amenities, such as accommodation, and from this a tourist resort is born.

Panama and the Gulf of Chiriqui

The Chiriqui province and the Gulf of Chiriqui in Panama are considered to be at the involvement stage of Butler's TALC. The Chiriqui province of Panama is a region that offers rainforests, waterfalls and indigenous villages.

The area is beginning to develop as an ecotourism destination, offering activities such as birdwatching, hiking, canopy zip lining and white-water rafting. Furthermore, the Gulf of Chiriqui offers whale watching activities.

DID YOU KNOW?

Standing at 293 metres, the JW Marriott Panama is the tallest building in Panama and Central America. Between its construction in 2011 and March 2018, the hotel was operated by Donald Trump's 'Trump Organization'.

Benidorm

Benidorm is an example of a destination that has transitioned through the stages of Butler's TALC model. In 1925, the port in Benidorm was extended and a few hotels were built. By the 1950s, Benidorm had become popular with Spanish residents visiting from inland Spain. By the 1960s, Benidorm had become popular with British holiday makers, who were able to access the resort thanks to cheap package holiday deals organised by UK-based tour operators.

However, by the 1980s, Benidorm had earned the reputation of a 'lager lout' destination, overrun by young drunk British men, and the image of the resort began to suffer. A strategy to try to improve the image of Benidorm and rejuvenate the resort was to try to attract more family visitors. Over the course of 15 years, between 1985 and 2000, a number of family-friendly 'parks' were opened. In 1985, Aqualandia amusement park was opened, followed by Terra Mitica, Aqua Natura and Terra Natura amusement parks in 2000. Furthermore, there were attempts to increase out-of-season winter-time tourism to Benidorm by attracting pensioners as a target market in order to reduce hotel closures in the winter months. Figure 2.14 highlights that eventually all destinations such as Benidorm will experience rejuvenation or decline after a period of stagnation.

◻ What stages of Butler's TALC model has Benidorm experienced?

ACTIVITY

Working in pairs, select a destination other than Benidorm (which has moved through the six TALC stages) and build a case study. Find a range of images from different dates and compare them. Identify the main differences in the development of the resort and write them down.

Next, create a factsheet for your destination, include the following:
- photographic images from different time periods
- data about visitor numbers over the years
- data about population in the resort
- information about popular attractions over the years.

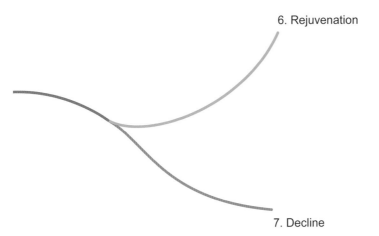

6. Rejuvenation

7. Decline

◻ Figure 2.14: Why do some people consider 'decline or rejuvenation' the most important stage of the TALC model?

CHECK MY LEARNING

Working as a small group, come up with five ideas about how a destination experiencing stagnation or decline could rejuvenate itself. For example, introducing a new theme park to try to encourage more family visitors.

Emerging destinations (1)

GETTING STARTED

Working in a small group, decide what characteristics you would expect to find in an emerging destination. Come up with a second list of characteristics that you would expect to find in a mature destination. Compare the two lists.

Emerging destinations are locations that have grown in popularity over the last ten years and report a growth rate of visitor arrivals of over 4 per cent year on year. Generally, emerging destinations are much less well known than mature destinations and offer a different kind of holiday experience compared with mass tourism. The challenge for the tourism industry is to learn from past mistakes and ensure that emerging destinations are managed in a more sustainable way.

Characteristics that emerging destinations may share

Visitors seek adventure

Visitors are attracted to emerging destinations because they offer an authentic experience that offers unspoilt cultural and natural features as the main attraction. Some emerging destinations are relatively undiscovered as there is limited awareness of these destinations globally, and this can add to the 'sense of adventure' for visitors.

DID YOU KNOW?

As of January 2019, there were around 30 new airports being constructed worldwide. Many of these airports are international airports, which will improve access for visitors from overseas.

Difficult to access from overseas

Some remote emerging destinations are very difficult to access for overseas visitors due to the lack of tourism infrastructure, which could include a very small airport with limited and non-direct flights, or the absence of an airport altogether. Therefore, visitors may be required to land at the nearest available airport and take another form of transport to get to the destination.

◨ Why is access important for the development of emerging destinations?

Underdeveloped transport links

Some emerging destinations do not have well-developed transport links within the destination; for example, a direct bus service to and from a local or regional airport. Some may even be 'off the beaten track', located away from a decent road or rail network and therefore difficult to access.

Basic infrastructure

Some emerging destinations in less developed parts of the world do not benefit from basic infrastructure such as energy sourced from a national grid, running water from a tap and waste disposal services.

ACTIVITY

Working in pairs, ask your teacher to allocate you, or select yourself, two destinations that could be classified as emerging. Compare the characteristics of the destination to the list that you produced at the start of the lesson. Decide if the destination that you are looking at is an emerging destination and be prepared to explain why.

Next, approach another pair and swap ideas. Share notes and write down the name and main characteristics of the other pair's destination.

Healthcare and education

Similar to basic infrastructure, the host communities from emerging destinations living in less developed parts of the world may not have access to basic healthcare and education. Some emerging destinations may lack basic services such as a local doctor's surgery and may be located a considerable distance from hospitals.

Unspoilt natural and cultural features

As emerging destinations have not experienced the impacts of mass tourism, many of the natural and cultural features found there remain unspoilt. Importantly, this means that visitors to emerging destinations are receiving an authentic experience.

Traditional lifestyles

In emerging destinations, it is likely that the host community follows traditional lifestyles that include centuries-old rituals and traditions that may be linked to religious beliefs. This is often an important part of the appeal of emerging destinations for visitors.

Seek to develop tourism

As income generated through visitor spending can boost local economies and raise living standards, the local communities in many emerging destinations may welcome tourism development.

Low volumes of visitors

One of the most important characteristics of emerging destinations is that they currently experience relatively low visitor numbers but are growing in popularity at a rate of 4 per cent year on year. One reason for this is that in many locations, visitors have to make their own travel arrangements, rather than being able to book a package holiday.

Limited awareness

Emerging destinations are not promoted and marketed to the extent that mature destinations are; they are often relatively unheard of compared with 'mass tourism' locations. This limited awareness is another reason why visitor numbers to emerging destinations are low. Furthermore, some destinations do not want 'mass tourism' and may deliberately avoid marketing locations as tourist destinations.

CHECK MY LEARNING

Create a revision checklist using the destinations that you have reviewed today. Come up with five key questions that will help you to identify if a destination is an emerging destination.

Emerging destinations (2)

GETTING STARTED

Working in pairs, recap the characteristics that you would expect to find in emerging destinations. Write the list of characteristics down and compare your list with another pair.

The names of many of the world's emerging destinations are unfamiliar to most; this is because most of these locations are relatively unknown as tourist destinations and experience low visitor number volumes. Importantly, these emerging destinations share similar characteristics, such as natural and cultural features that are unspoiled by tourism.

Destinations that have recently grown in popularity

Emerging destinations are destinations that have grown in popularity over the last ten years or so. Generally, you would expect an emerging destination to have a visitor arrival growth rate of over 4 per cent a year. Travel websites and blogs, such as Kayak, offer advice and lists of emerging destinations that are 'this season's must visits'. The following destinations have recently been featured.

Bequia, the Grenadines

Located next to the Caribbean destinations of St. Lucia and Antigua, Bequia is considered an emerging destination. The main appeal of the island lies with the quality of the relatively untouched beaches. Currently, the island is popular with scuba divers and sailors, who visit for the annual Easter Regatta. The island currently has about 12 small hotels and guesthouses; most of these have less than ten rooms.

◻ Why do you think Bequia is considered an emerging destination?

ACTIVITY

Working individually, select an emerging destination from this page to investigate further using the internet. Create a list of the main characteristics of the emerging destination that you have selected. Answer this question 'do these characteristics of an emerging destination match those you would expect to find using the TALC model?'

DID YOU KNOW?

In 2017, Baku hosted the first-ever Azerbaijan Grand Prix, a Formula One motor race.

Baku, Azerbaijan

Baku, the capital city of Azerbaijan, offers a mixture of modern-designed skyscrapers alongside a UNESCO listed old city. The city also offers a range of concert halls, museums and parks such as Baku Boulevard. Furthermore, a favourable exchange rate between the pound sterling and the Azerbaijani manat means that tourists visiting from the UK will find the cost of living relatively inexpensive.

Ischia, Italy

Ischia is an emerging destination located near to one of the most renowned tourist hot spots in Italy, the island of Capri. Ischia is another island in the Bay of Naples that is less well known, though shares similarly stunning views with Capri. One of the main draws of Ischia is the thermal springs and thermal baths available that supposedly offer a range of health benefits. Treatments include massages, mud masks and lymphatic drainage.

Caen, France

It is interesting that destinations in well-established and developed areas can still be considered emerging if they see an increase in popularity. An example of this is Caen, a city destination in the Normandy region of Northern France. Much of the appeal of Caen lies in the history of the area; medieval architecture features prominently within the city. The city suffered significant damage during the Battle of Normandy in the Second World War; the Caen Memorial Museum dedicated to the war is one of the most popular attractions within the city. Furthermore, there is a range of markets, patisseries, créperies and restaurants that specialise in seafood for tourists to enjoy when visiting the city.

LINK IT UP

In Component 1, you will have learned about the features that contribute to the appeal of a destination. What features do emerging destinations like Bequia, Baku, Ischia and Caen share? What is different about them?

ACTIVITY

Working in a small group, find an example of an emerging destination not featured on this page. Create a PowerPoint® presentation that explains the main characteristics of this emerging destination.

CHECK MY LEARNING

Working in pairs, answer the following questions about emerging destinations.

1 Can you identify an emerging destination and describe where it is located?

2 Can you describe why many emerging destinations are seeking to boost tourism?

3 Can you remember three characteristics of emerging destinations?

Mature destinations (1)

GETTING STARTED

Working in pairs, build on and add to your list of characteristics that you would expect to find in a mature destination. Compare your list with another pair and add any characteristics that you may have missed.

Most well-established European destinations, such as Ibiza, Tenerife and Kos, are classed as mature destinations. These destinations have all been popular for well over 20 years and have seen tourism develop and grow steadily over this time.

Characteristics that mature destinations may share

Mass tourism

Mature destinations experience a high volume of visitors who will probably have booked a package holiday with a tour operator. Mass tourism is often considered an unsustainable form of tourism due to the pressures placed on the local area.

Fully integrated transport links

Mass tourist destinations are well connected to the rest of the world. This includes having an international airport within easy reach of the destination. Usually a regular bus or rail service will exist between the destination and the airport.

Fully developed infrastructure

Mature destinations usually have full access to infrastructure, such as energy sourced from a national grid, clean, running water from a tap and waste disposal services. Visitors to mature destinations from wealthy countries like the UK, will usually experience similar infrastructure to that they would experience at home.

ACTIVITY

Working in pairs, decide on two tourist destinations to investigate. Compare the two destinations to your list of characteristics that you would expect to see in a mature destination; now decide if your selected destinations could be classed as 'mature'. Tick off all of the characteristics that are present.

Next, find another pair to compare your work with. Review each other's tick lists and agree if the destinations that have been researched are 'mature' or not.

Strain on resources

One of the main pressures on mature destinations is being able to maintain standards without placing too much strain on resources, such as water. Water shortages can become an issue if the destination experiences lower than expected levels of rainfall. In 2018 Cyprus, a popular destination in the Eastern Mediterranean, suffered from a third year of drought in succession and the island experienced severe water shortages.

Impacts on natural and cultural features

The main natural and cultural features of mature destinations can become damaged, diluted and overwhelmed by tourism. For example, many mature destinations feature major Western 'fast food' brands at the expense of local, traditional eateries. In Venice, Italy, the destination's World Heritage Status has come under threat due to concerns about the influence of mass tourism on the city.

Established season

Many mature destinations have an established tourist season; usually this is dictated by the weather. In European summer sun destinations, the tourist season tends to run from early spring to autumn (Figure 2.15). Seasonal unemployment for tourism workers is often an issue in mature destinations.

JANUARY								FEBRUARY								MARCH								APRIL						
S	M	T	W	T	F	S		S	M	T	W	T	F	S		S	M	T	W	T	F	S		S	M	T	W	T	F	S
	1	2	3	4	5								1	2							1	2			1	2	3	4	5	6
6	7	8	9	10	11	12		3	4	5	6	7	8	9		3	4	5	6	7	8	9		7	8	9	10	11	12	13
13	14	15	16	17	18	19		10	11	12	13	14	15	16		10	11	12	13	14	15	16		14	15	16	17	18	19	20
20	21	22	23	24	25	26		17	18	19	20	21	22	23		17	18	19	20	21	22	23		21	22	23	24	25	26	27
27	28	29	30	31				24	25	26	27	28				24	25	26	27	28	29	30		28	29	30				
																31													

MAY								JUNE								JULY								AUGUST						
S	M	T	W	T	F	S		S	M	T	W	T	F	S		S	M	T	W	T	F	S		S	M	T	W	T	F	S
		1	2	3	4									1			1	2	3	4	5	6							1	2	3
5	6	7	8	9	10	11		2	3	4	5	6	7	8		7	8	9	10	11	12	13		4	5	6	7	8	9	10
12	13	14	15	16	17	18		9	10	11	12	13	14	15		14	15	16	17	18	19	20		11	12	13	14	15	16	17
19	20	21	22	23	24	25		16	17	18	19	20	21	22		21	22	23	24	25	26	27		18	19	20	21	22	23	24
26	27	28	29	30	31			23	24	25	26	27	28	29		28	29	30	31					25	26	27	28	29	30	31
								30																						

SEPTEMBER								OCTOBER								NOVEMBER								DECEMBER						
S	M	T	W	T	F	S		S	M	T	W	T	F	S		S	M	T	W	T	F	S		S	M	T	W	T	F	S
1	2	3	4	5	6	7				1	2	3	4	5						1	2		1	2	3	4	5	6	7
8	9	10	11	12	13	14		6	7	8	9	10	11	12		3	4	5	6	7	8	9		8	9	10	11	12	13	14
15	16	17	18	19	20	21		13	14	15	16	17	18	19		10	11	12	13	14	15	16		15	16	17	18	19	20	21
22	23	24	25	26	27	28		20	21	22	23	24	25	26		17	18	19	20	21	22	23		22	23	24	25	26	27	28
29	30							27	28	29	30	31				24	25	26	27	28	29	30		29	30	31				

◨ Figure 2.15: How does having an established season impact on mature destinations?

Advertising and marketing

Mature destinations are well advertised and marketed; usually they are known globally. Advertising and marketing in mature destinations plays a key part in encouraging people to visit.

Appearance of visitor facilities

As mature destinations have experienced mass tourism for many decades, some of the older facilities may appear run down and dated. Many mature destinations invest extensively in updating facilities in order to maintain a positive image.

Economical reliance on tourism

In mature destinations many jobs are tourism-related, therefore the local economy relies on tourism revenue. However, many mature destinations experience issues with 'leakage' where money generated through tourism in the local area is lost to international organisations, such as tour operators and the owners of large all-inclusive resorts.

Conflict between the local community and visitors

In mature destinations, there is sometimes conflict between the local community and visitors. One of the main issues in many destinations is the sheer volume of tourists and visitors behaving in an antisocial or culturally ignorant manner.

In 2018, it was reported that the local community in destinations in locations such as Venice, Italy and Barcelona, Spain had become fed up with 'overtourism.' Residents in Barcelona referred to the volume of tourists visiting Barcelona as an 'invasion'. Residents in Venice protested about the volume of tourism using slogans such as 'Venice is not a theme park'.

LINK IT UP

You looked at how destinations might minimise leakage and make the most of the economic multiplier effect earlier in this component. How many strategies can you remember?

CHECK MY LEARNING

Create a set of revision checklist questions for each characteristic of a mature destination. For example: 'Does the destination experience mass tourism?'

Mature destinations (2)

GETTING STARTED

Working in pairs, recap the characteristics of a mature destination. Write down as many characteristics as you can remember.

Many mature destinations have been popular for decades; most of the original summer sun destinations that first experienced mass tourism from the UK in the 1960s and 1970s are still popular today. The Costa del Sol region in Spain was first developed for tourism as early as the 1950s and is still one of the most popular regions of the Mediterranean for visitors.

Destinations that have remained popular

To be classed as 'mature', the destination needs to have been popular for over 20 years and have experienced a 2 per cent annual growth rate of visitor arrivals year on year.

Marbella, Costa del Sol

Marbella, located on the Costa del Sol, has been a popular resort for many decades. Visitors, especially those from Northern Europe, are attracted to the warm Mediterranean climate, beaches and cultural attractions within the resort. More recently, Marbella has gained attention as a 'celebrity resort', attracting wealthy and sometimes famous visitors. For example, in 2015, *The Only Way is Essex* TV series launched with two special episodes filmed in Marbella.

■ Why do you think that Marbella has remained a popular resort for many decades?

Los Gigantes, Tenerife

Los Gigantes, located in the Canary Islands, is a resort town famous for its dramatic natural cliff formations. The area, along with the neighbouring Puerto Santiago, has been popular with UK holidaymakers for many years. This British influence has impacted on many areas of the resort; English is spoken in shops and restaurants throughout the town, many signposts and shop signs are written in English and many older British expatriates have moved to the area to retire.

Sant Antoni de Portmany, Ibiza

Sant Antoni de Portmany, also known as San Antonio, is a resort located in Ibiza, one of the Spanish Balearic Islands. The resort was initially part of the mass tourism revolution that happened throughout mainland Spain and surrounding islands in the late 1950s. Sant Antoni de Portmany became known as one of the main European 'clubbing' destinations as part of the dance music revolution that took place in the 1990s. The resort is home to the famous Café del Mar, one of the key music venues found in Ibiza.

Phuket, Thailand

Phuket, located in Southern Thailand, is the country's largest island and wealthiest region. The island is also one of Thailand's main tourist destinations and has been especially popular with visitors from English-speaking nations for many years. As Phuket is relatively hot and humid throughout the year, the island is popular with visitors from Europe in the winter months. One of the main impacts of tourism in the area has been the development of transport infrastructure, with the island benefiting from an airport. Phuket International Airport is located in the north of the island.

Before the airport was developed into a major international airport, visitors would land elsewhere and embark on a lengthy 200 km or more transfer by coach or taxi down the peninsular and across the Sarasin bridge, which links Phuket with the mainland (Figure 2.16).

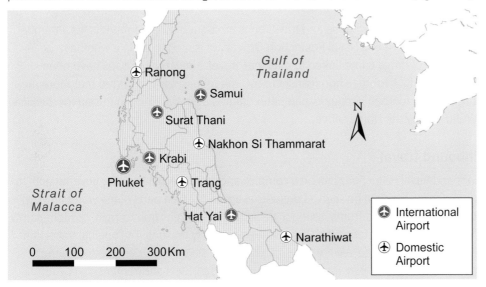

Figure 2.16: How has tourism impacted on the development of transport infrastructure in Phuket?

ACTIVITY

Working as a class, you will need to participate in a group discussion to answer the question: 'What are the dangers of mass tourism in mature destinations?'

As a class discuss the (positive and negative) economic, social and environmental impacts of tourism in mature destinations.

Barbados, Caribbean

Barbados, a former British colony, is an island resort located in the Caribbean. The island has been a popular tourist destination, especially with visitors from the UK, for many decades. In the 1980s, tourism became one of the most economically important industries in Barbados and remains so today. The island benefits from many attractive natural features including caves, bays and beaches; furthermore, Barbados benefits from a warm and pleasant climate.

ACTIVITY

Working in small groups, select a mature destination; you could use one of the examples from this page. Research information about your selected destination further using the internet and create a PowerPoint® presentation that outlines the main characteristics of your destination. Be prepared to present to the rest of the class, who will peer review your work.

DID YOU KNOW?

Barbados has over 3000 hours of sunshine each year. Between June and November, average temperatures in Barbados range from 23°C to 31°C.

LINK IT UP

In Component 1, you will have learned about the features that contribute to the appeal of a destination. What features do mature destinations like Sant Antoni de Portmany, Phuket and Barbados share? What is different about them?

CHECK MY LEARNING

Working individually, create some revision quiz questions about mature destinations – at least five. For example, can you explain how tourism promotes development in mature resorts?

Then swap your questions with those of another student and test each other. Who did the best? If there is time, swap and test again with another student.

The role of local and national governments in destination management

GETTING STARTED

Woking in pairs, list reasons why governments may want to encourage tourism. Think about the benefits that tourism can bring to an area.

Governments have a very important part to play in encouraging and developing tourism through destination management. Local and national governments have a central role in travel restrictions and security, improving and managing transport, infrastructure, and communications, approving and controlling development, attracting and providing funding, and ensuring sustainability.

Travel restrictions and security

The movement of people, especially across national borders, must be controlled carefully in order to maintain security within a country or region. Most countries have passport or visa requirements, which may differ according to which country visitors are travelling from.

Outbound travel

Outbound travel restrictions and travel bans are issued by governments for a number of reasons. In the UK, Travel Restriction Orders are issued to people who have been convicted of drugs crime linked to overseas travel. Similar travel bans have been issued to British football hooligans; in 2018 the *Independent* reported that more than 1200 British football hooligans had been banned from travelling to Russia for the FIFA World Cup by the Home Office.

Inbound travel

Inbound travel restrictions can be a complex and controversial topic for governments to deal with, as they can be seen as prejudicial against certain parts of the world. In 2017, US President, Donald Trump issued a 'travel ban' on citizens from certain, predominantly Muslim, countries entering the US for national security reasons. The original travel ban has since been revised several times; however, the seven countries affected by the original ban include: Iran, Iraq, Libya, Somalia, Sudan, Syria and Yemen.

ACTIVITY

Working in a small group, select one emerging destination and one mature destination to research. Find out the safety and security measures used by each destination including:
- travel restrictions
- security measures
- entry requirements.

Security measures

Airports

Since the September 11th attacks in New York and Washington, DC in 2001, governments have worked hard to tighten security at airports. The high volumes of people passing through airports and using air travel on a daily basis makes airports and commercial aircraft a potential target for terrorism.

Airport security is enforced by a range of personnel, often including police with police dogs, security guards and sometimes the military. In some countries, airports are protected at a national level by government-controlled agencies, while in other countries airport security is enforced by local or regional government.

Specific equipment used to screen travellers includes metal detectors, wave scanners, explosive detection machines and X-ray machines. In some cases, airports will also use specially trained personnel to converse with travellers in order to detect suspicious behaviour.

◻ Why are security measures used by airports?

Seaports

In the US, seaport security is managed nationally by the Coast Guard and US Customs and Border Protection; at a local and regional level, the FBI is also involved in seaport security. One reason security at seaports is a priority for the US government is that they are vulnerable to potential terrorist attacks.

Seaports are also used by criminals to smuggle illegal and black-market goods in and out of the country. Many port authorities use sniffer-dogs to try to detect any contraband that is being hidden on ships that use the seaport.

Entry requirements

Most countries will allow entry to valid passport holders from other countries; however, some countries will also require a visa, especially if the visit is for months rather than weeks. Many countries will require that citizens renew their passports every 5–10 years, depending on the age of the passport holder.

The International Civil Aviation Organization (ICAO) sets passport standards that are issued as guidance to governments. These standards include instructions about the required size of the passport and the information that must be contained in it, such as date of birth and country of origin.

DID YOU KNOW?

Investment in global airport security is set to reach US$12.67 billion by 2023. The key driver of this level of investment has been an increase in the number of people using airports.

LINK IT UP

Check back to Figure 2.10 to see some of the common time limits for UK citizens travelling abroad. How long could you stay in the USA?

CHECK MY LEARNING

Create a revision mind map about how governments manage the safety and security of travellers in destinations. Remember to include:
- travel restrictions
- security measures
- entry requirements.

ACTIVITY

Working as a group, discuss the question 'How do travel restrictions help to maintain safety and security in a destination?'

Transport links and infrastructure

GETTING STARTED

Working in pairs, list as many examples as you can of tourism infrastructure in a destination. This list can also include the facilities that tourists use.

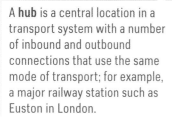

KEY TERM

A **hub** is a central location in a transport system with a number of inbound and outbound connections that use the same mode of transport; for example, a major railway station such as Euston in London.

LINK IT UP

Gateway and terminal, other related key terms, were defined in Component 1.

One of the key characteristics that separates mature destinations from emerging destinations is that they tend to have better transport links and infrastructure in place. Governments are usually aware that transport links and infrastructure can play a massive role in encouraging economic growth in an area, especially through the development of tourism. As a part of transport infrastructure gateways, **hubs** play a vital role in the development of tourism and in increasing visitor numbers to a destination.

Improving transport links and networks

Road

The role of government is crucial in developing road networks. Planning and funding for most road projects in the UK is coordinated by the government through schemes such as the 'Road Investment Strategy', which commits to spending £11 billion on road improvements between 2015 and 2020. However, in some places, private organisations are also involved in the development of road infrastructure, especially in some Asian countries and the USA.

Rail

Rail networks are often operated and developed through public–private partnerships, which involve governments working with the private sector to operate rail services and maintain the railway network. In the USA and Canada, the major railroad service called Amtrak, is classed as a state-owned enterprise, which means that the government has a share in the organisation, along with private organisations.

In the UK, Crossrail is a new rail venture. The Elizabeth Line, as it will be known, will connect central London to Reading and Heathrow in the west and Shenfield and Abbey Wood in the east. The project has been funded by Transport for London and the Department for Transport alongside contributions from private sector organisations such as Heathrow Airport, Canary Wharf Group plc and Berkeley Homes.

Air

Similar to numerous rail networks, many of the world's airports are operated and funded through a combination of public and private investment. Phuket International Airport benefitted from a 5.14 billion baht (£126 million) improvement which was completed in 2016; the airport is operated by Airports of Thailand PCL of which the Thai government holds a 70 per cent share.

The government is also a key stakeholder when it comes to granting permission for airport expansion. In 2018, the UK government voted in favour of a controversial plan to build a third runway at Heathrow airport. Heathrow is the busiest airport hub in Europe and it is argued that expansion is needed to maintain this position.

Sea

In some cases, other institutions, such as the EU, can support transport infrastructure developments with funding. In 2015, the EU provided funding of over £100 million to improve the crucial ferry route between Dover and Calais. The money is being used to support the Calais Port development project and Dover Western Docks revival project, which as of 2018 is ongoing. The route is essential for both tourism and trade between the UK and Continental Europe.

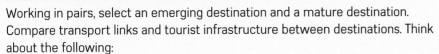

ACTIVITY

Working in pairs, select an emerging destination and a mature destination. Compare transport links and tourist infrastructure between destinations. Think about the following:
- quality of the road networks
- size of the airport
- other transport links, such as rail networks and seaports
- access to energy and water.

Supporting the development of infrastructure

Energy and water supply

Government-funded initiatives are essential for the development of infrastructure to support the general population and industries such as tourism. Major projects such as dam construction can support the development of areas by meeting both energy and water needs. A classic example of this was the US government-funded construction of the Hoover Dam, along the Colorado River on the border of Nevada and Arizona. Built in the 1930s, Hoover Dam generated the energy, and supplied the water, that allowed Las Vegas to develop into one of the world's most-visited destinations. Furthermore, the Hoover Dam itself and Lake Mead, a reservoir created by the damming of the Colorado River, are themselves very popular tourist attractions today.

LINK IT UP

Approving and controlling the development of tourism projects such as infrastructure construction is important for governments. This is discussed under 'sustainability' in previous lessons.

Waste disposal in Venice

As with most popular destinations, the local government in Venice, Italy, has issues with managing waste disposal, including raw sewage, due to the very large numbers of people visiting and producing waste. Historically, Venice has benefitted from tidal processes to remove raw sewage from the canals of the city.

Areas in and around Venice, such as St. Helena, Giudecca, Santa Marta and Murano, benefit from modern sewerage infrastructure including networks for sewage disposal. There is also a central treatment plant; however, it is quite a distance from the centre of Venice. Some of the older sewer networks still enter directly into the canals and lagoons of Venice. Private sector organisations, such as hotels, are required to have their own septic tanks to help to alleviate the issue of waste disposal in the city.

ACTIVITY

Working in the same pairs, discuss how tourism can improve transport links and infrastructure. Consider why governments need to support infrastructure projects.

CHECK MY LEARNING

Working in pairs, complete the following activity about proposals for managing tourism in Venice.

The authorities in Venice are considering three proposals to minimise the negative impact of tourism.
- Proposal 1: Introducing a limit on the number of tourists permitted to enter the city.
- Proposal 2: Limiting the amount and size of cruise ships that are allowed to use the canals nearest to the city centre.
- Proposal 3: Developing a new port area on the outskirts of the city.

Explain how each of these three proposals could help to minimise the negative impacts of tourism in Venice.

Communication links

GETTING STARTED

Working individually, answer the question: 'Why is communication important to tourist destination development?'

Technological developments have improved global communication links. It is now possible to communicate instantly with people in different parts of the world via a range of technologies, such as tablets, game consoles, mobile devices and computers. Many people rely on such technology to function on a day-to-day basis; destinations recognise this and as a result many places have improved their **connectivity** over recent years.

Access to the internet

KEY TERM

Connectivity is the ability to link and communicate with other electronic devices, computer systems and the internet.

Access to the internet provides destinations with a competitive advantage because they are able to market and advertise products and services, respond to enquiries and take bookings. This is a major reason why governments are generally supportive of schemes to improve internet services.

Currently, about 50 per cent of the world's population has access to the internet; with the majority of people not yet using the internet coming from the world's poorest countries. One of the main difficulties is that the world's poorest people often live in challenging and remote locations that are difficult to access for the purpose of installing internet services; for example, in the middle of a rainforest or on a remote island. However, such locations are often the ones most sought after by tourists.

The role of government in securing internet access

Governments can play a part in how Wi-Fi is provided by investing directly in the fibre optic broadband infrastructure that enables Wi-Fi to be provided effectively, or by issuing legislation that compels private organisations to provide access to broadband.

In the UK, the government has introduced a 'Universal Service Obligation', so that by 2020 everyone that lives in the UK will have a 'clear, enforceable right to request high speed broadband.'

Which came first, the tourist or the internet?

One of the issues for governments in such places is that it is more cost-effective and efficient for them to contribute to the development of internet services in densely populated urban areas, rather than isolated rural areas. However, providing internet services to remote, rural areas could potentially aid the development of industries such as tourism.

One possible way to connect people in remote locations to the internet is via satellite technology, rather than ground-installed cabling. However, this technology can be expensive. Antarctica currently benefits from internet connectivity thanks to the European satellite navigation system, Galileo.

◨ It is possible to access the internet in some places as remote as Antarctica. What are the benefits of this for tourists?

Local government's role in improving internet access

In the UK, local government is also involved in improving internet access, especially in more remote areas. For example, Essex County Council is responsible for coordinating the rolling out of superfast broadband to rural areas, which includes tourist destinations such as picturesque villages like Finchingfield, through their Superfast Essex programme in partnership with several network operators.

Wi-Fi

Wi-Fi is the technology that enables electronic devices, such as tablets and mobile telephones, to connect to the internet at high speeds without the need for physical wires and cables. A small hub is required to transmit radio waves which are then received by the electronic device; most hubs have a range of about 20 metres indoors.

Providing Wi-Fi in tourist destinations can be a huge draw for tourists, as this can enable them to maintain communications with home. Furthermore, business travellers may require Wi-Fi access for work-related purposes.

ACTIVITY

Working in pairs, research and review the online presence and quality of websites that promote developing countries and remote areas. Think about how this might impact on the image of the destination. Examples of countries and areas for research could include:
- Kenya
- Cambodia
- Bangladesh
- Vietnam
- Outer Hebrides (Scotland).

ACTIVITY

Working in pairs, make a list of ways in which tourists might use the internet while visiting a destination. Think about why governments might want to support the development of communication links for tourism.

DID YOU KNOW?

It is estimated that in 2019, 2.8 billion people in Asia will use a mobile telephone.

LINK IT UP

In Component 3, you will learn about customers' needs, including unstated needs. Why do you think access to the internet and Wi-Fi could be considered an important unstated customer need?

CHECK MY LEARNING

Working individually, write a short summary about the importance of the government's role in developing technological communication links. Include five points that you have learned.

Attracting and providing funding

GETTING STARTED

Working in pairs, come up with an idea for an exciting new infrastructure initiative that could attract funding from the private and public sector in your town or local area. You may wish to cover:
- where the proposed infrastructure project would be located
- the possible costs incurred
- the economic benefits that your proposal could bring to the UK or global travel and tourism sector.

DID YOU KNOW?

In the UK, 27.04 million people were employed in the private sector in 2017.

Governments often work in partnership with other sectors to gain funding for major projects and initiatives. This is a complex area, as the way funding is generated and public money spent can depend on the political ideology of whoever is in charge of the country at the time. Generally speaking, public–private partnerships are an effective way of sharing expertise in order to move projects forward.

Attracting funding from the private sector

One of the benefits of attracting investment and support from the private sector is that private organisations are sometimes seen as being more efficient and innovative than public sector organisations. In 2016, the UK government announced that it wanted the private sector to fund over half of the £483 billion planned infrastructure investment by 2021.

The UK government was involved in securing a £200 million investment in infrastructure by a number of insurance companies, including Aviva, and Legal and General. This investment provided new trains on the Thameslink cross-London rail service.

Return on investment

The main key incentive for the private sector to invest in such projects is the promise of a return on their investments, where potential profits to be made outweigh the initial risks of funding such infrastructure projects.

However, one of the main issues is that when both the tax payer and private investors fund projects, private organisations often take what could be considered an unfair return on investments. Ensuring that tax payers get value for money is an important part of any public–private partnership.

ACTIVITY

Working in pairs, visit https://en.unesco.org, search for Guide 9 Securing Funding and Investment. Using advice from the website, create a guidance factsheet about attracting funding for tourism.

Providing funding for new initiatives

Transport

Along with the planned extension to Heathrow Airport, probably the biggest transport infrastructure project that the UK government is involved with is the High Speed 2, or HS2, rail scheme. The scheme involves the construction of 330 miles of new rail track that will link London, the West Midlands, Manchester and Leeds. Estimates made in 2018 suggest that the UK government could end up spending £99 billion on HS2.

Part of the rationale for this initiative is to create a 'Northern Powerhouse' that will enable decades of economic growth for local communities in the north of England, such as in Manchester, Newcastle, Leeds and Sheffield. Furthermore, HS2 ltd has listened to local communities' concerns about the impacts of the rail scheme and has adjusted the route to limit the number of people affected; for example, large parts of the phase 1 route will be completely enclosed in a tunnel, which will dramatically reduce noise pollution.

Events

National governments often contribute significantly when funding major global events such as the World Cup and Olympic Games. The Brazilian government contributed about 40 per cent of the funds towards the construction cost of venues for the 2016 Summer Olympics in Rio de Janeiro. The total cost of the project was estimated to be R$7.07 billion; therefore, government funding was around R$2.82 billion. However, this amount of government funding was considered controversial, given that living standards among the poorest people in Brazil are very low.

Similar to Rio, the London Olympics in 2012 required significant investment from both the public and private sector. In total, the London Olympics cost £8.7 billion. However, while some people expressed concerns about local communities suffering from forced evictions, police violence and wasted spending in the build-up to the Olympics in Rio, the organisers of the London Olympics have publicised in great detail the benefits of the London Olympics for the local communities around the East End of London, particularly Stratford. Some of the benefits have included improved leisure facilities, a new shopping centre, better transport links and sports venues, such as a velodrome than can host future world events.

Training

In 2016, the Greek government introduced new laws to try to stimulate tourism growth in the country. The law included plans for the government to subsidise a range of infrastructure projects including new tourism training centres. The main aim of the new laws was to try to encourage fresh investment in the Greek tourism sector and to try to encourage new jobs and growth for tourism-related industries. The tourism sector is essential to local communities in Greece, as both direct and indirect jobs contributed to 24.8 per cent of all jobs; this is around one in four jobs in Greece.

Government subsidies are also used to try to encourage employers to provide training opportunities to staff. In January 2019, the UK government offered 187 schemes that enabled employers and employees access to finance for training initiatives.

Infrastructure

Government agencies are generally more willing to invest in tourism projects that are sustainable. These projects can meet a number of objectives for governments, such as promoting community cohesion and celebrating local culture. Funding for the Museum of Liverpool, constructed in 2011, came from a number of sources, including The European Regional Development Fund, Heritage Lottery Fund and Department for Digital, Culture, Media & Sport. The museum is free for both visitors and local communities to visit, which promotes community cohesion. The main focus of the museum is to celebrate the global significance of the local area, including Liverpool's maritime infrastructure, which has been awarded World Heritage Status by UNESCO.

KEY TERM

A **government subsidy** is a form of financial aid provided with the aim of promoting a particular policy, such as stimulating tourism growth.

ACTIVITY

Working in a small group, select an emerging destination and a mature destination. For each destination, use the internet to research any projects related to transport, events, training or infrastructure that the government has contributed funding to. Create a poster presentation that includes:
- the names of the destinations
- what projects the government has funded
- how the funding has been used.

CHECK MY LEARNING

Working individually, create a series of revision questions about the role of government in attracting or providing funding. For example, 'How do private organisations contribute to publically funded projects?'

Ensuring tourism development is sustainable

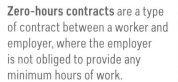

GETTING STARTED

Working in pairs, write a definition of sustainable development or sustainable tourism. Can you remember what the principles of sustainable tourism are and how sustainable tourism can benefit local communities?

KEY TERMS

Zero-hours contracts are a type of contract between a worker and employer, where the employer is not obliged to provide any minimum hours of work.

Jobseeker's Allowance is an unemployment benefit that people can claim when they are looking for work.

Tax credits are extra payments from the government paid to people in lower-paid work and/ or who have children that may require paid childcare.

For governments, promoting sustainable tourism will usually underpin any tourism strategy that they have. The idea of ensuring that tourism developments are sustainable is logical because sustainable tourism developments can bring about lasting social, economic and environmental benefits to local communities living in a destination. Furthermore, sustainable tourism development reduces the possible negative impacts of tourism.

Employment

According to VisitBritain, since 2010, tourism has been the fastest-growing employment sector in the UK, accounting for nearly 10 per cent of all jobs in the country. One of the key principles of sustainable tourism is that jobs are paid fairly and are secure. Governments can play a part by creating legislation that supports workers' rights; for example, by ending **zero-hours contracts**.

Government data shows that employment rates in local communities living in the Lake District National Park are higher than the national average, with only 1 per cent of residents in the Lake District registered as unemployed. Overall 15,000 of the 41,000 people who live in the Lake District National Park are employed in tourism-related jobs; this figure demonstrates the important and sustainable role that tourism can play in providing employment to local communities.

However, you may be aware that one of the problems for governments all over the world is that jobs in tourism are often low paid and seasonal. In the UK, this means that the government will often be required to 'top up' low-paid tourism employees' wages with **tax credits** and **Jobseeker's Allowance** when workers find themselves seasonally unemployed. Furthermore, in 2015, just under half of all jobs in the hospitality sector made use of zero-hours contracts.

Business initiatives

In 2016, the government announced the recipients of the First Discover England fund, a £40 million investment intended to boost tourism, including sustainable tourism initiatives, across England. The funds were awarded to projects that help encourage tourism outside London. The recipients included a range of attractions and events including music festivals, championship golf courses and restaurants intending to serve world-class cuisine.

One of the projects called 'England's GREAT South West Peninsula' led by Visit Cornwall, focuses on delivering family and friendship group based tours. The sustainable basis of the initiative is to encourage more visitors from Australia and the USA to experience the main natural and cultural attractions in the area and make use of local accommodation, bringing benefits to the host communities who rely on tourism income to support the local economy and create and maintain jobs in the local area.

Promoting 'support local' schemes

The government also launched its Tourism Action Plan in 2016. One of the key initiatives of the action plan was to support smaller local businesses, such as B&Bs, by helping to make their business models more sustainable, through changing legislation. For example, letting B&Bs offer customers an alcoholic welcome drink on arrival and allowing them to pick up visitors from local train stations.

Supporting local businesses is of vital importance to any sustainable tourism model. Experiencing local produce can form part of the overall experience and benefit both visitors and local communities. For example, a visitor to Marbella, Spain would gain a much more authentic experience by opting to eat in a traditional locally owned Spanish restaurant than in an internationally owned restaurant chain. Furthermore, opting to spend in local businesses benefits the economy of the local area, as 'leakage' of revenue generated through tourism out of the host community is avoided.

ACTIVITY

Working in pairs, access www.biospheretourism.com/en, search for 17 Sustainable Tourism Examples. Explore the examples on the website and use them, along with your own knowledge, to create a list of sustainable tourism practices. Now use the internet to research how two other destinations approach sustainable tourism. Add to your list of sustainable tourism practices.

Next, create a PowerPoint® presentation about sustainable tourism practices. Include lots of examples from the list that you generated earlier in the lesson.

Reducing negative impacts of tourism

Both local and national governments have the power to pass legislation that reduces the negative impacts of tourism in order to make tourism more sustainable. In 2016, the local government in Magaluf banned street drinking, nakedness and other forms of antisocial behaviour, such as shouting and fighting. Street signs were erected in English to warn tourists about the consequences of their bad behaviour. The signs warned of fines of up to €400 for people who failed to follow the rules of the resort.

Hamburg, Germany

Research shows that in areas where tourism is well developed, such as Hamburg in Germany, there are two key causes of conflict between tourists and the local community. These causes are the number of tourists in relation to the number of local residents and the behaviour of visitors. Some proposed solutions to this issue that aim to reduce the negative impacts of tourism include the following.
- Developing ways to improve the distribution of visitors to avoid overcrowding of certain areas of the city.
- Developing ways to better manage time distribution, to avoid overcrowding at peak times.
- Create city experiences for visitors that involve benefits for local residents.
- Better communication with local stakeholders.
- Improvement of infrastructure in and around the city.

CHECK MY LEARNING

Working in the same pair, present your PowerPoint® presentation to the rest of the class. Agree as a group which places adopt the best sustainable tourism practices.

How do governments encourage sustainable tourist behaviour that reduces the negative impacts of tourism?

DID YOU KNOW?

Magaluf is located on the island of Majorca where tourism contributes to a massive 80 per cent of the destination's GDP.

LINK IT UP

In Component 3, you will learn that customers will express desirable preferences about what they want from a holiday. Why do you think more and more tourists want their holiday to be sustainable?

Taxes, rules and legislation

GETTING STARTED

Working in pairs, think of any examples of taxes, rules or legislation that have an impact on tourism development. Can you explain why such taxes, rules and legislation have an impact on tourism?

Local and national governments can manage the way tourism impacts on destinations by setting taxes, passing legislation and providing guidance related to tourist activities. This can often be a fine balancing act between setting taxes, rules and legislation that bring about maximum benefits for the resort without exploiting tourists or discouraging tourists from visiting.

Taxes

Levying tourism taxes is often at the discretion of local government at the destinations themselves. Similar to 'sustainable tourism' taxes levied in the Spanish Balearic Islands, in 2018 the City of Edinburgh council launched a consultation about the possibility of introducing a charge of £2 per room, per night, to guests in all forms of accommodation. The council suggested that the funds raised through the tax could be invested in growing tourism in the city and managing its impact.

◘ How might the introduction of a 'tourism' tax benefit Edinburgh?

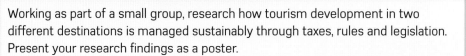

ACTIVITY

Working as part of a small group, research how tourism development in two different destinations is managed sustainably through taxes, rules and legislation. Present your research findings as a poster.

Rules

Rules and laws are quite different from a legal perspective. Rules are generally guidance about conduct, whereas laws are legally enforceable; breaking the law may result in fines or imprisonment.

You may be familiar with rules in an everyday setting; for example, schools and colleges have rules. Another example of rules that you may also be familiar with is guidance given at rides at theme parks. These might include rules about minimum height requirements, riding with a health issue and wearing appropriate footwear when riding.

Many other destinations also have rules that ensure tourism remains as sustainable as possible. For example, you may be familiar with the Countryside Code, a set of rules of conduct for visiting the countryside (Figure 2.17). This includes rules about keeping gates shut to avoid letting farm animals out and staying to the footpath route that has been provided to reduce erosion in other parts of the countryside.

Respect other people	• Consider the local community and other people enjoying the outdoors • Leave gates and property as you find them and follow paths unless wider access is available
Protect the natural environment	• Leave no trace of your visit and take your litter home • Keep dogs under effective control
Enjoy the outdoors	• Plan ahead and be prepared • Follow advice and local signs

◘ Figure 2.17: How do the rules within the Countryside Code promote sustainable tourism?

ACTIVITY

Case study: Egypt – Bringing Tourists Back

Between January and September 2017, 5.9 million tourists visited Egypt, with the majority coming from European countries. A benefit for the Egyptian government has been an increase in tax revenue due to an increased number of visits compared with 2016, when only 3.8 million tourists visited.

The Egyptian government has worked with the private sector to launch initiatives to promote tourism and set policies and rules to encourage tourism development.

One of the main initiatives has been to pass rules to encourage the construction of new infrastructure and the restoration of infrastructure that has been deteriorating due to neglect.

Another main initiative has been to promote Egypt as a MICE (meeting, incentive, conference and events) destination. To launch this initiative in 2017, the World Youth Forum held a conference with 3,000 attendees. The event attracted funding from sponsors, including banks, hotels and Egypt Air.

Working individually, read the above case study about Egypt. Use the above and your own research to create a detailed information file about the destination. Include the following headings that relate to the role of local and national government in destination management.
- Travel restrictions.
- Improving transport links and infrastructure.
- Improving communication links.
- Attracting investment and providing funding.
- Ensuring development is sustainable.
- Managing development through taxes, rules and legislation.

Legislation

UNESCO is keen to ensure that tourism developments are managed carefully. It explains that stakeholders with responsibility for the management of World Heritage Sites are under international obligation to maintain the integrity of the site, without altering it unnecessarily for the benefit of tourism. One way it encourages sustainable approaches to tourism development is through the undertaking of an environmental impact assessment (EIA), the process of evaluating the likely impact of a proposed development.

As of 2018 in Liverpool, the Liverpool Waters development is under construction around Princes Dock, Central Docks and Northern Docks. The development will see the introduction of residential apartments along with tourism facilities. UNESCO is against the development and has threatened to remove Word Heritage Status from Liverpool's Maritime Mercantile City. Despite this threat, the city council has legislated for the development by awarding planning permission to the project. This highlights that managing tourism development is challenging, especially when various key stakeholders have conflicting interests of economic growth against the preservation of heritage sites.

CHECK MY LEARNING

Working individually, create five revision questions about the role of local and national government in destination management.

Importance of partnerships in destination management (1)

GETTING STARTED

Working in pairs, recap the definition of the following sectors:
- public sector
- private sector
- voluntary sector.

Next, describe what you think a public and private sector partnership is.

Partnerships between different types of organisations play a significant role in ensuring destinations are managed effectively. Organisations form partnerships for different reasons and there are advantages and disadvantages to working collaboratively.

Public and private sector partnerships

Public–private sector partnerships, known as PPPs, are essential for supporting and developing the global tourism sector. Partnerships are an effective way of encouraging collaboration in order to secure best practice, to secure funding and to share costs.

New tourism developments

Planning and constructing new hotels is not possible without the public sector and private sector working together. Commonly, new hotel developments are funded and constructed via the private sector, however, legal permission to begin work is often granted by local government.

For example, in 2018, Benidorm City Council gave permission for a new hotel to be built in Benidorm Old Town on the seafront close to the Parque de Elche. The new hotel will have capacity for 200 guests across eight floors and two basements. This is the first hotel development to be constructed in Benidorm Old Town for about 10 years. This project would not be possible without the public sector and private sector working together.

Transport links and infrastructure

Public–private partnerships are essential for the construction of new transport links and infrastructure. Often funding for major projects, such as new roads and airports, will be provided by a combination of public and private sector investment and loans, while the actual physical construction is usually undertaken by private sector organisations.

For example, in order to construct the Mersey Gateway Bridge between the towns of Runcorn and Widnes, Halton Borough Council (public sector) invited bids from private sector organisations to construct and manage the project. The council selected Merseylink as the preferred bidder for the project, which was completed in October 2017.

ACTIVITY

Working in a small group, use the internet to find an example of a public–private sector partnership. Prepare a five-minute presentation and then share your findings with the rest of the class.

Local authority issues

Restricting design, size and scale

Local authorities will always be key stakeholders when it comes to new tourism-related developments. One of the key roles of the local authority is to ensure that the design, size and scale of any new construction projects are sympathetic to the existing area and won't have a negative impact on the quality of the built environment.

Part of the Liverpool Waters proposal is the construction of a skyscraper predicted to be around 200 metres high, called the Shanghai Tower. If planning permission is approved for the building, it is estimate to be completed in 2025. However, UNESCO and English Heritage have objected to the plans on the grounds that the building would lead to a 'serious loss of historical authenticity'.

Revitalising town centres

One area that has proved a recent issue for local authorities has been the deterioration of town centres in the UK. Major private sector brands such as Marks & Spencer have been withdrawing from UK town centres over a number of years. This is due to the general loss of footfall in town centres due to competition from internet shopping services and out-of-town shopping centres.

In 2018, private sector retailers appealed to the UK government to work in partnership with them to reduce the business rate taxes that apply to organisations with physical retail units. According to the British Retail Consortium, reduced business rates could encourage more retail business to operate high street units in towns and cities and help to improve the overall retail offering in many town centres.

In response to the decline of town centres, in 2018, the Local Government Association released a handbook that offers guidance to local authorities about how town centres can be revitalised. One of the key areas of guidance encourages local authorities to embrace the heritage of town centres to create a more desirable experience.

LINK IT UP

In Component 1, you will have learned about public and private sector partnerships, such as VisitBritain working with global travel providers to promote the UK as a destination. Why are partnerships like this important?

■ How can town centre revitalisation encourage more people to visit?

ACTIVITY

Working individually, create a factsheet about public–private sector partnerships using the examples that you studied from earlier in the lesson.

CHECK MY LEARNING

Working individually, create a mind map about the benefits of public–private partnerships within the travel and tourism sector. Include examples that you have covered this lesson.

Importance of partnerships in destination management (2)

GETTING STARTED

Working in pairs, list examples of voluntary and public organisations from within the travel and tourism sector.

Voluntary sector partnerships

The voluntary sector relies on partnerships with public and private sector organisations. Such partnerships can raise awareness of a cause and perhaps most importantly, raise much needed funding. Some voluntary organisations, such as the National Trust and English Heritage operate travel and tourism visitor attractions; however, other non-travel and tourism voluntary organisations still rely on the support of the sector for raising awareness and funding.

Promoting good causes

Private sector organisations often partner with voluntary organisations to promote good causes. Specific support, such as assisting with the costs of marketing or running an event can lead to positive publicity and raise the profile of all organisations involved. Many larger private sector organisations will have departments that deal specifically with sponsorship. For example, Thomas Cook Children's Charity provides support to voluntary sector organisations including (Figure 2.18):
- WheelPower – a charity that promotes British wheelchair sport
- Save the Children – a charity that campaigns to improve children's lives
- SOS Children's Village – a global charity that supports children without parental care
- Red Cross – a global volunteer network that responds to conflicts and natural disasters
- Just a Drop – an international water development charity.

◻ Figure 2.18: How does providing support to the voluntary sector benefit organisations such as Thomas Cook?

ACTIVITY

Working in pairs, find examples of voluntary–public sector and voluntary–private sector partnerships. Provide a very brief description of:
- the organisations involved
- the type of partnership
- the benefits of the partnership for all organisations involved.

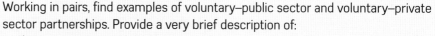

Raising funding

One way the voluntary sector raises funding in partnership with the travel and tourism sector is by encouraging individuals to raise money to take part in international challenges such as trekking to the top of a mountain or participating in a cross-continental bike ride, on behalf of a charity. Often such challenges are organised by specialist tour operators working with voluntary sector organisations.

For example, Fearne Cotton, Ben Shephard, Chris Moyles and Gary Barlow and other celebrities took part in a trek to the top of Mount Kilimanjaro, Africa's highest peak. The trek raised funding of £1.4 million for Comic Relief, mainly through donations from members of the public.

DID YOU KNOW?

Between 1985 and 2015, Comic Relief raised over £1 billion for charity.

How can the global travel and tourism sector work in partnership to raise funds for good causes?

> **ACTIVITY**
>
> Working in small groups, research an event that involves a voluntary sector organisation working with other sectors for reasons such as raising awareness of an issue or raising funding. Discuss why other sectors might want to get involved in such a scheme and what the benefits to the different partners could be. Share your findings with the rest of the class.

Sharing skills and resources

A key benefit of voluntary and public or private sector partnerships is sharing skills and resources. A report by the Charity Commission highlighted that many smaller voluntary sector charities get into difficulties due to a lack of understanding of legal compliance, lack of ethical policies and failure of monitoring and self-evaluation. Such voluntary organisations could benefit from partnerships with private sector organisations which could provide advice about legal matters, policy and self-evaluation.

LINK IT UP

Refer back to the Chalalan Ecolodge earlier in this section for an example of a private–voluntary partnership and to the previous lesson where you looked at public–private partnerships to help you with the Check My Learning activity.

National Trust

One of the key ways that the National Trust works in partnership with local governments is by securing funding from them in the form of grants. In 2017–2018 the National Trust secured £18 million in funding from a range of bodies, including both local and central government. This funding has then been spent on the conservation of historic homes and gardens and protecting and providing access to the coast and countryside in the UK.

Travel Foundation

The Travel Foundation has a very specific partnership with TUI, called the TUI Care Foundation. This partnership supports the development of sustainable tourism initiatives. Some current projects supported by the TUI Care Foundation, working in partnership with the Travel Foundation, are based in Jamaica, Cape Verde and Croatia. For example, in Jamaica, it is aiming to encourage tourists to spend beyond their hotels so that they spread the economic benefits of their visit to local communities. TUI Care Foundation donations also contribute to a range of other Travel Foundation activities.

CHECK MY LEARNING

Working individually, create a factsheet with examples of partnerships across different sectors and the benefits that these partnerships bring to all key stakeholders. Include at least one example of each of the following;
- public–private partnerships
- private–voluntary partnerships
- voluntary–public partnerships

> **ACTIVITY**
>
> Working individually, list reasons why voluntary and public sector organisations might form a partnership to try to improve a destination.

What are destination management organisations?

GETTING STARTED

Working in pairs, research and list some examples of DMOs that operate in Britain and overseas. You may find the following websites useful:

https://www.visitbritain.org/destination-management-organisations-england

www.tourism.australia.com/en

www.discoverqueensland.com.au/

KEY TERM

Destination management organisations are generally inbound organisations that promote, manage and help to develop tourism in their area.

Destination management organisations, or DMOs, are partnerships between a range of tourism agencies and stakeholders that play an important role in the development of tourism within a destination. They are found both in the UK and in overseas destinations. In the UK, DMOs include:

- UK National DMOs – VisitBritain
- UK Regional DMOs – Visit Cheshire
- UK Local DMOs – Visit Liverpool.

Overseas, for example in Australia, DMOs include:

- National DMO – Tourism Australia
- Regional DMO – Discover Queensland
- Local DMO – Destination Gold Coast.

What they do

In general, DMOs are concerned with marketing and promoting the destination that they represent. This can include working with a range of partners to promote different tourism activities, facilities and events within a local area.

Visit California

Visit California provides a free visitor guide that includes articles about tourism in California and many adverts that feature attractions in the area, such as Universal Studios Hollywood, Disneyland Park and SeaWorld.

These attractions work in partnership with Visit California by paying a fee to advertise in their visitor guide. The visitor guide is available as an e-download from the website or as a printed magazine sent free of charge.

◼ How do high-quality marketing materials persuade people to visit California?

ACTIVITY

Working in a small group, research examples of DMOs in two different destinations. Discuss how a DMO such as VisitBritain:
- raises the profile of the destination
- supports the launch of new products
- provides marketing, funding and sponsorship
- helps with the organisation of major events.

Partnerships

VisitBritain has been involved in a range of global partnerships with both public and private organisations. One of the main aims of such partnerships is to increase the volume of inbound visitors to the UK. These partnerships include the following.

- Showcasing London to the US market with British Airways.
- Inspiring more Chinese visitors to explore Great Britain in partnership with Ctrip.
- A European city campaign in partnership with easyJet.
- British Airways promoting UK travel in China.
- Partnership with StudioCanal as part of a film tourism campaign for Paddington 2.

Major projects and events

VisitBritain has been involved in a £100 million marketing campaign which has promoted Britain to a global market through a number of themes including culture heritage, sport, music, the countryside and shopping.

Part of this four-year initiative was promoting a major event; the 2012 London Olympics. This included a series of adverts featuring 'British' celebrities shown on TV and digital channels around the world. A pre-games image campaign involved wrapping a New York subway train with the Union Jack flag and decorating 100 Delhi taxis with themed branding.

DID YOU KNOW?

London is the first city to host the Olympic Games three times: in 1908, 1948 and 2012.

ACTIVITY

Working individually, write a detailed comparison of how two different DMOs raise their profile and launch new products. Judge which DMO is more effective by considering the profile of each DMO and how well marketed new products and services are by that DMO.

Temporary projects and events

Many DMOs will offer services to support the development of smaller projects or one-off events. Visit Cheshire offers a full event management service that includes organising events such as conferences, award ceremonies and gala dinners. It makes use of the local knowledge of its employees to select suitable venues for such events.

CHECK MY LEARNING

Working individually, create a quiz about DMOs. Questions could be about the type of DMO, how they are funded, or the partnerships they engage with.

What are the main benefits of destination management organisations?

GETTING STARTED

Working individually, based on your learning from last lesson can you define what a DMO is?

Effective DMOs can bring about many benefits for destinations and organisations. National DMOs play an important role in raising the profile of the country abroad and increasing visitor numbers. Regional and local DMOs can help to promote individual attractions and facilities.

Raising the profile of the destination

One of the main aims of DMOs at national, regional and local levels is to raise the profile of the destination. Many DMOs have relatively large marketing budgets that are spent on raising the profile of the destination. National and regional DMOs tend to focus on raising the profile of the destination abroad to attract a greater volume of inbound visitors. Depending on the size and profile of the local area, local DMOs tend to advertise destinations and attractions to the domestic market within their own country. However, some local DMOs that represent a major city also target overseas visitors. For example, Visit Liverpool promotes events such as the Liverpool International Horse Show to overseas visitors.

How can raising the profile of a destination such as Liverpool promoting events such as their International Horse Show help to increase visitor numbers?

Launching new products

DMOs can be an effective platform to inform people about new products or services. Some DMOs allow you to find out about, book or purchase a new product through their website. For example, VisitBritain had a specific web page dedicated to 'what's new and happening in Britain in 2018'. The web page featured a month-by-month guide to new events happening across Britain. For example, in December 2018, Christmas at Kew and The Great Christmas Pudding Race were featured along with weblinks that connected directly to the websites for the events.

DID YOU KNOW?

According to VisitBritain, the British tourism industry will be worth over £257 billion and support over 3.8 million jobs by 2025.

Marketing

As you will be aware, marketing is one of the most important roles of DMOs. Effective marketing can create genuine interest in a destination and help to shape the image of the place.

Examples of marketing activities with the aim of raising the profile of destinations include:

- production and distribution of marketing brochures; for example, Visit Brisbane produces a printable 'Brisbane Visitor Guide' for visitors to use
- International and domestic advertising; for example, in 2017 four short commercials were created by VisitBritain and BBC StoryWorks to promote the landscapes, fashion, culture and history of Britain to an American audience
- operation of a website; most DMOs will have a website to promote tourism, for example www.visitfrance.co.uk
- travel exhibitions, fairs and trade shows; for example, the VisitScotland Expo is an exhibition for Scotland-based organisations to show off their products and services
- Customer Relationships Management (CRM); many DMOs will have specific job roles linked to CRM, for example VisitBritain has a Senior Social Media Manager position.

ACTIVITY

Working in pairs, compare notes about DMOs from last lesson. Create and present a PowerPoint® presentation that details each DMO and compares their effectiveness.

Funding and sponsorship

DMOs rely on funding from a range of partnership sources; these include the following:

- national government
- regional, state or local government
- hotel tax or other specific tax
- membership fees from tourism organisations
- advertising income from other from tourism organisations.

This list highlights that DMOs work with both public and private organisations to secure funding. National and local governments support the existence of DMOs because they recognise that income from tourism can massively boost the economy of an area. Furthermore, private organisations, such as visitor attractions, recognise that advertising in DMO-produced visitor guides and websites can increase visitor numbers and therefore improve profitability.

Providing funding

Some DMOs also provide funding to smaller schemes and projects. For example, VisitBritain oversees a £40-million Discover England Fund that is intended for small-scale and larger-scale collaborative projects linked to offering world-class English tourism products. One of the main aims of the Discover England Fund is to encourage more tourism to take place outside London. Some of the pilot projects that were launched in 2017 include the following.

- Golf tourism England
- Telling the Stories of England: Developing Cultural Tourism Products across England
- Gardens and Gourmet
- South West Coast Path – Amazing Experiences and Making Memories
- England's Seafood Coast.

CHECK MY LEARNING

Working as a class, answer the key question: 'Why are DMOs important for destination management?'

The advantages and disadvantages of partnerships

GETTING STARTED

Working in pairs, think of examples of real partnerships involving travel and tourism organisations that you know about and write a list. For example, Manchester City Football Club and Etihad Airways have a sponsorship deal.

Partnerships are essential for travel and tourism organisations of all shapes and sizes. Effective partnerships can help an organisation to gain a competitive advantage over others through sharing costs and collaborating on projects and ideas. However, not all partnerships are effective; some can be quite unconstructive.

Advantages of partnerships

Shared resources, skills and expertise

One of the main advantages of a partnership or collaboration is that resources, skills and expertise can be shared. For example, one organisation in the partnership may have experience of marketing products through television advertising. This organisation can then share its experiences, including the costs and benefits of television advertising, with its partner organisation.

New ideas

Creating an organisational ethos where every member of an organisation feels confident enough to share new ideas can be very beneficial. This is also true of partnerships; when honesty trust and integrity exist between organisations, new ideas are more likely to be introduced, and tried and tested.

For example, a travel organisation called GetGoing introduced a unique scheme involving partnerships with airlines, whereby customers enter two preferred holiday locations and then wait to find out which destination has been selected for them to visit. This scheme means that empty airline seats can be filled and customers benefit from a 40 per cent discount on their holiday.

ACTIVITY

Working individually, create a table with two columns; advantages and disadvantages of partnerships. Using examples from real organisations, complete the table.

Next, use the evidence that you have collected about the advantages and disadvantages of partnerships to answer the following question in detail:

Are partnerships beneficial to global travel and tourism organisations?

Remember to include some examples from real organisations to back up your argument.

Shared costs

One of the key benefits of partnerships is that costs can be shared. This can include marketing costs, which are often one of the biggest investments that organisations make. For example, two of the world's biggest global brands, Disney and McDonald's, have worked together to promote the Disneyland Paris resort and the McDonald's Happy Meal® as part of a joint marketing campaign.

DID YOU KNOW?

McDonald's and Disney offered an Incredibles 2 Happy Meal in 2018; this comes over a decade after Disney cut ties with McDonald's over concerns about promoting childhood obesity.

Increased publicity

Effective partnerships can increase publicity for organisations. One example is the sponsorship of advertising hoarding around Spanish La Liga and English Premier League football pitches. Adverts featured are often related to travel organisations, such as airlines like Emirates. Furthermore, a technology exists, called digital replacement technology, which allows adverts to be altered depending on what country they are being seen in, meaning that partnerships can easily be global.

Disadvantages of partnerships

Conflicting aims and priorities

One disadvantage of working in partnership is that if the aims of each organisation are not aligned and/or are at odds with the will of the local community then this can lead to conflict, negative publicity and a loss of business. In 1997, McDonald's was successful in collaborating with local authorities to gain planning permission to construct a new restaurant in Tavistock, Devon. However, the local community was unhappy about the restaurant and set up a campaign to boycott the local McDonald's. By 2006, the McDonald's restaurant was forced to close due to a lack of business. In 2018, it was reported that the town has since become 'the top destination for lovers of boutique, organic, independent eateries'. This highlights that visitors often prefer authentic styles of food and eating in locally owned restaurants compared with corporately owned fast-food chains.

Less flexibility

Partnerships can also lead to less flexibility within an organisation. For example, two organisations may form a shared marketing agreement that then prevents one organisation from working with any similar organisation that provides a similar product or service. Similar to this, some organisations may incentivise other businesses to stock their own or their partners' products as part of a deal. For example, Sky Sports has a partnership with Molson Coors brewery, where pubs and hotels that serve Molson Coors drinks get a 30 per cent discount on the cost of a Sky Sports subscription package. This discourages pubs and hotels from choosing rival breweries to supply their drinks.

Slows down decision making

Working in partnerships can often slow down decision making because more people are involved in the process. For example, if planning a music festival with multiple partnerships, the more acts and events involved can increase the complexity of planning and slow the overall decision making.

Difficulty in responding to change

Responding to change can be difficult for organisations locked into partnership with each other. For example, a premium tour operator that works with airlines, accommodation and transport operators to provide a package holiday may struggle to respond to competition from organisations which specialise in one area, such as budget airlines, which can offer a similar but much cheaper service.

LINK IT UP

In Component 1, you will have learned about how travel and tourism organisations work together and often form partnerships. Can you remember what the term 'interdependencies' means?

CHECK MY LEARNING

Create a mind map about the importance of partnerships in destination management. The following questions will help you to plan your mind map.
- What are DMOs?
- How do partnerships benefit destinations?
- What are the disadvantages of partnerships for travel and tourism organisations?

Learning aim C: assessment practice

How you will be assessed

Although the topics from the whole component could occur in any of the questions across the assessment, some examples of the types of question that may be asked in relation to topics in Section B are shown here. Before answering the following questions, refer to the command words words found on page XXX. The external assessment may assess your understanding of Section C: Destination management. This may include:

- explaining how destinations change over time and how this is managed
- assessing the characteristics of emerging and mature destinations
- evaluating the importance of partnerships in managing and developing destinations.

CHECKPOINT

Review your learning of this section by answering the following questions; this will help you to prepare for the external assessment.

Strengthen

- Identify three characteristics of emerging destinations.
- Identify three characteristics of mature destinations.
- Describe how tourism may have impacted on the culture of a mature destination.
- Explain the appeal of emerging destinations for tourists.

Challenge

- Assess how partnerships can benefit destinations. Evaluate the impact of Destination Management Organisations (DMOs) on destinations.

ASSESSMENT ACTIVITY 1 | LEARNING AIM C

Situated in the Costa Blanca, Benidorm is one of the original Spanish beach resorts. The destination has been heavily influenced by British culture over the years and features many English language signs, British shops and pubs and British-style restaurants such as fish and chip shops.

Look at the timeline which outlines the evolution of tourism in Benidorm.

1956 – First general urban development plan for a tourism-devoted town.

1959 – Four major hotels opened in Benidorm.

1963 – Second general urban development plan for Benidorm allowed the construction of skyscrapers.

1970 – Alicante airport was opened.

1985 – Aqualandia amusement park was opened.

1999 – Foreign tourist numbers to Benidorm peaked at over 6 million visits per year.

2000 – Opening of Terra Mitica, Aqua Natura and Terra Natura amusement parks.

2011 – Foreign tourist numbers to Benidorm declined to around 5 million visits per year.

TIP

Make sure that you understand the difference between a mature and emerging destination and can give an example of each. This reminder might help:

emerging destinations – these are less well known and are generally untouched by tourism, e.g. **Ischia, Italy**

mature destinations – these are very well-known tourist destinations that have well developed tourism infrastructure in place, e.g. **Benidorm, Spain.**

Now answer the following:

- Mass tourism with organised package holidays is one characteristic of a mature destination like Benidorm. Give **one** other characteristic of a mature destination.
- Improved infrastructure, such as the opening of airports like Alicante, is one impact of tourism. Describe **two** ways that improved infrastructure can benefit the local community.
- A destination such as Benidorm experiencing stagnation or decline may try to rejuvenate itself. Give **two** impacts of a destination in decline.
- Explain how mass tourism can impact on local culture in mature destinations like Benidorm. Refer to the timeline in your answer.
- Evaluate why foreign tourist numbers to Benidorm may have declined between 1999 and 2011.
- Assess the importance of key stakeholders working together to manage tourism in Benidorm.
- To what extent do you agree that mass tourism has damaged the culture of Benidorm?

ASSESSMENT ACTIVITY 2 | LEARNING AIM C

Read the following article about VisitBritain:

VisitBritain is an example of a destination management organisation (DMO) which receives funding from the Department for Digital, Culture, Media & Sport (DCMS). It plays a role in raising Britain's profile worldwide and increasing the volume and value of tourism in Britain.

Now answer the following:

- Raising the value of tourism in Britain is one role of VisitBritain. Give **one** other role of VisitBritain.
- VisitBritain is an example of a national DMO. Give **one** example of a local or regional DMO.
- VisitBritain is funded by the DCMS – a government department. Explain why the UK government wants to encourage tourism in Britain.
- Explain the role that a DMO like VisitBritain can play in raising the profile of a destination.
- To what extent do you agree that DMOs like VisitBritain are needed to promote tourism?

TIP

In preparation for the external assessment remember to learn some real examples of partnerships that exist within the travel and tourism sector. For example, how local government works with the private sector on infrastructure projects.

TAKE IT FURTHER

Have you checked that you are familiar with all of the stages of the TALC model? Are you aware of the roles that local and national government play in destination management? Remember to familiarise yourself with different partnerships and the advantages and disadvantages of these.

03 Customer Needs in Travel and Tourism

Introduction

Keeping track of what's hot and what's not is what gives travel companies the edge. Traditional methods of market research along with a more modern approach using hashtags and social media platforms help travel companies to stay ahead of the game. People love to boast about where they are and what they are doing, and this is a great market research tool.

The travel and tourism environment is constantly changing to meet the needs and preferences of its customers. So, how important is it that travel and tourism industries develop their products and services to meet these needs?

In this component, you will investigate how travel and tourism organisations use market research to identify trends to match products and services to meet customer needs. You will explore the impact that global influences have on travel and tourism industries and how they respond to these trends and factors to meet customer needs and preferences.

Think about it, if a travel company is struggling to find new ideas and ways to develop its travel products and services, what better way to start than by asking its customers what they want?

This component will provide you with the opportunity to apply learning from Components 1 and 2 and link this learning to the context of meeting customer needs.

LEARNING AIMS

In this component you will:

A	Investigate how organisations identify travel and tourism trends
B	Explore how to meet the needs and preferences of travel and tourism customers.

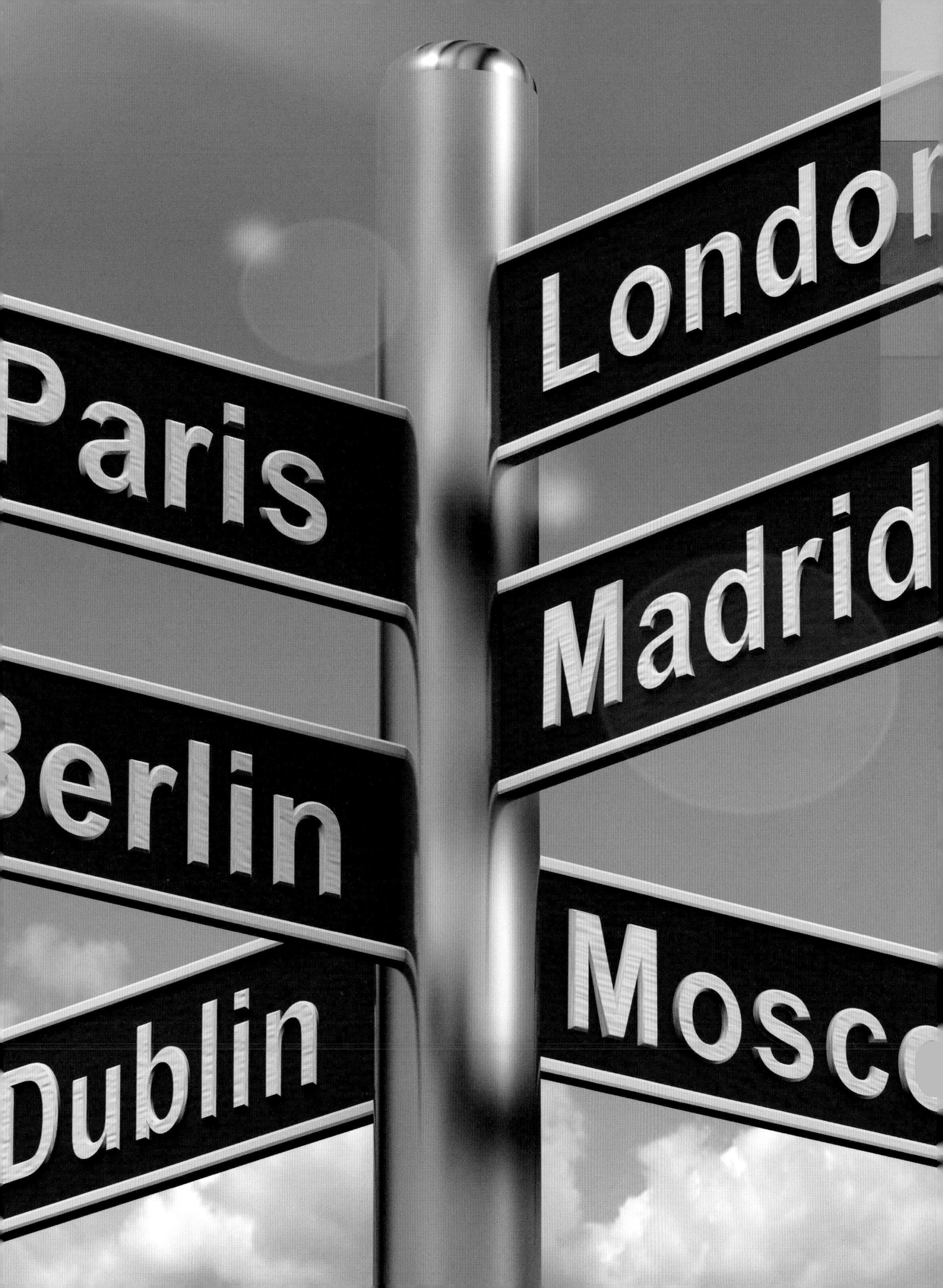
London
Paris
Madrid
Berlin
Dublin

Types of market research (1)

GETTING STARTED

Working in small groups, discuss what is meant by the term 'market research'. What is it? How can travel and tourism organisations use it to gather information about their customers?

Remember, the travel and tourism industry is made up of many different types of organisations so try to think about this in your discussions.

Market research is used by travel and tourism organisations to develop their products and services to ensure that they meet the needs and preferences of their customers. There are different types of research, primary and secondary, and different types of data, qualitative and quantitative, that are used to gather different types of information for different purposes.

Primary research

Primary research is new research that asks specific questions relating to a business, products or services. Travel and tourism organisations may carry out this research themselves or they may employ a specialist organisation to do this for them. There are several common methods of gathering data (Figure 3.1).

LINK IT UP

In Component 1, you learned about the many different organisations that are involved in the travel and tourism sector, not just airlines and travel agents. How many examples of these different organisations can you recall? Use these organisations as you explore market research activities across the sector.

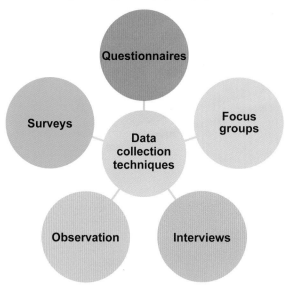

◘ Figure 3.1: Have you used any of these techniques before?

KEY TERMS

Primary research is research that directly collects new data or facts to address a certain problem, validate a decision taken or answer specific questions.

Questionnaires have a predefined set of questions, designed to collect data about specific things, most often in the form of a customer satisfaction questionnaire. Sometimes confused with a survey.

Surveys include the whole process of collecting data, through the use of questionnaires among other means, and then analysing the returned data to work out the significance of the responses and to draw conclusions from them. Sometimes confused with a questionnaire.

Questionnaires

Travel and tourism organisations often use **questionnaires** as part of **surveys** (see next lesson) as a primary research technique to gather customer information. These questionnaires are most often delivered by post or email and are completed by returning the questionnaire form or answering online. Customers may be asked to complete a questionnaire at the end of a holiday or when they leave a visitor attraction to tell the organisation about their experience (Figure 3.2). These can be used to improve and develop the products and services that the organisation offers. Customers may be asked to complete these by hand or to submit them online.

Interviews

Interviews can be carried out over the telephone or in person. They are more expensive than questionnaires and other forms of data gathering because of the people and time needed. However, interviews provide an excellent opportunity to get detailed insights and to engage in a dialogue with customers.

Travel Explore, Peregrine Square, Ware SG00 1AB

We use your feedback to develop our holidays and improve the service that we offer. We would be grateful if you could help us by completing the following questionnaire to tell us about your recent holiday experience.

1. Your details

| Title | First name | | Last name |
| Postcode | E-mail | | Booking reference |

2. Who did you travel with?

| Alone ☐ | Family ☐ |
| A partner ☐ | As a group ☐ |

3. How did you hear about Travel Explore?

Returning customer ☐	Social media ☐
Recommendation ☐	TV advertising ☐
Search engine ☐	Other (please state)

4. Why did you choose Travel Explore?

Price ☐	Service ☐
Special offer ☐	Reputation ☐
Recommendation ☐	Range of holidays and destinations ☐

5. How did you book your holiday?

| Direct with Travel Explore ☐ | Through a travel agent ☐ |
| Internet ☐ | |

6. Your holiday resort

Which holiday resort did you visit?

How would you rate your holiday resort?

Excellent ☐ Good ☐ Average ☐ Poor ☐

Comments and feedback

7. Your accommodation

What was the name of your accommodation?

How did you rate the following:

	Excellent	Good	Average	Poor
Service of staff	☐	☐	☐	☐
Cleanliness	☐	☐	☐	☐
Condition and maintenance	☐	☐	☐	☐
Food and drinks	☐	☐	☐	☐
Daytime activities (if applicable)	☐	☐	☐	☐
Evening activities (if applicable)	☐	☐	☐	☐

8. What did you enjoy the most about your holiday?

Relaxing by the pool ☐	Sightseeing ☐
Going to the beach ☐	Organised activities ☐
Exploring independently ☐	Children's clubs ☐

9. Our service

Information and service before your holiday

Excellent ☐ Good ☐ Average ☐ Poor ☐

Comments and feedback

Information and service during your holiday

Excellent ☐ Good ☐ Average ☐ Poor ☐

Comments and feedback

▣ **Figure 3.2:** Has Travel Explore asked the right questions? Are they useful?

ACTIVITY

Travel Explore wishes to find out the types of customer who are booking its holidays and what customers think about their holiday experience. Working in pairs, review the purpose of Travel Explore's questionnaire (Figure 3.2). Answering the following questions will help you.

1 How can the organisation use the information about the customers' details in question 1?

2 What is the reason for asking who the customer travelled with in question 2?

3 How can the organisation use the information from questions 3, 4 and 5 to market and advertise future holidays?

4 What future decisions might the organisation make based on the information gathered from customers in question 6?

5 Which of the questions in the questionnaire could help the organisation to identify trends?

6 How could the two parts to question 9 help the organisation?

7 Which of the questions do you think are the most and least useful and why?

Types of market research (2)

Observation

Observation can be used as a method of collecting information. This is a method that is best used in a natural environment and involves someone observing customer behaviour and recording this information, usually by taking notes, photographs or videos. The best results can be gained when people are not aware that they are being observed. If someone knows they are being observed, then they may act differently.

This method can be used to get a snapshot view of a situation and provide an insight into the bigger picture. Travel organisations can use this method to observe customers and staff to help them to see how people behave or handle different customer situations.

Mystery shoppers

Mystery shoppers, a form of reverse observation, can also be used as a method of gathering information, to measure levels of service provided by the organisation and its staff. Mystery shoppers can be people employed within the organisation or people from outside. Their role is to pretend to be an ordinary customer while observing and reporting back on their experience.

Focus groups

A focus group is where a selected small group of people are invited to come together to discuss a topic. This discussion is managed by someone from the commissioning organisation, who will direct the conversation to make sure that it does not move away from the subject. They are often used in the travel and tourism industry to get people's views and opinions on a brand or a product.

Similar to interviews, they are a good way to obtain in-depth responses and have the benefit of involving more than one respondent; eight to 12 participants is considered the best number of people for a focus group.

◘ What skills do you need to run a successful focus group?

> **ACTIVITY**
>
> Working in pairs, use the internet to carry out research and find out as much as you can about focus groups and how they are used across the travel and tourism sector. Try to find examples of how specific organisations have used them. What did they use them for? List the advantages and disadvantages of using focus groups.

Surveys

Market researchers will use the data gathered through the above methods to complete a survey, the findings of which will help the organisation adapt and develop the products and services that they offer. Surveys usually follow a standard series of steps (Table 3.1).

◘ Table 3.1: Common survey stages

Stage	Description
Research methods	Common research methods include: Postal questionnaires – these can often get a low response rate and therefore a large sample is required. Face-to-face interviews – these can be done by approaching people in the street or by calling door to door. The researcher asks questions and notes the answers. Interviews can get a higher response rate but take more time and cost more money. However, the researcher can select who they interview to get a broader range of people. Telephone interviews – these are cheaper and quicker than face-to-face interviews but people may be more likely to refuse to take part.
Designing research tools	Whatever the chosen method, the questions must be carefully planned. The design, wording, form and order of questions can affect the type of responses you receive.
Sample	It is not possible to collect information from all the population; therefore, a sample of the population must be selected. This is called a sampling frame. The sample size will depend on the research method. For example, for a focus group, the sample size needed will be smaller than if using questionnaires.
Data collection	Data collection must be thorough, fair and clearly recorded.
Data analysis	This should summarise the data so that it is easy to understand and provide answers to the original questions.
Reporting/conclusion	The overall aim of carrying out research is to share the information, record it and use it to make decisions.

Open and closed questions

Good use of open and closed questions can be the key to creating great market research. Both are used as part of each of the four primary research methods detailed above. By asking the right questions, organisations get better information, and this leads to better communication between the customer and the organisation in developing the right products and services.

Closed questions can be answered with a single-word answer and this will usually be 'yes' or 'no'. Closed questions are quick and easy to answer and can be used to confirm information (Figure 3.3).

For example, would you like me to go ahead and book this holiday for you? Would you visit this attraction again?

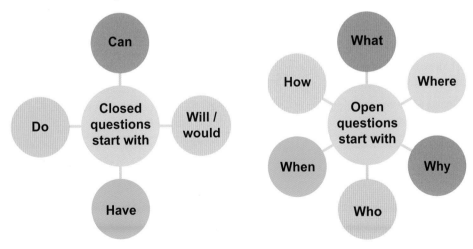

◘ Figure 3.3: Does the question you ask make a difference to the information you receive?

Open questions will provide more information. They will take more thought and time to answer. They allow researchers to build on the answer to gather more information (Figure 3.3).

For example, what type of holiday are you looking for? How did you find out about this attraction?

CHECK MY LEARNING ■■■

Working in pairs, write a list of all the situations in which you would use closed questions and all the situations in which you would use open questions and why.

Secondary research

GETTING STARTED

There are some great ways to access information about a topic and help with research. These include newspapers, websites, trade organisations and journals. Can you think of examples of these secondary research sources that can be used by travel and tourism industries?

Organisations cannot always carry out market research themselves. They will often use information that another organisation has gathered to identify travel trends and customer preferences.

Why use someone else's research?

Have you ever read reviews before deciding to buy something? This is an example of **secondary research**. Secondary research uses information that already exists; primary research that has already been carried out by somebody else. Travel organisations will often use research that has already been carried out by government agencies, trade associations and other media sources. Much of this information is available to the public and can be used for free. Some of this information can be accessed through membership to a trade or educational organisation and must be paid for.

KEY TERM

Secondary research is research that builds on and uses existing primary research, sometimes by bringing together similar data from different sources or analysing their findings.

Advantages of secondary research:
- someone else has already done the work and carried out the research
- it saves the organisation time
- it saves the organisation money.

Disadvantages of secondary research:
- the source could be unreliable
- the information could be out of date
- it may not be specific enough to your needs.

LINK IT UP

Later in this component, you will be carrying out your own secondary research using the data and findings in ABTA reports to analyse trends.

ACTIVITY

Working in pairs, first both choose a different holiday type (beach, countryside, activity, etc.), then working independently and using secondary research on the internet find out information about your classmate's chosen holiday type.

You should identify tour operators, main destinations, best times of year to visit, transport options, travel advice and entry requirements if applicable. Make a list of information and images that you used or found useful and make a note of the websites you used and how you used them.

Finally, present the information you have found back to your classmate and discuss what each of you has found out, how and where from.

DID YOU KNOW?

Plagiarism is the term used when someone attempts to pass off other people's work or ideas as their own. This can result in legal action due to infringement of copyright laws. Get into the habit of keeping a reference list whenever you use secondary research so that you can reference this accurately in your own work.

Sources of relevant tourism research

Many travel organisations carry out research that can be used for secondary research purposes. Table 3.2 provides some detailed examples from five key organisations.

LINK IT UP

In Component 1, you explored a range of different organisations that promote tourism to raise awareness and to encourage more people to travel and visit different destinations. Consider how you might use such reports and data for secondary research.

◘ Table 3.2: Sources and examples of research

Organisation	What it does	Examples of research
VisitBritain www.visitbritain.org	VisitBritain promotes Britain to the rest of the world. It is funded by the government to help grow the British tourism market and encourage visitors and tourism. It also produces statistics and data in monthly and annual survey reports. This information is in the public domain and can be used by organisations to identify customer travel trends.	The Great Britain Tourism Survey The Great Britain Day Visits Survey England/UK Occupancy Survey Annual Survey of Visits to Visitor Attractions
Association of Leading Visitor Attractions (ALVA) www.alva.org.uk	The ALVA represents its members to government, the media, business and the broader tourism and cultural sectors. It shares information, insights and experience to help their members continually improve their visitor experience.	Latest visitor figures of visits made to UK visitor attractions
Office for National Statistics www.ons.gov.uk	The Office for National Statistics has a responsibility to collect and analyse information about the UK economy and society. This includes visitor numbers to the UK, reasons for visiting and the amount of money spent. It also looks at statistics on UK residents travelling abroad.	Travel trends estimates – UK residents' visits abroad
United Nations World Tourism Organization (UNWTO) www2.unwto.org	The UNWTO promotes sustainable tourism policies. It produces publications, statistics and market trends reports.	Tourism Highlights Tourism and the Sustainable Development Goals
Association of British Travel Agents (ABTA) www.abta.com	ABTA offers information and advice to the travelling public and to travel organisations to help deliver high standards of customer service. It publishes annual reports to identify trends and habits affecting the industry.	Annual Holiday Habits and Travel Trends Reports

ACTIVITY

Working individually and using Table 3.2, choose one example of research from two organisations. Take some time to explore this research and see what information it provides. Consider how organisations use this information.

An example of data from this type of research is trends in visitor numbers to the UK. VisitBritain, in 2016, reported that the growth trend in the number of visitors to Britain over the 5-year period from 2012 to 2016 had moved steadily upwards. It forecasted that the trend would continue for the following two years (Figure 3.4).

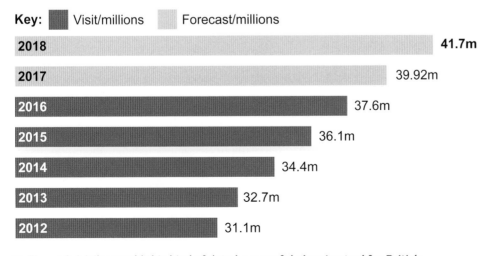

Key: ■ Visit/millions ▨ Forecast/millions

2018	41.7m
2017	39.92m
2016	37.6m
2015	36.1m
2014	34.4m
2013	32.7m
2012	31.1m

◘ Figure 3.4: Why would this kind of data be a useful planning tool for British travel organisations?

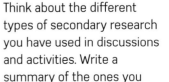

CHECK MY LEARNING

Think about the different types of secondary research you have used in discussions and activities. Write a summary of the ones you found to be the most useful and explain why.

Qualitative and quantitative research

GETTING STARTED

Working in small groups discuss the terms 'qualitative' and 'quantitative'. Can you list some examples of qualitative and quantitative data that travel organisations would find useful? These organisations could include hotel chains, tour operators, visitor attractions or transport providers.

KEY TERMS

Qualitative research seeks to understand the reasons, opinions and motivations of respondents and their behaviour. It targets why people do a certain thing. It is sometimes used to identify ideas for follow-up quantitative research.

Quantitative research collects objective, measurable data, that can be used for statistical analysis. It targets how many people do a certain thing.

Eco-tourism is sustainable tourism that has as little impact as possible on the natural locations offered; it often also encompasses support of local conservation work.

DID YOU KNOW?

Studies show that connecting a brand to a consumer on an emotional level is one of the most powerful advertising techniques. Take some time to look at adverts for holidays and see how they connect their brand with emotional benefits. For example, TUI: 'Discover Your Smile'.

Both primary and secondary research use different ways to collect data, depending on the aim of the research. There are two different types of data that can be gathered, known as qualitative and quantitative, and each give organisations different types of information that can be used in different ways.

Qualitative research

Qualitative research provides information that is detailed. It is based on a customer's perception and allows them to express an opinion. This may be based on their feelings or emotions. This research will usually measure the quality of something and aims to capture how and why people behave in a certain way (in contrast to **quantitative research**).

For example, the open question 'what can we do to improve our customer service?' will produce qualitative data as the answer will likely include customers' thoughts and feelings.

Travel organisations will often use qualitative research to understand travel behaviours. It asks the question 'why?'

Think back to Component 2, which explored sustainable tourism. This is a good example of an area where, through their market research, travel and tourism organisations are becoming more aware of sustainability and customers' interest in **eco-tourism** holidays. In response to their research these organisations can then create holidays that are more responsible and environmentally friendly.

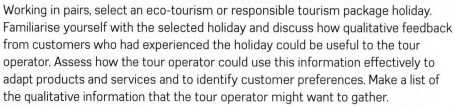

ACTIVITY

Working in pairs, select an eco-tourism or responsible tourism package holiday. Familiarise yourself with the selected holiday and discuss how qualitative feedback from customers who had experienced the holiday could be useful to the tour operator. Assess how the tour operator could use this information effectively to adapt products and services and to identify customer preferences. Make a list of the qualitative information that the tour operator might want to gather.

Useful websites:

www.responsibletravel.com

www.exodus.co.uk

www.brazilnaturetours.com

Travel behaviours are often linked to customers' emotions and feelings about an experience. Many customers will choose a brand because of how it makes them feel. Travel and tourism organisations rely on customer loyalty for growth and success. They want customers to keep choosing their brand. It is important that travel and tourism organisations use qualitative research to explore customers' feelings and emotions to develop their products and make improvements.

Quantitative research

Quantitative research provides statistical data and information that can be analysed numerically. This will usually measure the quantity of something and assess its value or importance.

For example, the closed question 'how many holidays have you taken this year?' will produce quantitative data as the answers will likely only contain a number.

Travel organisations will often use quantitative research to plan and forecast by finding out which destinations are growing in popularity and which destinations are in decline.

Putting the data to use

Tourist organisations use quantitative data as evidence to support or challenge an idea. Think about adverts that use phrases like '8 out of 10 customers'. This is an example of using quantitative data to support the advertised popularity of a product.

Once an organisation has collected the data, they need to analyse it by putting it into some sort of order or format so that they can understand it. Data will often be sorted into a table or shown on a graph. For example, VisitBritain uses quantitative research to produce official statistics. It will often produce these using graphs and tables.

Combining qualitative and quantitative research

Qualitative and quantitative research can complement each other, as shown in the example below.

1 How do you prefer to travel to your holiday destination? (tick your preferred option)

   a Car ☐

   b Train ☐

   c Bus ☐

   d Plane ☐

   e Other ☐ Please specify: ....

2 Why do you prefer this method of transport? ....

By combining these types of research, travel organisations can gain a better understanding of what their customers are doing and why. The data then provides a more complete picture of travel behaviours.

LINK IT UP

In Component 2, you learned about stages of tourism development as suggested by Butler's Tourism Area Life Cycle.

ACTIVITY

Sort the key words below into the table in the correct columns. There are two spare rows: can you think of any other relevant key words? If so, complete the table.

Calculations   Frequency

Descriptions   Measured

Emotions   Numbers

Feelings   Opinions

Qualitative	Quantitative

CHECK MY LEARNING

Return to Travel Explore's questionnaire (Figure 3.2). Remember that qualitative = quality, and quantitative = quantity.

1 Identify which of the questions will gather qualitative information and which will gather quantitative data.

2 Write four new questions for the questionnaire. Two should be qualitative and two quantitative.

3 If you worked for the company, would you include a question asking if the respondents would consent to being contacted about their answers? How might this be useful?

Using research to identify customers and their needs

GETTING STARTED

Working in pairs, identify a local visitor attraction or hotel. Make a list of the types of customer that the organisation would appeal to. Discuss the reasons why you think the organisation would appeal to these visitor types.

The travel and tourism sector is competitive. It is important that organisations across the industry get to know their customers if they want to keep them. By asking the right questions, market research can be used by travel and tourism organisations to identify who their customers are and recognise their needs.

Identifying customers and their needs

Think back to earlier lessons where you explored how organisations find out about customer needs. Consider the ways that they collected information about customers. Once organisations know what their customers want, they are on their way to making their customers happy and to encouraging customer loyalty.

One way that travel and tourism organisations can do this is to offer different products and services to cater for a range of different customer types. These customer types can be classified in many ways; for example, by their age, lifestyle, income or reasons for travel. For example, tour operators will offer different types of holiday to meet the needs of different types of customer, such as families, solo travellers or couples.

Families

Families with children will generally look for facilities and services that can cater for the whole family, across all ages, before booking a holiday or a day out at a visitor attraction. They will look for family-friendly destinations, transport and travel times, and accommodation with facilities for children, such as a swimming pool or entertainment. Nowadays, families are often looking for more than just the offer of a cot or extra fold-out bed. Families are not all the same and organisations need to be aware of this (Table 3.3).

Travel and tourism trend reports suggest that the family travel market is growing and changing. According to an article in *Travel Weekly* (February 2018), family bookings have fuelled sales growth for a seventh year in a row, with sales increasing at twice the rate for non-families (13 per cent vs 7 per cent in 2016). Family holidays now account for 40 per cent of the summer market. The report notes that for 2018, advance sales for seven-night holidays rose by 15 per cent but 14-night stays were down by 7 per cent. It also comments that the average selling price for family holidays is 23 per cent lower than for non-families, which is partially explained by the predominance (61 per cent of bookings) of cheaper all-inclusive trips.

Lone travellers

Solo travel is another growing market across the travel and tourism industry. People often don't want to compromise on where they go and what they do and travelling alone means that they can choose to do exactly what they want. As it is now more acceptable for people to travel alone, people feel more comfortable eating alone, visiting places alone and going on holiday alone. Travelling alone is no longer limited to backpacking and staying in youth hostels, with holidays designed for single, divorced and widowed travellers of all ages available.

Lone travellers will consider comfort, safety, entertainment, activities and cost. Visiting destinations alone whether it be for a day, a weekend or a longer holiday no longer carries the stigma it once did and more people are travelling by themselves, as reported by the

□ **Table 3.3: Examples of how families have different requirements**

Family type	Specific needs
With pre-school children	Children's clubs, early suppers, babysitting services and activities for young children
With teenagers	Facilities that allow some independence for older children within a safe environment, e.g. youth clubs, discos, games rooms, juice bars/cafes, shops
One-parent	Accommodation that doesn't charge under-occupancy supplements
Multi-generational	Flexible accommodation including adjoining rooms, suites or multi-bedroom apartments, activities for all age ranges

ABTA Holiday Habits Report in 2018 with 15 per cent travelling solo compared with 12 per cent in 2017. Reasons to travel solo vary, with 76 per cent doing so to 'have the opportunity to do what they want', up 3 per cent on 2017 and coming out as the top reason. Other reported motivations included taking time out of everyday life or meeting new people, both of which saw a fall: 63 per cent vs 71 per cent and 31 per cent vs 41 per cent, respectively.

Business travellers

The needs of business travellers are quite unique as their reasons for travelling are very different from those of leisure travellers. Business travellers will consider facilities that allow them to work while travelling, value for money to meet the company budget (though this doesn't necessarily mean cheap), space to work, location, accessibility, reliability and convenience are all considerations. They will consider transport and accommodation that can provide this and often use a business travel agent to make these arrangements for them. Businesses will operate to different budgets and this will determine the amount of money that business travellers have to spend. Some business travellers will travel in economy class and stay in budget hotels whereas others will travel business class and stay in smarter, more luxurious hotels.

ACTIVITY

Working in a small group, select a travel and tourism service. This could be a holiday, a hotel or a visitor attraction. Using one of the following scenarios, discuss their needs in relation to the travel and tourism service. You may consider transport, facilities and entertainment.

Ana, 22, is a student from Brazil. She is travelling alone and will be spending three days with a cousin in London but then wants to visit the Lake District. She doesn't have a large budget, she cannot drive, but she enjoys meeting other young people.

Anil has to present at a large international one-day conference in Bangkok. The conference includes overnight accommodation the night before his presentation, in a five-star hotel. Anil must leave from his home in Glasgow and would prefer to fly in business class. He wishes to take three days leave and stay on to see the city, but needs a different, cheaper hotel.

Mike and Sue have three children aged 9, 11 and 14. They want a holiday in Europe with facilities and daytime activities for the children so that they can relax by the pool. They have a reasonable budget and would like a three- or four-star hotel with all-inclusive facilities. They would like some evening entertainment but would also like to be in a resort so that they can go out in the evening if they wish.

Create a poster to present your customer type and illustrate their needs in relation to the selected travel and tourism service.

Importance of researching customer needs

So why is it important that travel and tourism organisations carry out research to find out what their customers need? Customers have choices and they have expectations. If these expectations are not met, then customers are disappointed. They may complain, or they may just simply not come back. Organisations have key financial and strategic aims that are linked to making a profit and they must work hard to keep encouraging customers to buy their goods and services. It is therefore important that organisations carry out research to identify what their customers' needs are, and then make sure they meet or exceed them.

LINK IT UP

In Component 1, you explored retail travel agents and business travel agents. How many reasons for business travel can you recall?

LINK IT UP

Think back to Component 1, where you explored the key financial and strategic aims of many travel and tourism organisations and how they interrelate. Where does customer needs research fit in to these aims?

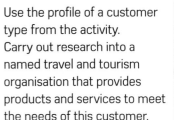

CHECK MY LEARNING

Use the profile of a customer type from the activity. Carry out research into a named travel and tourism organisation that provides products and services to meet the needs of this customer.

What products and services does the operator provide?

How does it meet the needs of this particular customer type?

Informing product and service development

GETTING STARTED

Do you think all families with children are the same? Do all business travellers want to stay in the same kind of hotel? Do lone travellers all enjoy the same kind of entertainment? In small groups, pick one of these customer groups and come up with three different 'sub-groups', explaining what the differences might be.

Travel and tourism organisations, having identified their customers and their needs, must make use of this information to develop specific products and services for the various sub-groups that make up the main customer types. What would happen to an organisation that found out that the majority of its potential customers were families, but did not update its accommodation to provide more family and interconnecting rooms?

Target market and market segmentation

The term 'target market' is used to refer to the group of people that an organisation aims to sell its products and services to. Within a target market there are different groups of people who will buy different types of products and services. For example, tour operators sell different types of holidays to cater for different types of customers, such as families, this is **market segmentation**.

KEY TERMS

Market segmentation is dividing a market into groups (segments) by characteristics; the segments comprise potential customers with similar characteristics and who are likely to respond to the same type of marketing and buy the same type of products and services.

Socio-demographics is a combination of the social and demographic characteristics of a population.

Organisations need to know their target market and market segments before they can decide on the best ways to market their products and services and make them attractive to these groups. The market can be split by behaviours or by **socio-demographics** such as age, gender, income or lifestyle. Splitting their market helps travel and tourism organisations to target their products and services to relevant customers.

Segmentation example: geographical areas

Organisations will often carry out research to find out which geographical areas visitors come from. Alton Towers Resort uses this information to market and develop products and services to existing customers and broaden their appeal to other market areas (Figure 3.5).

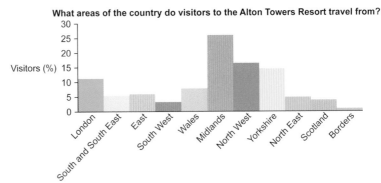

What areas of the country do visitors to the Alton Towers Resort travel from?

■ Figure 3.5: Where would you target your marketing? In your heartland of the Midlands and the North West, or in more distant, less-represented areas to try to secure new visitors?

Matching products and services

Market segmentation is used to develop products and services to meet customers' needs and preferences and to keep the organisation ahead of the **competition**. It helps organisations to target their products and services to specific groups of people. This is where market research activities come in useful.

Travel and tourism organisations will match products and services to meet the needs of people in a specific sector of the population, for example, younger people. Can you think of any travel and tourism products that cater for younger people? This could be a type of holiday or a visitor attraction.

KEY TERM

Competition is companies selling similar products and services to the same target groups.

Age

TUI Travel operated a youth clubbing brand marketed as '2wentys'. It operated successfully for 30 years but, in 2014, TUI decided it was time to reinvent itself. This brand is now marketed as 'Scene'. The target market remains the same. There are two collections: Scene Hub, which appeals to young people looking for budget hotels, bar crawls and holiday reps to help get the party started, and Scene Style, which still offers nightlife but with a focus on chic hotels and stylish beach clubs with a broader range of destinations. This is a good example of where a travel organisation has used market research to identify customer trends and adapted its products and services to meet the changing preferences of its customers.

Accessible holidays

Accessible holidays is another growing market segment. Thomas Cook now offers Disabled Access Holidays to meet the needs of this growing market. It offers accessible accommodation and arranges flights with special assistance where needed, adapted rooms, transfers in adapted vehicles and arranges mobility equipment.

TUI: one company, many holiday types

Organisations may also consider different lifestyles and budgets and tailor products to meet these needs. Large travel and tourism organisations, such as TUI, may have a strong brand, recognised by customers, with differentiated products and services that cater for specific market segments (Table 3.4).

◘ **Table 3.4: How can these different hotel brands help customers to make choices about what sort of holiday to choose?**

Product	Market segment
Sensatori	5-star luxury holidays with high-quality dining, activities and entertainment, for adults and families
Magic	All-inclusive 24-hour, all-inclusive holidays in beach-front locations with sports programmes and entertainment
Blue	Luxurious holidays, authentic with high-class service and tailor-made experiences
Family Life Holidays	Bringing generations together (creches, children's clubs, hang-outs for teenagers, health and fitness facilities for adults)
Couples	Adult-only, offering great locations, fine dining and relaxation

TUI also offers other types of holidays within its portfolio such as TUI Scene, noted above, and Skytours, value-for-money holidays in a range of destinations for both families and couples.

Take some time to explore these TUI brands and holiday types and consider the types of people that would book these types of holiday.

CHECK MY LEARNING

Alton Towers Resort is located in Staffordshire in the West Midlands. Refer to the Alton Towers region graph (Figure 3.5) and consider how this data would assist the theme park in planning its marketing and advertising. For example, which of the regions are day tickets most likely to appeal to and which regions would overnight or weekend tickets most appeal to and why?

ACTIVITY

Working in small groups, use the customer examples below to work out which of the TUI holiday segments (Table 3.4), TUI Scene or Skytours, would suit them **best**. Create a table with the holiday segments in one column and add the customers against them in the second column.

1 A group of friends in their 20s who want a beach holiday with nightlife and clubs for chilled days and lively nights.

2 A professional couple in their 30s who would like a relaxing holiday in five-star accommodation by the sea.

3 A family with children aged 6, 8 and 12, who would like a holiday with a hotel that offers childcare, children's clubs, sports and entertainment.

4 Two friends travelling together who want a relaxing holiday in a hotel with an international feel and a focus on well being, fine food and drink.

5 A multi-generational family looking for an all-inclusive hotel offering activities, entertainment, food and drink at no extra cost.

6 A couple looking for adult-only accommodation in tranquil, relaxing surroundings.

7 A family, with young children, on a budget, looking for value-for-money accommodation.

Once the table is complete with customers assigned to their **best**-fitting holiday, you could then consider if any of the customers would fit with another holiday segment.

New and changing customer needs

GETTING STARTED

Consider the following questions. What would be your ideal holiday? What facilities would you expect there to be? How about your parents or grandparents, what would they want and expect now, and ten or 20 years ago? Consider the differences in how you would go about booking your holiday and how your parents or grandparents would have ten or 20 years ago. Who would use a travel agent and who the internet?

An organisation may have a strong brand presence with the products and services that they offer but customer needs and trends are constantly changing. It is important that travel and tourism organisations change with their customers to stay ahead in a competitive market if they are to retain customer loyalty and secure repeat business. Think about hotel accommodation. Have customers' needs and expectations changed over recent years? Think about facilities that customers expect, price and value for money.

New and changing customer needs

You may sometimes hear reference to the **customer journey**. This refers to the contact that the customer has with the organisation from the beginning to the end of their experience. Organisations need to see that journey as an opportunity to have contact with their customers and contribute positively to their overall experience.

Customers expect to be listened to and understood, and that means that travel and tourism organisations must pay attention and adapt their products and services to keep up with customer needs and expectations if they are to succeed and stand out from their competitors. It is not just about the product, it is also about the service. Excellent customer service can make the difference between keeping customers and losing them to a competitor.

KEY TERMS

The **customer journey** is the full experience a customer has using an organisation's products and services, viewed holistically, but made up of each individual interaction: booking, airport, transfer to hotel and so on.

Intellectual property (IP) means intangible property, the results of human creativity, encompassing copyrights, patents, literary and artistic works.

Embracing, broadening and evolving

Customer needs and behaviours are changing. PwC is a consulting company that helps organisations to reach their objectives. It carried out a survey in 2017 to identify how the UK attractions sector is responding to customers who are becoming better informed and more aware of their needs and expectations. It identified that visitor attractions need to respond to these changing needs and expectations by:

- embracing technology – 93 per cent of attractions have a website, but only 29 per cent offer online booking
- broadening their appeal – using **intellectual property (IP)** from television, films and gaming, and partnerships
- evolving their offer – by adding new and complementary products to their existing attractions.

Merlin Entertainments

Merlin Entertainments plc own many UK visitor attractions including LEGOLAND, Alton Towers Resort, Madame Tussauds and the London Eye. They are embracing technology to meet customer expectations by developing 3D models and robotics to bring stories alive at their theme parks. They have also introduced free, high-density Wi-Fi to provide a continuous connection for visitors during their ride on the London Eye.

Merlin are investing in products to grow their customer base and attract customers from different market segments. One way that they do this is to develop partnerships with film, TV and gaming providers and use their intellectual property to market their own products. For example, Alton Towers have CBeebies Land and LEGOLAND have Star Wars exhibitions. These themes tap into different markets and broaden the appeal to different customers.

Merlin Entertainments recognises that products need to develop and evolve and has also recently submitted plans in Birmingham for a brand new indoor and outdoor attraction called Project Thor, to include skydiving and high ropes.

ACTIVITY

1 Working in pairs or small groups, discuss why Wi-Fi on the London Eye would appeal to visitors?

2 How can using themes help to attract different customers?

3 What sort of things will influence Merlin Entertainments when it looks for new themes for its attractions?

Butlin's

Butlin's opened its first holiday park in Skegness in 1936. Founded by Billy Butlin, the holiday park included chalet accommodation, meals, and entertainment provided by staff known as 'Redcoats'. The company has survived the test of time and evolved to keep its place in the UK holiday camp market by meeting the changing needs and expectations of its customers. An example of this is the way that Butlin's now allows potential customers to book online and create an account on its website or download a phone app. It also uses social media to promote and advertise.

In the 1950s, Butlin's introduced indoor, heated pools. The 1960s saw the introduction of monorails, pools with underwater-viewing windows and revolving bars. In the 1980s, indoor waterparks were introduced at the camps. In the 1990s, some of the parks were sold and the three remaining camps saw the building of Skyline Pavilions to cater for guests if the weather was bad. The millennium saw the introduction of its first hotels and, in the 2010s, Butlin's developed products 'Just for Tots' in partnership with Great Ormond Street Hospital, science and 'Horrible Histories' weekends, and new seaside apartments.

■ What has Butlin's done to survive over time? How has it developed its products to cater for different customers through the decades?

ACTIVITY

Working in pairs consider the following questions.

1 List two things that you think has helped Butlin's to stand the test of time.

2 Who are Butlin's main target market and market segment?

3 What is the key driver behind Butlin's product development?

CHECK MY LEARNING

Split into two teams. Each team should come up with five questions (and two in reserve in case these are repeated) based on the information covered in this lesson. Select a team leader to represent your team and take it in turns to ask the opposing team a question.

Measuring customer satisfaction

GETTING STARTED

Working in pairs, take a moment to write down a response to the following two questions.

How do organisations know how they are doing?

How do they know if they are meeting their customers' needs?

LINK IT UP

Refer back to your work in the first four lessons, covering primary and secondary research and qualitative and quantitative methods, for a refresher on how organisations may gather data.

ACTIVITY

Working in pairs, select a well-known airline or tour operator and carry out research using TripAdvisor to explore customer reviews. Identify any common themes of satisfied and dissatisfied customers.

1 How could your selected organisation use these reviews to its advantage?

2 How could it respond to these reviews?

Develop a brief customer satisfaction questionnaire based on these reviews that would help the organisation to identify common themes and use the information to respond and develop its products and services.

Refer to your notes from previous lessons to help you to develop your questionnaire to gather qualitative and quantitative information.

It is not enough to have customers who are satisfied. Organisations need to go one step further and try to exceed expectations.

Customer reviews can help to generate sales for travel and tourism organisations. They are a trusted source of information for potential customers who will read reviews on sites such as TripAdvisor, Google and Facebook before visiting a visitor attraction, booking a hotel or a holiday. Businesses can link to these websites to give themselves a stronger online presence.

Importance of measuring satisfaction

Keeping customers happy is important for the customer and for the organisation. If a customer is satisfied with a product or service received, why would they go somewhere else?

- A statistic that is often quoted is that it costs five times as much to attract a new customer as it does to retain an existing one. Satisfied customers are more likely to be returning customers. Organisations which can keep their customers make more money and are more likely to have a positive company image and reputation. This is an effective tool in marketing.
- Customers who are happy and satisfied are likely to recommend an organisation to other people they encounter, even more so if their expectations have been exceeded. In other words, give customers more than they expect.
- Consider the customer journey, discussed in the previous lesson, and try to think of ways that travel and tourism organisations can exceed customer expectations by giving them something that costs little or nothing. This could be by offering a personal touch, remembering a name or following up on something they have said.

Collecting customer feedback

Customer satisfaction cannot be achieved without knowing what customers want and expect in the first place. It is equally important for organisations to gather information from customers following their experience so that they can measure how effectively they are meeting those needs. Customers like to feel valued and organisations have an opportunity to capture levels of customer satisfaction by asking them directly about their experience and responding to this feedback.

This feedback can be captured using a variety of methods depending on the type and size of the organisation. The owners of a small hotel may speak directly to their customers or use a guestbook to gather feedback and respond. A larger hotel chain may use a written questionnaire that it asks customers to complete when they check out or sends to them electronically. Customers may choose to use social media such as Facebook or review sites such as TripAdvisor as a platform to leave feedback. Whatever the method used, these are opportunities for organisations to improve their products and services based on what their customers are telling them. This can also be an opportunity to celebrate the things that they are doing well.

Poppy Cottages

Poppy Cottages is a well-established accommodation provider situated in the village of Carleton-in-Craven, just two miles from the market town of Skipton, known as the

'Gateway to the Dales'. The cottages offer stylish, luxury self-catering accommodation for couples and small groups.

The owners, Sally and Steve, pride themselves on providing the highest standard of service and monitor feedback closely, responding positively to customer needs and expectations. They rely heavily on repeat business and customer recommendations to generate future business, so service and standards mean everything. Attention to detail is what makes this accommodation different from the rest and customer feedback is crucial to its success.

Feedback in person

Initially operating as a Bed and Breakfast, Sally and Steve were in direct contact with their customers and feedback was first-hand. They were able to respond almost instantly to customer needs and expectations. Now, running a self-catering accommodation, this is more difficult as direct customer contact can be limited.

With the change to self-catering, they have found that customers prefer to be left alone so, other than a welcome text, customers are left to their own devices with the owners living next door if they need to be contacted.

Online review sites

Sally and Steve were first introduced to TripAdvisor when a customer wanted to leave feedback online. From that point forward they realised how important these reviews were to promote the business and they continuously push themselves through the fear of receiving a bad review.

The business has its own website, which is handled by a third party with 22 distribution channels, including Airbnb, TripAdvisor Rentals, Expedia and Booking.com. The company which handles the website can also collect analytical data such as where people come from and how many times they have booked this accommodation, or accommodation in the area. Steve and Sally can then access this data.

They also have a Facebook page which is a good tool for promoting the cottages, allowing them to give regular updates of late availability, reduced rates and general news to customers old and new. These updates generate a good deal of interest and are a good way to push any late availability.

Controlling and responding to reviews

With TripAdvisor, feedback alerts are sent to the owners via email when a review has been received and these can be viewed and responded to before it shows on the website. Sally and Steve reply to all reviews, good or bad, and see this as essential.

Occasionally, reviews are left on Facebook and these are instantly visible unless the owners ask them to be removed. To date they have all been positive, but if that changed the lack of control and ability to respond prior to posting could cause a problem. They always take time to leave a comment on the review.

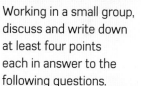

ACTIVITY

Working in a small group, discuss and write down at least four points each in answer to the following questions.

1 How are social media and review sites useful to the business?

2 How could Poppy Cottages use the analytical data collected by the website facilitator to grow the business and encourage repeat business?

DID YOU KNOW?

It is said that 96 per cent of unhappy customers won't complain to the offending business, but they will tell 15 of their friends and 91 per cent of these customers will simply never return.

CHECK MY LEARNING

Swap your completed customer survey with another pair and carry out a review. Highlight examples of good questions and discuss why these are good examples. Identify any questions that you think could be improved and discuss how these could be improved.

Travel and tourism customer trends

GETTING STARTED

Working in pairs, discuss why some holiday destinations may suddenly become popular.

LINK IT UP

In Component 2, you investigated the appeal and characteristics of global destinations that change over time. You learned why some destinations increase or decrease in popularity.

ABTA was introduced to you in Component 1 as a provider of a financial protection scheme for bookings made through agents registered with them, giving travellers peace of mind.

Have you ever wondered what makes something popular and trendy? What makes a holiday destination more popular than another? It is very important for travel and tourism organisations to be aware of customer habits and upcoming trends in the market, so that they can change existing, or introduce new, products in response.

Travel trends

ABTA, the trade association (see later in this lesson), publishes very useful annual reports, including Holiday Habits and Travel Trends. Table 3.5 details the top five travel trends for 2019 according to the 2019 ABTA Travel Trends Report.

▫ **Table 3.5: Top five 2019 travel trends**

Trend	Detail
Sustainability and responsible tourism	Holidaymakers are now more aware of the impact that they have when they visit a destination and want to make a more positive impact and minimise the negative effects that they have on a destination's environment, culture and economy. It was found that 45 per cent of people say that sustainability is an important element when booking a holiday, this is up 6 per cent from 2017. It was found that 36 per cent of people would choose one travel company over another if they have a better environmental record – up 6 per cent since 2017.
Using a travel professional to book a holiday	ABTA research shows that one of the main reasons holidaymakers book with a travel professional is because they feel more confident. It was found that 45 per cent of holidaymakers chose to book through a travel professional because they can offer well-selected holidays that meet the customer's specific requirements, while also giving advice and support throughout the booking process.
Wellness travel	More people than ever are seeking new ways to alleviate stress, reduce illness and boost wellbeing. Global wellbeing trips are up 20 per cent since 2015 and mainstream travel companies are adapting their products to include activities such as yoga and including hotels that offer health and wellness food menus.
Tailor-made package holidays	Ease of booking, value for money and consumer protection have long been core benefits of the package holiday. Increasing numbers of holidaymakers look to a package holiday for a good value break – in 2018, 60 per cent booked a package because it was the best value option for the price, up 3 per cent on 2017. Travel companies are finding more ways to provide flexible and personalised holidays to meet the demand for tailor-made holidays.
Using technology to support the holiday experience	Service-based technology is making travellers' lives easier – from the moment they leave their front door to the moment they return home. Facial recognition technology is replacing the need for passports at some airports. Hotels are offering sun cream booths that offer head-to-toe coverage in only ten seconds. Holidaymakers can also choose a sunbed location in advance and some tour operators have hotels where customers can check in their bags for their flight, leaving them luggage-free on the last day of their holiday.

How organisations identify trends

A **trend** is the direction in which something is changing or developing. In the world of travel and tourism, this could be a holiday type, a growing market segment, preferred transport type, a destination or a way of arranging travel.

Whatever the trend, it is crucial that travel and tourism organisations identify these trends and cater for them to meet the demands of their customers. This can be challenging as these trends are constantly changing, good-quality data can be hard to find, and organisations need to find the time, the budget and the resources to identify these trends. So how do organisations identify these trends? The four sub-sections below detail the main ways businesses can do this.

ACTIVITY

Choose one of the roles below and work out which of the five trends in Table 3.5 is most significant to you. Write down why and what would you would do in response to this trend.

- Owner of an independent travel agency.
- Manager of a tour operator that has built its business on providing 'fun in the sun' holidays to those aged 18–35.

Pair up with a partner who took the other role and discuss your thoughts.

Own market research

For organisations to truly understand their own customers, they must carry out their own market research. This will help them to understand why their existing customers choose their product over their competitors. This will also help travel and tourism organisations to identify which of their existing products customers prefer and deliver the best possible service to maintain customer loyalty and increase their customer base through recommendations. The following are good examples of how travel and tourism organisations developed new products or services in light of their own research.

- Butlin's has introduced a Premier Club. This is an exclusive club for all guests who have stayed with Butlin's three times or more in a three-year period. Membership is automatic and members receive treats such as early check-in, discounts and vouchers.
- Hilton Hotels has a loyalty scheme, called Hilton Honors, where customers earn Honors Points when they stay in a Hilton Hotel or Resort. Points build up and can be redeemed for free hotel stays.

National statistics

Organisations such as the Office for National Statistics (ONS) and VisitBritain collect and produce statistics. They provide the travel and tourism industry with research to help with marketing and product development by providing them with information about visitor numbers and spending. The data they collect is analysed to produce statistics that are reliable, professional and **ethical**. This includes the Office for National Statistics' annual Travel Trends Articles.

Published information from competitors

Travel and tourism organisations have a responsibility to produce annual financial reports. Not only do these help the organisation to make decisions, they are also available to the public, including other travel organisations, and these reports can also help inform their own decisions. Organisations also produce annual reports that give details of their activities. Both types of reports are published on company websites. For example, Thomas Cook provides various data and reports on its corporate website: www.thomascookgroup.com/investors

Public organisations and trade associations

Most travel and tourism organisations are in the private sector. Public sector organisations are funded by local or national government. They provide information to educate and inform people. These include tourist boards and the Department for Digital, Culture, Media & Sport, which, for example, produces statistics on monthly visits to museums and galleries in the UK. It produces reports that are useful to private travel and tourism organisations and that help them to make informed decisions in marketing and product development. Trade associations, including ABTA, are funded by the businesses that operate in that industry and fulfil a similar role.

KEY TERMS

A **trend** is something that changes or develops in a general direction over time.

Ethical means something that is morally right or correct.

LINK IT UP

See Table 3.2 for some examples of ONS and VisitBritain research and reports.

CHECK MY LEARNING

Think back to the list of trends from the beginning of the lesson. Now rank the trends in the order that you feel are most significant to the industry as a whole and explain why you think this is. Support your explanations, using the information you have gathered from this lesson.

ACTIVITY

Working in pairs, discuss the four different methods of research that organisations may use to identify customer trends. Consider how easy it is to collect good data using each method and how beneficial it is to an organisation.

Trends: reasons for travel

GETTING STARTED

Working in pairs, have a discussion to recap and identify why people travel and why these reasons for travel might change. Feed back these reasons to the rest of the class.

People travel for different reasons, whether it be for leisure, visiting friends and family or for business. The reasons why people travel within the leisure travel market will change over time. For example, a child may start by going on family holidays, then when they are young adults they may enjoy party holidays, and as they get older may start to go on more relaxing or longer holidays, especially in retirement.

Business travel

Organisations that expect their employees to travel for business have a responsibility to keep them safe and this often means using a reputable travel company to make their arrangements.

Business travel is an expense for an organisation but is also essential to develop and grow a business. Time and efficiency are therefore important so that the organisation gets the maximum benefit from this expense.

Changing business trends

Trends in business travel are often influenced by factors such as fuel costs, accommodation prices, availability, safety and security, changes in legislation, such as data protection, and technology. Cost and safety are the main drivers and trends in business travel. Some changing business trends have included the following.

- Improvements in technology infrastructure and in conference and video meeting services mean that virtual meetings have become very common, reducing the need to travel to meet face to face.
- It is now becoming more acceptable to combine business travel with leisure by extending the duration of a business trip or by taking a family member or friend on a business trip at their own expense. With a more modern-day approach to flexible working, known as **bleisure** trips, this can be a positive way for employers to offer perks to their employees.
- Business trips that last for more than three days are 30 per cent more likely to be followed by an additional leisure trip.
- In a recent survey, 59 per cent of respondents said that cost-saving is a driving factor to engage in bleisure travel.
- Due to the money saved on travel, 66 per cent of bleisure travellers spend more money on leisure activities.

KEY TERM

Bleisure is a way of combining business with leisure travel.

Leisure travel

Within the leisure travel market, the types of holidays on offer are changing all the time. The traditional short-haul beach holiday is still popular among UK holidaymakers. These package holidays can cater for most budgets throughout the year, which is probably why they remain popular.

However, many customers are looking for something more than lying on a beach and eating out. Different market segments are growing within the leisure travel market and organisations are developing their leisure travel products and services to cater for these growing markets (Table 3.6).

■ Table 3.6: Reasons why customers may choose a certain holiday type

Holiday type	Reasons why customers may choose these holidays	
Adventure	Provides a challenge Experience something new Develop a hobby or an interest	Mix with like-minded people Create new memories Provides exercise, fitness and wellness
Volunteering and conservation	Explore a new country Learn new skills Make new friends	Provides a cultural experience Make a positive contribution Social and environmental awareness
Domestic	Cost Ease of travel, particularly if using own transport	Changes in weather leading to hotter summers in the UK Familiarity Choice of transport
Cruise	All-inclusive Several destinations and cultures in one trip	Facilities

ACTIVITY

Review Table 3.6 and then think about other reasons that motivate people to go on these types of holidays. Add one reason to each of the four holiday types.

Can you think of at least one other holiday type within the leisure sector that is becoming popular and the reasons why?

Changing leisure trends

■ Table 3.7: Top five trends identified by ABTA, 2015–2019

2015	2016	2017	2018	2019
People who are more well off are driving the market, taking more holidays	Western Mediterranean, particularly Spain, is growing in popularity	Weaker pound influences destination choice	Sustainability and responsible tourism	Sustainability and responsible tourism
Challenge and activity holidays	People who are well off continue to drive the market, taking more holidays	Long-haul city breaks	Alternative destinations	Using a travel professional to book a holiday
Trying new destinations	Destinations are regenerating to attract different market groups	Micro-adventures: active short breaks	Package holidays	Wellness Travel
Living like a local	Long-haul holidays	Virtual reality technology: try before you buy	Low-cost long haul	Tailor-made package holidays
Destination celebrations	Adventure holidays for over 55s	Sustainability and responsible tourism	Luxury meets escapism	Using technology to support the holiday experience

ACTIVITY

Working in pairs, study the top five trends lists in Table 3.7.

1 Are any common to all years, or do any feature in more than one year?

2 Now cross-reference the trends with the holiday types in Table 3.6. Which holiday types will have become more popular and less popular considering the trends?

3 Prepare and practise a five-minute presentation to deliver your findings to the rest of the class.

CHECK MY LEARNING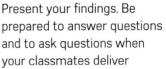

Present your findings. Be prepared to answer questions and to ask questions when your classmates deliver their presentations.

Trends: visitor numbers

GETTING STARTED

How can looking at trends in visitor numbers help travel and tourism organisations make decisions about the products and services they offer?

The number of visitors taking trips, visiting tourist attractions and going on holiday to different destinations changes year on year. There are many factors that will influence popularity and trends. Some of these trends and factors can be predicted but there will always be those factors that can change these predictions, such as climate.

Holiday habits

Habits tend to be things that we do on a regular basis without really thinking too much about it. When it comes to holidays, some people tend to stick to the same thing; for example, going to the same destination or resort, booking with the same organisation or buying the same holiday product, such as an all-inclusive package or a cruise.

Other people may choose a different destination every time they go on holiday or change the type of holiday that they book. Some customers prefer to use the same travel agent while others may prefer to book holidays themselves using different booking platforms to get the best possible price. Whatever the trends and behaviours of travel customers, they often consider their holiday something they don't want to give up.

ABTA's Holiday Habits Reports

Every year ABTA analyses data and statistics to produce a Holiday Habits Report. This helps to give the travel sector an understanding of what consumers are booking, how they are booking and who they are travelling with. It also helps to make predictions in travel trends for the year ahead based around customer behaviours and attitudes.

The 2018 report shows that people are still taking holidays (Figure 3.6). The report shows that 60 per cent of the population went on a foreign holiday in the past 12 months, which is the highest figure since 2011. Package holidays proved popular, with value for money rising up the list of priorities for people choosing this type of holiday.

ACTIVITY

Working in pairs, access the three most recent ABTA Holiday Habits Reports and complete a factsheet to identify and record key data, to produce a summary of information about Britons' holiday habits.

Include average number of holidays taken, holiday types, booking preferences and predictions for the future across the three reports.

	AVERAGE	UNDER 45 (no kids at home)	YOUNG FAMILY (any children under 5)	OLDER FAMILY (any children over 5)	OVER 45 (no kids at home)
UK HOLIDAYS	1.8	1.7	2.2	1.9	1.8
HOLIDAYS ABROAD	1.6	1.6	1.8	1.6	1.6
TOTAL HOLIDAYS	3.4	3.3	4	3.5	3.4

◼ Figure 3.6: Top travellers – which group of people took the most holidays?

Emerging destinations

An emerging destination is one that is growing and developing. There are several factors that contribute to the emergence of a destination.

Travel is now more accessible to mass market tourists, and people are always looking for something new, but in recent years the trend to undertake a unique, authentic experience has risen. There is often an element of mystery linked to an emerging destination, possibly because they are often relatively undiscovered by tourists and travellers.

The ABTA Travel Trends Report 2017 expected the weakening and fluctuating value of the pound to drive a trend for UK travellers to seek out destinations where their money

LINK IT UP

In Component 2, you investigated the characteristics of emerging destinations.

would buy more, such as Argentina. One of the attractions of emerging destinations is that they can be relatively cheaper than those that are more established.

Why the new attention?

Emerging destinations may previously have had tight visa restrictions that have been recently lifted (such as Kazakstan, now allowing EU citizens to visit for 30 days without a visa) or have been affected by political unrest or civil war that has ended, such as Sri Lanka which is seeing the return of tourists following the end of a 26-year civil war and a disastrous tsunami in 2014. It was a popular destination in 2018. Destinations such as these are often largely unaffected by tourism but are developing quickly so people want to visit them while they are still relatively unspoiled.

Identifying emerging destinations

Travel and tourism organisations are keen to be 'on trend' and to be ahead of the competition in marketing the next 'new' destinations and to inspire people to visit. However, there are risks to be considered. Organisations such as tour operators will need to look closely at factors such as the infrastructure, political stability and the economy before making operational decisions, such as deciding when or whether to return to a destination following a major incident such as a terrorist attack (Figure 3.7).

■ Figure 3.7: Do emerging destinations offer opportunities or challenges?

Emerging destinations can be influenced by trends that make destinations more attractive. Some of these recent trends include economies that provide visitors value for money. TV and media can also stimulate interest in travellers wanting to visit somewhere for a specific interest, such as trekking or wildlife. Trends linked to health and wellbeing can also stimulate travel.

CHECK MY LEARNING

Summarise in your own words what factors contribute to an emerging destination. Identify a destination that is emerging and list the reasons why this is becoming popular with tourists.

ACTIVITY

According to the latest ABTA Travel Trends Report 2019, the following is a list of the 12 emerging destinations to watch, given in alphabetical order:

1 Bulgaria
2 Costa Rica
3 Denver
4 Durban
5 Galicia
6 Japan
7 Jordan
8 Madeira
9 Poland
10 Thessaloniki
11 Uzbekistan
12 Western Australia

Create a table with 3 columns:

1 destination
2 why you think it may be popular (research online)
3 which trend you think each destination reflects. Refer to Table 3.7 which lists the top five trends from recent years and choose the most relevant trend for each destination. If you can't match it to one from Table 3.7, add your own idea.

To take this further you could read the Travel Trends Report from a different year and compare that year's list to 2019's. What similarities and differences can you spot in the lists of destinations?

Trends: holiday types and methods of booking

GETTING STARTED

Think of as many different holiday types as you can, for example all inclusive. Also think about how people plan and book their holidays. Do you think that the way people book a holiday depends on the type of holiday they book? Contribute to a class list by putting forward your answers.

DID YOU KNOW?

Thomas Cook is sometimes credited with organising the first day trip for a group of people and for putting together the first package holiday, closely followed by Vladimir Raitz, who founded Horizon Holidays.

KEY TERM

Differentiation is distinguishing between the needs and expectations of two or more groups of people.

The types of holiday that people take and the methods they use to plan and book their holidays change constantly. Customer demands and expectations are rising, and they are looking to find products that are tailored to meet their needs. Developments in technology mean that customers have more choice when it comes to making travel arrangements. Both trends need to be monitored closely by sector organisations.

Holiday types

Many destinations have now developed to cater for mass tourism, realising its economic value. But we are now starting to see a clear shift in travel behaviours and in the way tourism is now promoted to encourage a more responsible approach within the travel and tourism industry, a trend bolstered by 2017 being the UN Year of Sustainable Tourism for Development.

Customers also now have different preferences, whether it be a day trip out or a holiday away from home, and they tend to take a more individual approach to the type of experience they want. The industry must move with these changes in customer needs and preferences to develop products and services to meet their demands. Customers don't just want a holiday, they want an experience.

Differentiation and packages

Differentiation is a key driver behind the development of holiday types to cater for different customers and meeting their expectations. Tour operators are reinventing the package holiday with a focus on quality and culture. This can be seen in the way that tour operators are tailor-making package holidays to meet customer needs. Kuoni's new brand, Meraki Travel, allows holidaymakers to book a tailor-made package online. Solo travel specialist Just You is offering more options to customise their trips through its 'Make Your Own Way' service.

ABTA's Holiday Habits Report 2018 identifies that ease of booking, value for money and consumer protection have long been core benefits of the package holiday. Increasing numbers of holidaymakers look to a package holiday for a good value break – in 2018, 60 per cent booked a package holiday because it was the best value option for the price, up 3 per cent on 2017.

Trending types

City breaks seem to be the nation's favourite type of holiday. Beach holidays continue to be the second most popular type of holiday. Sightseeing holidays are also growing in popularity. In 2019, ABTA expected value for money to be a priority, with more people planning all-inclusive holidays. Cruise holidays also looked to remain popular. Their research also showed that almost 70 per cent of people now believe that travel companies should ensure their holidays help the local people and economy. Programmes such as the BBC's *Blue Planet II* may well have influenced this, it being the most-watched programme of 2017, and adding significant weight to the campaign to address our plastic use and its effect on the oceans.

Booking preferences

Travel agents were once the only available platform for customers to book a holiday or an organised day out. Now, of course, customers have many different booking choices available to them that mean they are no longer reliant on a travel agent to make travel arrangements for them.

Booking trends

Many people still prefer the face-to-face personal contact of using a travel agent, whether it be for convenience, out of loyalty or for security and peace of mind. Online travel agents are becoming more popular, which gives customers another option of using an agent to plan and book travel arrangements and holidays without having to leave the house (Table 3.8).

According to the ABTA Holiday Habits Report 2018, the trend towards booking holidays online seems to have stabilised, with younger people preferring to let someone else book the holiday for them. Interestingly, the number of people using tablets and phones to book holidays has also dropped. Desktop computers and laptops are the preferred means of booking holidays online.

◨ Table 3.8: Advantages and disadvantages of using a travel agent and booking independently online

Travel agent		Booking online	
Advantages	**Disadvantages**	**Advantages**	**Disadvantages**
Specialist expertise	Need to leave the house	Flexible	Time-consuming
Personal service	May have limited choices	Make comparisons	Risk of things going wrong
Saves time	Can be more expensive	Own research	
Security		Sense of achievement	

◨ Would you prefer the freedom of booking online yourself or the reassurance of having a professional travel agent do it for you?

ACTIVITY

Responsible tourism is a growing trend. As tourist numbers increase, travel and tourism organisations have a responsibility to do everything they can to minimise the negative impacts of organised travel and maximise the positive impacts. This is what customers want. This is reflected in research and reports carried out by organisations such as ABTA and Responsible Travel.

Work in pairs or small groups and discuss how tour operators are responding to this area of growth. You may find it useful to look at one of the major tour operators such as TUI or Thomas Cook and identify what they are doing to provide responsible tourism products and services to meet customers' expectations. How effective do you consider these changes to be?

CHECK MY LEARNING ■■

Working in pairs, interview each other about the different types of technology for booking holidays that are used now compared with technology that was available five years ago. Discuss this topic with older family members and friends to see how this has changed over time.

Trends: age group preferences, average costs and employment patterns

GETTING STARTED

Working in pairs, discuss a type of holiday you would like to go on. What do you think the most popular holiday choice for your age group would be? Think about the destination and the facilities. How different is your answer today from what it would have been five years ago?

Now think about an older relative or friend; someone who is five or ten years older than you. How do you think their choices would be different from yours, and others your age, and why?

ACTIVITY

Working in small groups, you will be allocated one of the following market segments:

- a young and lively group, aged 18–25
- a family with young children under 10
- a retired couple, both aged 60, looking for adventure
- a group of friends in their 20s looking for a cultural city break.

Use the internet to search different tour operator websites and research suitable destinations that are popular with your given age group.

Compare the prices for **low season** and **high season**.

Different age groups have discernible preferences; trends in these and in the link between holiday costs and employment patterns, have a strong effect on the types of holiday and destination that become popular.

Different age groups

People's holiday habits will often change depending on their life stage; for example, if they have a young family or if they are retired. They also change depending on their age. Young people who are taking their first independent holiday tend to want a different type of holiday from a family with young children.

Young adults

Traditionally, holidays for young adults have centred around a beach during the day with lively nightlife, often staying in budget accommodation. While younger people may still like a lively destination in a beach resort, this market is also seeing a change. There is a clear trend among young adults, dubbed 'generation sensible', that sees a move away from drinking, drug taking and smoking.

This change has contributed to a fall in popularity of Club 18-30 and 2wenty's holidays, with Thomas Cook's Club 18-30 closing in 2018. Tour operators are now offering better-quality holidays with activities that don't centre entirely around drinking and partying. TUI Travel has now adapted its youth market holidays and rebranded to TUI Scene.

Families

Families with young children are also a growing market. Holidays for some families are an opportunity to spend more time together in a world where people are working longer hours and commuting further.

These holidays often include family members across generations. Facilities for families are becoming something that families expect when they book a family holiday. All-inclusive holidays seem to be a growing market that attracts families to quieter resorts in destinations that are relatively quick and easy to get to with daytime flight times.

Mature travellers

People are living longer and travelling further. People aged 45 and over are a growing market in the travel and tourism industry. Holidays for over 50s, once associated with coach trip holidays or winter sun on the Spanish Costas, are now more likely to be associated with adventure travel, solo holidays and grown-up gap years, travelling across the world with a more adventurous attitude to travel and discovery.

Holiday costs and employment patterns

The average British family holidays twice a year, spending more than £6,000, which represents a quarter of the average household's annual disposable income. When the price of something rises, it is expected that people will buy less of it. This is true of holidays too. Articles and research would suggest that household spending on holidays is increasing.

However, remember, holidays are an experience that people often do not want to give up. In 2018, a report by the building society Nationwide revealed that half of UK residents (of 2000 surveyed) would not consider giving up their holiday. Four in 10 paid for their last holiday using savings and a quarter said they had to borrow money to go on holiday, including through credit cards (15 per cent) and a personal loan (4 per cent), while 3 per cent said they borrowed money from family and friends.

Prices

When the economy is good, prices tend to increase. This affects holiday prices, too. There are other factors linked to price changes in the cost of holidays. Tour operators will increase the price of holidays during school holidays when they know that the demand is high. This is important to the family as they try to find an affordable holiday when they are forced to take holidays during school holiday time. According to the ABTA Travel Trends report 2018, looking at 2019, value for money is expected to be a priority, with more people planning all-inclusive holidays.

Despite uncertainty over BREXIT, rising prices and the lower value of the pound, UK residents are taking more overseas holidays than ever before.

According to official data from the Office for National Statistics published in 2019, UK residents took 46.5 million overseas holidays in 2018 – this is an increase of one million compared with data published ten years ago.

Employment

When employment rates are high, this is usually a sign that the UK economy is performing well. When people are employed, they are more likely to spend money. They will have more disposable income and are more likely to spend this money on things such as holidays.

Within the UK, the labour force refers to people aged between 16 and 64 who *can* work. The employment rate refers to the percentage of those people who are *in* work.

Figure 3.8 shows the employment rates in the UK from 1971 to 2017. Over time the number of women in work has risen, while that of men has fallen. The combined rate has shown, 2008 aside, steady improvement. The effect of the 2008 recession is clear to see in both employment rates and the number of overseas trips, with both dipping. Overall, the general trend in employment has been upwards between 1997 and 2017, and there is a corresponding upward trend in the number of overseas trips taken.

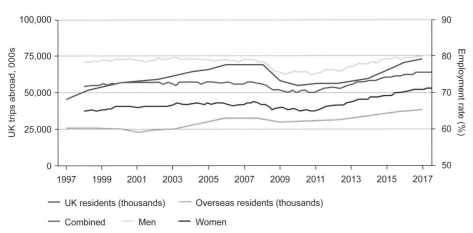

UK employment rates (ages 16 to 64 years), seasonally adjusted and UK trips abroad, 1997–2017

- UK residents (thousands) — Overseas residents (thousands)
- Combined — Men — Women

▣ **Figure 3.8: Would more women being in work affect holiday trends?**

KEY TERMS

Low season is those periods of the year when destinations attract fewer visitors and the cost of travel and holiday accommodation falls.

High season is those periods of the year when destinations attract the most visitors and the cost of travel and holiday accommodation rise.

ACTIVITY

Other political issues can affect the UK and the global economy, and this can also have an impact on the cost of holidays. Can you think of any current or recent political issues that could affect the UK economy and impact the cost of holidays?

CHECK MY LEARNING

Reflect on your learning in this lesson and take some time to answer the following questions.

1 What factors have led to the development and reinvention of youth-branded holidays?

2 What is meant by the term 'multi-generational family'?

3 What factors have led to a growth in the holiday market for more mature people?

4 What economic factors could impact on the number of holidays people take and the amount of money they spend?

Trends: holiday volumes by age group, regional variations and impact on destinations

GETTING STARTED

How would you expect the number of holidays people take each year to change as they get older?

Would you expect where people live to affect the number and type of holidays they go on each year? If so, in what way?

Why do you think organisations are 'going green'?

Identifying trends linked to the number of holidays taken by different age groups and the regions that they come from can help travel and tourism organisations to market their products and services more effectively. This lesson will explore how these trends can be identified. You will also examine how environmental impacts affect customer trends.

Number of holidays taken by different age groups

The number of holidays taken over a year will vary depending on the life stage that people are in, as this will often affect the amount of disposable income and the amount of free leisure time that they have.

It can be useful for organisations to identify travel trends linked to age and frequency of holidays to assist with marketing and product development. Identifying growing markets and gaps in the market can help to inform business decisions.

Young people

Younger people generally have less disposable income as they are just starting out in new jobs and living independently. Buying or renting property and paying bills will leave little for recreational spending. However, this generation is said to be more likely to borrow money for holidays.

There would appear to be a change to the preferences and choices that younger people are making when choosing a holiday, with 36 per cent of people aged 18–35 who say they still enjoy a party holiday and 71 per cent who would prefer a city break.

◼ Do you think that attitudes of younger people towards drinking and clubbing holidays are changing? What influences these changes?

Couples without children

Couples in their 20s to 40s with two incomes and no children are ideally placed to take advantage of higher disposable incomes than younger single adults, and they are also free to travel outside of school holidays, when the costs are lower.

Older people

People who are retired and mortgage-free have more free leisure time and are more likely to have more disposable income. Many people in this age range downsize to smaller properties to enable them to access funds and enjoy retirement. Others have healthy pension pots, which they can draw on to fund leisure and travel.

The over-50s hold 76 per cent of the nation's wealth and 40 per cent of over-50s spend more than £3,000 a year on holidays.

Regional variations

So how can identifying regional trends help travel and tourism organisations with product development and marketing activities? Do people from different regions have different buying behaviours? The ABTA Holiday Habits Reports identify some of these behaviours; for instance, there are regional variations in the number of holidays taken per person. People in the North West took the most holidays per person (5.6) overall, while those in the West Midlands took the most domestic breaks (2.7).

Holidays were the most popular reason for UK residents to travel abroad in 2015, accounting for 68 per cent of visits from residents of England (excluding London), 71 per cent of Scottish and 75 per cent of Welsh residents. Only 23 per cent of London residents were likely to choose an all-inclusive holiday, compared with more than 40 per cent for all other areas. These 2.3 million visits accounted for 23 per cent of the money spent abroad by Londoners (£2.0 billion).

Visits overseas by London's residents were more likely to be to countries outside Europe or North America than visits by residents of other UK regions; 19 per cent of visits by Londoners were to these areas of the world compared with between 11 and 14 per cent from other regions.

Impact of tourism on destinations: environmental considerations

More than two-fifths (45 per cent) of people say the sustainability credentials of their travel provider are important when booking a holiday – this number has almost doubled over the last four years (it was 24 per cent in 2014).

According to a survey conducted by Booking.com, one in three tourists intended to choose options that were more respectful towards the planet during 2017. TV programmes such as *Blue Planet* have raised awareness and encouraged holidaymakers to think about the impact that their holiday has on the environment.

The Travel Foundation

The Travel Foundation works with businesses and governments to bring benefits of tourism to people and the environment. Sustainable tourism is about making better places to live and visit. Travel organisations have a responsibility to incorporate sustainable tourism policies and practices into their holidays. So what does this look like? It can include things like using carbon-efficient aircraft, becoming involved in conservation projects, recycling, employing local people and buying from local producers and businesses. Thomas Cook has pledged to remove excursions, such as elephant rides and swimming with dolphins, from its holidays in the interests of animal welfare.

ACTIVITY

Working in pairs or small groups, research online to create a factsheet to show what tour operators can do to work in partnership with local communities and businesses to have a positive impact on the environment and the economy.

CHECK MY LEARNING

Describe to your partner what is meant by disposable income and explain how this can influence the number and types of holidays people take.

Ask an older member of your family to tell you about the way the types of holiday they have taken have changed throughout their life.

Customer travel and holiday needs: dates, travel requirements and accessibility

GETTING STARTED

Working in pairs, discuss the needs, preferences and lifestyle considerations that you think might influence a customer's choice of how and when to travel. Make a list of these things. Highlight how these considerations might be different for different customer types.

What are the reasons that customers select one travel product or service over another? What influences their decision to book a holiday or hotel? This lesson will explore how dates of travel and accessibility can influence a customer's decision.

Dates of travel

Whether customers select a tour operator for their holiday or whether they book the components themselves, time of year is important. Different destinations operate high and low seasons with prices that reflect this. Many things can influence this but one of the main considerations is the climate. A ski holiday needs snow and a beach holiday needs sun. Within Europe the seasons tend to be similar to the UK. Across other continents the considerations are different and thought needs to be given to other climatic issues such as the rainy season, humidity and extreme heat (Figure 3.9). Seasons and hemispheres can also influence customer choice and dates of travel. A season is a time of year that is distinguished by climate conditions. The seasons in the northern hemisphere are the opposite of the seasons in the southern hemisphere, so winter in Europe is summer in Australia.

High and low season prices are an important consideration and can be the deciding factor for many people when selecting the time of year that they choose to take their holiday. Families are often restricted to school holidays, particularly with recent changes in the law that make it difficult for parents to take their children out of school for holidays. Holiday prices can double during school holidays, making it very expensive to take a family holiday at this time. People who have retired and have more free leisure time have much more flexibility to shop around and get the best deals that are often last minute.

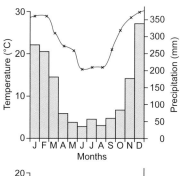

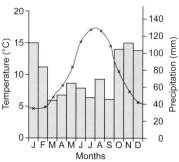

■ Figure 3.9: How would you use regional climate graphs, such as these for Madagascar and the New Forest, UK?

ACTIVITY

Working in pairs, take some time to study the following customer profiles.

- A family with two children under the age of 5. They would like to travel within Europe and travel on daytime flights. They would like a seven-night holiday. They have a budget of £3,000 and would like an element of luxury with some childcare facilities.
- A couple in their 50s who would like a cultural experience in South East Asia. They are not restricted by budget and would like a multi-centre holiday with some organised tours and activities. They can travel at any time of the year and would like to be away for about three weeks.
- A female traveller in her 30s who would like to relax and explore South America. She can travel any time between May and September. She has a budget of £1,000 and would like to meet like-minded people.
- A family with two children, aged 7 and 10, would like an all-inclusive holiday with daytime activities and evening entertainment. They would like a short flight time. They have a budget of £2,500.

Discuss the profiles and carry out research to suggest suitable destinations, giving reasons for your choice. Your research should include looking at temperature charts (Figure 3.9), high and low seasons, prices and transport.

Changing climates

It is also worth considering that climates are not as reliable as they used to be. Winter 2018–19 saw severe snowfall across Europe causing chaos in ski resorts and the summer of 2018 saw record-breaking temperatures, drought and wildfires across the Continent. This can also have an impact on domestic tourism figures with higher temperatures and hotter summers experienced and predicted for the UK. Spring is becoming warmer and, being less crowded and with cheaper travel, Europe is becoming more popular at this time of year. August is the busiest month of the year in Europe when most Europeans take a holiday, and this can mean crowds, queues and high prices. Other factors affecting dates of travel include special events such as the Tour de France, Oktoberfest and St Patrick's Day. If you want to experience a special event in a particular country, then you have to be in that destination at a particular time.

Travel requirements and accessibility

People have very different needs and preferences when it comes to travel requirements and accessibility, getting to and moving around a destination. Transport options to a destination will very much depend on the destination itself as it may be reached by road, air, rail or a cruise.

Road travel can be popular with families who need to carry more luggage and prefer to make stops that are convenient to them. Cruise holidays are becoming increasingly popular and offer full accessibility for all ages and requirements, with adapted cabins and assistance. Luxury train travel across the world is also on the increase, allowing passengers to enjoy the scenery and the travel experience rather than seeing it only as a way to get from one place to another (ABTA Travel Trends 2018).

People who don't like flying may select a domestic holiday or a European destination that can be reached by rail or sea. Families with young children may consider a destination with a short flight time. People who require special assistance will look closely at the transport provider to make sure that they get the assistance they need.

Information is key to planning a great holiday. Using a tour operator and/or travel agent to book a holiday can help to ensure that travel requirements are met, provided accurate information is given at the time of booking.

Cost will also be a consideration when making travel arrangements. People taking a holiday overseas will need to consider how to get from the airport to the accommodation. Transfers can vary in price depending on the selected method. Cost may be the deciding factor when it comes to selecting this; alternatively, comfort and speed may influence the decision. Some people will be influenced heavily by the need for assistance or to have accessible transport to make travel manageable and comfortable.

With increased security around the world, another consideration for travellers is accessibility and entry into a country. Visa requirements and ease of applying for visas is a consideration for many. Political factors can change and influence restrictions and requirements.

DID YOU KNOW?

Oktoberfest starts in September not October – days in September were added to take advantage of the warmer weather.

CHECK MY LEARNING

Team up with another pair in your class. They may have selected different destinations for each of the different customer types. Discuss your findings and exchange information based on the research that you carried out.

ACTIVITY

Working in the same pairs and using the same destinations, create a table to show the transport options available to access each of your selected destinations. Include details of travel times and average costs.

Discuss how these factors could influence the customer's choice when selecting these destinations for a holiday.

Customer travel and holiday needs: accommodation types

GETTING STARTED

Working in pairs, make a list of as many different types of accommodation that you can. Include details of the facilities, products and levels of service that customers can expect from each accommodation type.

LINK IT UP

In Component 1, you explored the different types of accommodation available to customers and the different levels of service, facilities and products they offer. How many have you stayed in?

Accommodation is another consideration for customers when booking a holiday. The range of accommodation is vast, with many different choices of accommodation type and standard available.

Accommodation types

The choice of accommodation available to customers is broader than ever before. Organisations such as Airbnb have introduced a new concept to booking not only accommodation but a whole different accommodation experience. People can book entire houses, boutique rooms, a boat or a tree house for their holiday. Airbnb was conceived in 2008 when someone with space to spare hosted some travellers looking for a place to stay, and now millions of hosts and travellers use the site each year. The concept connects buyer and supplier directly.

Camping is another developing market with the option to go 'glamping' for those who desire a more luxurious camping trip. Yurts are very popular, with full-size beds and log-burning stoves. Many glamping holidays come with pools and leisure facilities. Some see it as a way to experience the benefits and flexibility of camping without forgoing all conveniences. Glamping options have become popular at multi-day music festivals, offering accommodation to the more discerning festival-goer.

▢ **Seasonality has a particular effect on the Ice Hotel, Quebec, Canada. What do you think it is?**

Accommodation requirements

Accommodation needs will vary depending on customers' needs (Figure 3.10). For instance, a solo traveller working their way around the world will most likely look for cheap and no-frills accommodation, possibly sharing with similar travellers. In contrast, a business traveller visiting a city, who must work, host meetings with prospective clients and create a good impression, will look for a top-quality hotel in or near the business district, with dedicated working space and meeting and hospitality rooms.

■ Figure 3.10: Can you add to these factors that affect accommodation choice?

Alternatively, the length of stay and budget will influence choice. A young couple celebrating their wedding anniversary might, if away for a weekend, opt for a top-quality five-star hotel, to celebrate in luxury. Whereas if they were to stay away for longer, a week perhaps, they may have to budget further and so choose a two- or three-star hotel.

The reason for the trip or holiday away will influence the choice of accommodation. A family away for a weekend at a theme park may prefer budget accommodation, such as a caravan or a bed and breakfast, because the focus of their visit is to spend time and money in the theme park and therefore the accommodation is secondary.

Standard and meal arrangements

Accommodation can be serviced or non-serviced; in other words, you can choose to be looked after by other people during your stay or you can choose to look after yourself. Serviced accommodation can include housekeeping and cleaning. Hotels are classed as serviced accommodation and can offer different standards of facilities and luxury. Hotels will offer choices when it comes to board basis. This could be room only; bed and breakfast; half-board, which is usually breakfast and evening meal; full-board, which is usually three meals a day; or all-inclusive, where all food and drink is included for one price. Tour operators, such as Thomas Cook and TUI, now provide information to help customers decide which is the best board basis for them.

All-inclusive holidays are on the increase but with this comes the social issue of the decline of local bars and restaurants. Tour operators and hotels offer a range of different board options to give customers a choice. Self-catering holidays are becoming more popular as people want the freedom to experience culture on holiday, including local food and drink. All-inclusive may work out to be cheaper all round for some, but self-catering accommodation can provide more freedom and choice.

ACTIVITY

Working in pairs or small groups, discuss the pros and cons of different accommodation types that fall under the headings 'serviced' and 'non-serviced' and the different customer types that these accommodation types could appeal to.

CHECK MY LEARNING

Working in the same pairs, create a PowerPoint® presentation to present your findings to the rest of the class.

Customer travel and holiday needs: budget and purpose of travel

GETTING STARTED

Working in pairs, discuss the following holiday destinations. What would attract people to these destinations? Rank them in order of most expensive to least expensive to visit.
- Skiing in the French Alps.
- Beach holiday in the Costa del Sol.
- Theme park holiday at Alton Towers Resort.
- All-inclusive holiday in Cyprus.
- Caribbean cruise.

We would all like to book a holiday without considering the price. Imagine being able to select a destination, accommodation and duration of stay without having to consider a budget. The reality is that most people will need to think about how much they can afford when it comes to booking a holiday and have to ensure that they stick to their budget.

Budget

Deciding what you can afford before you book a holiday will narrow down choices and give easier access to what is available. Mass market tour operators offer a range of products under their brand to cater for different budgets. For example, TUI offers a range of accommodation types and products to suit different budgets. People appear to be willing to pay for quality holidays and have rising expectations with a demand for more luxury and quality. This is reflected in the products and services offered by tour operators.

The type of accommodation selected can change the price of a holiday in terms of its quality rating and board basis. Travel times, distance and method of transport will also impact on cost. Long-haul flights using scheduled airlines will cost more than using a budget airline to a short-haul destination.

Booking and supplementary charges

The booking method can also have an impact on cost. Making your own travel arrangements can work out cheaper if you are prepared to shop around and look for discounts, but quite often a good travel agent can find a bargain, especially if you give them a budget to work from.

Families or single travellers can often pay increased supplements for family rooms or sole occupancy, so this is another consideration.

Discounting

For people who are flexible and can travel at the last minute, last-minute deals can offer a healthy discount. This is because tour operators have already chartered the aircraft and if they don't sell the seats, they will lose money. They may have accommodation booked but if not, they can make late reservations with accommodation providers. Equally, tour operators such as Thomas Cook will offer early bird discounts for people who can book early. Free child places are also offered by tour operators to encourage bookings.

Then there is the destination itself. Political events and the economy can affect the popularity of a destination. Think of destinations that have been affected negatively by recent events. This could have been triggered by an event or negative press reporting. If destinations are considered by the public to be unsafe or unattractive to tourists, then they tend to become cheaper to visit, offering discounted prices to attract tourism back to the area and maximise bookings for tour operators for contracts that are already in place.

Counting the pennies

Disposable income and budget will decide the type of holiday that people can afford. Other factors, such as the local economy, can also influence decisions. While people may travel for a particular reason, such as a relaxing beach holiday, skiing or to get married, the destination they select and travel organisation they use may depend on their budget.

ABTA research shows that 60 per cent of the population took a foreign holiday in 2018 – the highest figure since 2011 – with longer overseas breaks. They also show that people managed their budgets by reducing the number of UK breaks and shorter overseas breaks and by cutting back on their spending while they are away. This suggests that holidaymakers are budgeting more carefully while away, rather than choosing not to go on holiday at all.

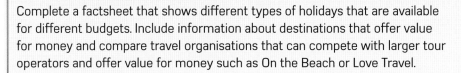

ACTIVITY

Complete a factsheet that shows different types of holidays that are available for different budgets. Include information about destinations that offer value for money and compare travel organisations that can compete with larger tour operators and offer value for money such as On the Beach or Love Travel.

Purpose of travel

There are many different holiday types to choose from to give customers a choice of holidays linked to their reason for travel.

- Activity – these types of holidays and breaks are becoming more popular with people wanting to experience something new on holidays and to be more active. This could include a specific activity such as trekking or walking or it could simply include some water sports or hiring bikes to explore.
- Adventure – adventure holidays are another growing market where people want to experience and explore somewhere new. This could be trekking in the Himalayas or rafting on the Colorado River.
- Celebrations – many people choose to go on holiday to celebrate a special occasion. This could be a wedding, an anniversary or a special birthday.
- Clubbing – popular destinations such as Ibiza and Ayia Napa remain popular with younger people who like to enjoy club scene holidays.
- Culture – a cultural holiday can appeal to people who want to learn about a destination's heritage and traditions. This can also include sampling local food and wine.
- Festivals – festivals including music, food, drink and art are growing in popularity and give people the opportunity to enjoy a theme they are interested in within a new environment.
- Relaxation – this could be a beach or pool holiday and could include some relaxation activities such as spa hotels.
- Sport – sporting holidays such as golfing, cycling and horse riding give people the opportunity to discover destinations while participating in the sport they love.
- Volunteering – volunteering holidays provide a real opportunity to discover a new destination and give something back to the local community by being involved in community projects.
- Wellbeing – these types of holidays are becoming increasingly popular with people who want to take time out of their busy lives to relax and take time for themselves. These holidays can include healthy diet and exercise classes such as Pilates and yoga.

People now base their holiday around their reasons for travel. Holidays have been reinvented to cater for all needs, ages, interests and budgets. People will look to find a destination and holiday type that will meet their own needs.

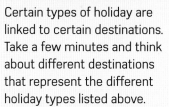

ACTIVITY

Certain types of holiday are linked to certain destinations. Take a few minutes and think about different destinations that represent the different holiday types listed above.

CHECK MY LEARNING

A group of four friends want a skiing holiday for a week towards the end of January, flying from Manchester. Carry out some research and select two holidays. Use a well-known tour operator such as Neilson to cost a week in France and compare this to a week in Bulgaria using an organisation such as Travel Supermarket. What is the price difference and why do you think this is?

Customer travel and holiday needs: unstated and specific

GETTING STARTED

Sometimes customers may state exactly what they want and sometimes they will make assumptions that their needs will be met without having to make them obvious. For example, a person with mobility needs may tell a travel agent that they want to book a hotel but may assume that the travel agent will know that they need a ground floor room.

Can you think of stated and unstated needs of different customer types, such as families or couples?

Whether customers are travelling for business or pleasure, travel and tourism organisations have a responsibility to offer products and services that meet the needs of customers with specific needs and make reasonable adjustments where they can.

Stated and unstated needs

Stated needs are those that customers tell you about directly. Unstated needs are those that a customer may not necessarily tell you about but that they will expect to be met. These are not always easy to identify. Customers may not tell you about some of their needs because they don't think it is important, they may be embarrassed, or they may expect you to know what they are.

- An example of stated needs could be if a customer tells you they need disabled access when they book a hotel room or that they need a wake-up call or a morning newspaper.
- An example of unstated needs could be if a customer assumes and expects that their room will be cleaned, and they will get clean towels and bedding.

Specific needs

It is important to understand that not all specific needs are linked to mobility and not all disabilities are visible. Figure 3.11 provides examples of some of the wide range of specific needs travellers may have.

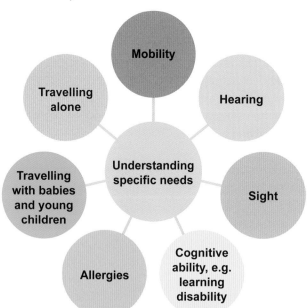

▫ **Figure 3.11: Have you travelled with family or friends who had a specific need, or seen how staff have assisted a fellow traveller?**

Providers of travel and tourism products have a responsibility and duty of care to make reasonable adjustments to cater for the specific needs of different customers. The following are some of the things that transport providers and accommodation providers are doing to make things more accessible.

Transport providers:
- accessible journey through airports with assistance where necessary
- assistance with boarding and disembarking aircraft
- ramps on trains and coaches.

Accommodation providers:
- automatic doors
- wider doors to bathrooms, raised toilets and walk-in showers
- low level light switches, wardrobe hanging and door handles
- vibrating pillow alarms
- flashing fire alarms
- ground-level accommodation.

Facilities managers (in addition to sharing most of the accommodation points above):
- large format/Braille books and guides in museums and attractions
- time set aside as 'quiet' to allow autistic visitors to shop or enjoy an attraction.

Specific needs case study

Hoe Grange, in the Peak District, provides accessible log cabins as part of the self-catering accommodation on a working farm. Owners David and Felicity Brown realised that the demand for accessible accommodation is growing and that this market has great spending power. They took design advice and applied for grants to incorporate accessible accommodation alongside glamping pods and other log cabins.

Their cabins cater for a wide range of needs. They have invested in equipment, including profile beds, shower stools and chairs, bath boards, toilet seat risers, bed rails, bed blocks and a mobile hoist. Door frames, skirting boards, door handles and handrails are in contrasting colours to help guests with visual impairments. They have alarm clocks with flashing lights/vibrating modes, a portable door chime and all televisions have subtitle facilities. They have also invested in a 'Boma 7' all-terrain wheelchair so that less-mobile guests can cross the farm fields and get onto the local trails with family and friends.

They also welcome assistance dogs, have an accessible website and use social media to encourage conversations about access issues.

ACTIVITY

A family with children aged 3, 7 and 10 years old would like to visit Blackpool. The younger child still sometimes uses a pushchair. They will be travelling from Bradford. They have a car but would also consider travelling by train. They would like to stay in Blackpool for two nights and would like to know about leisure and entertainment activities suitable for their family.

Carry out research to find information about:
- suitable methods of transport and ways to get to and around Blackpool
- suitable options for accommodation – they will need a family or adjoining rooms
- suitable leisure activities.

1. Refer to your research and select which options you think would best suit their stated and unstated needs.

2. How suitable is Blackpool as a destination for these visitors?

CHECK MY LEARNING

Select a large visitor attraction in the UK. Look at its website and identify how it caters for visitors with different needs. Include accessibility for different types of visitor and write notes to make a judgement on how well you think it caters for the stated and unstated needs of these visitors.

Desirable preferences: responsible tourism and convenience of travel

GETTING STARTED

Customer needs are the things that a customer wants or expects from a travel product or service.

Customers' desirable preferences are the things that add to the customers' needs and experience. For example, a customer needs transport from the airport to the hotel but they would prefer it to be a private taxi that goes directly to the hotel rather than a shared coach.

Think about:
- a family who want to go on an all-inclusive holiday to Spain
- a couple who want to go on a romantic break in Europe.

Identify the customer needs and the desired preferences of each customer type.

For example, the family need flights to their destination and their desirable preference could be daytime flights as they are travelling with children.

As customer expectations are rising, so travel and tourism organisations need to look at innovative ways that they can exceed these expectations to give customers what they desire, to try to meet customers' desired preferences. These things may not be essential customer needs but providing these is a way to keep ahead of the competition; for example, through responsible tourism and minimising **carbon footprints**.

Responsible tourism

People are more aware than ever before of social and environmental responsibility. Tour operators and providers of travel and tourism products need to be equally aware and need to act to minimise negative impacts and maximise positive impacts of tourism. Responsible tourism is about making changes for the long-term benefit of local people, tourists and travel companies.

While customers may be driven mainly by price and location, the responsible travel market is growing. Customers can select a responsible travel company to book a holiday with and many prefer to use an organisation with a responsible travel policy in place.

People who have a preference and interest in being a responsible traveller may:
- ask to see the organisation's responsible travel policy
- check accommodation to see what they do to support responsible tourism in the destination
- consider the carbon footprint of the organisations they book with
- make travel arrangements that minimise emissions (their own carbon footprint)
- ask to see the organisation's accessibility policy.

TUI's sustainable tourism strategy

TUI Travel has three main principles in its sustainable tourism strategy, Better Holidays, Better World (Figure 3.12).

KEY TERM

Carbon footprint is a measure of the amount of carbon dioxide released by an individual or organisation.

Step lightly	• TUI is taking responsibility for its airline, hotels, cruise ships, coaches, shops and offices and is trying to reduce the environmental impact of its operations. • TUI aims to operate Europe's most carbon-efficient airline and reduce the carbon emissions of its operations by 10 per cent by 2020.
Make a difference	• TUI strives to involve its customers and colleagues in sustainable tourism by creating greener and fairer holidays.
Lead the way	• TUI plays a key role in leading the way when it comes to sustainable tourism. • TUI has created the TUI Care Foundation which supports projects to create opportunities for the young across its destinations.

◘ Figure 3.12: Why should tour operators have a responsible tourism strategy and incorporate such practices into their package holidays?

Convenience of travel

Ease of travel is becoming more important to customers. The expansion of regional airports and frequency of flights means that customers have more choice of where to travel from and to and who they travel with. According to the ABTA Travel Trends Report 2018, other forms of transport are increasing in popularity, with some predicting an increase in people choosing to travel by train, particularly luxury train travel.

Driving and rail and coach options compete with air travel, and what is convenient for one destination or visitor type will not be convenient for others. Customers travelling from London to Paris will find rail, road and air travel links between these two European capital cities. But what is convenient for a school party on a four-day visit to Paris and surrounding attractions, such as Versailles and Disneyland Paris, will be rather different from that of a business traveller needing to reach a meeting in central Paris by 11 a.m. and needing to be back in Manchester the same evening.

Flying

Flying remains popular as the preferred method of transport for people taking a holiday overseas. More people are flying, and more frequently to more destinations which means that airports are more congested and the airport experience is becoming less attractive.

On-board services that were once complementary often now need to be paid for and this means that airlines must look to differentiate themselves by either price or by service.

Choosing convenience

Convenience of travel is important in a society where time is precious. This is not easy to achieve with a focus on security rather than convenience. Convenience in getting to and around the destination is important and can have a major influence on the selection of a destination or holiday. Passengers may consider the following.

- Destination routes, with passengers potentially preferring to fly from airports near to them and this helping to determine the destination that they select.
- Departure times and frequency of flights are important to maximise the time visitors spend in the holiday destination. This may also be a consideration for passengers with specific needs, such as having babies or young children who prefer daytime flights.
- On-board services, such as catering and working facilities, on planes and trains are important to some passengers depending on the flight time and the duration of the flight.
- Transfer times and methods of destination transport can be a consideration. Families with young children may not want to sit on a transfer coach for a long period of time, so a range of transport options for passengers to get to their accommodation is important. Train stations are mostly in central city and town locations and therefore can save valuable transfer time, especially for travellers on a short city break or business trip.
- Destination infrastructure can be a deciding factor when selecting a holiday destination. Standards of health and hygiene, being able to get around and having access to facilities is an important factor to some people.

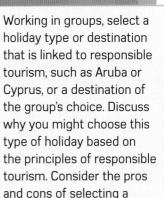

ACTIVITY

Working in groups, select a holiday type or destination that is linked to responsible tourism, such as Aruba or Cyprus, or a destination of the group's choice. Discuss why you might choose this type of holiday based on the principles of responsible tourism. Consider the pros and cons of selecting a holiday that incorporates responsible tourism into its products and services.

You may find the following website useful: www.responsibletravel.com

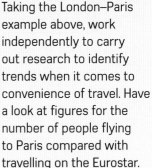

ACTIVITY

Taking the London–Paris example above, work independently to carry out research to identify trends when it comes to convenience of travel. Have a look at figures for the number of people flying to Paris compared with travelling on the Eurostar.

Think about the benefits of these two and other modes of transport and link these to visitor types. Take some time to identify the transport operators that provide transport to and from Paris.

How would you get to Paris from where you live?

Create a factsheet or presentation to reflect your findings.

CHECK MY LEARNING

Review why customers may book an environmentally friendly or responsible package holiday. Find out some names of tour operators that specialise in these types of holiday.

Desirable preferences: flexibility and practical assistance

GETTING STARTED

Working in small groups, discuss the customer types which would find it beneficial to have flexibility in the services that they receive. For example, can you think of the flexible preferences for business travellers or families with small children?

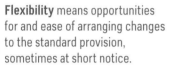

KEY TERMS

Flexibility means opportunities for and ease of arranging changes to the standard provision, sometimes at short notice.

Practical assistance is help, often physical, to enable travellers to do something, be that moving from an airport lounge to departures and on to a plane, or negotiating self-service technology.

Depending on the reasons that people are travelling and who they are travelling with, their preference for **flexibility** may be quite important and could be a deciding factor in making travel arrangements. The level of **practical assistance** required, and the ease of securing it, will be an important consideration for some travellers.

Flexibility for different customer types

Organisations that offer flexibility and practical assistance can lead the way in securing a competitive advantage and retaining customer loyalty.

Families and business travellers

Families, especially those with young children, may consider flexibility of service a factor that influences their choice when they make travel arrangements or book a holiday. Family-friendly facilities that offer flexibility in mealtimes and flight times could make a difference to their holiday experience.

Business travellers may not always run to time or may be on a tight schedule where they need to make changes to arrangements for breaks and meals. They may require a change to a room layout for a meeting or need to extend their stay. This type of flexibility could be a deciding factor when picking which hotels and venues to book.

Groups and those with specific needs

Groups of people on a tour may need to keep to a very tight schedule that demands that part of the itinerary is changed or altered to fit around plans that change.

People with specific needs, such as those arising from a disability, may require both flexibility and assistance while travelling or on holiday. Organisations that meet the needs of these customers may gain customer loyalty.

Practical assistance

There is an opportunity for travel operators to develop products and services for this growing market and to support the trend towards inclusive travel for all.

Dignity

It is very important for organisations to maintain the dignity of those needing assistance, not to exclude them or make them feel different, and to provide an appropriate level of assistance. Organisations that consider some of the principles of good social care will be able to develop good relationships with those needing assistance. The principles include: allowing those needing assistance to make their own choices; always speaking respectfully; listening; respecting personal space; ensuring that personal information is kept confidential; allowing those needing assistance to maintain their personal hygiene standards.

Disability awareness

Disability awareness is growing. In 2018, Gatwick led the way in becoming the UK's first autism-friendly airport and introduced a hidden disability lanyard to alert staff members that a passenger might need additional assistance.

There are currently more than 11 million disabled people in the UK. More inclusive travel not only offers people with accessibility needs greater choice of where to travel, but it also provides more opportunities for travel companies.

Virgin Holidays SATs

Virgin Holidays has Special Assistance Teams (SATs) that claim to lead the way in providing holidays to everyone. This includes offering support to those with mobility restrictions and other medical requirements, including hidden disabilities. Virgin has an experienced and dedicated team of knowledgeable staff who are on hand to help customers. They have integrated accessibility and specialist services into the relevant sections of their website to assist those searching for the perfect holiday for customers with a disability.

Enable Holidays

Enable Holidays specialises in planning and arranging accessible holidays for people with a disability. The staff assess most resorts, hotels and apartments to make sure that they are suitable. They can arrange and book special assistance at the airport and during flights and transfers to the accommodation, and they offer a range of services tailored to those needing practical assistance (Figure 3.13).

Royal Caribbean International

Royal Caribbean International offers accessible cruises. It offers help with embarkation and disembarkation; adapted cabins and onboard assistance; assistance to passengers with hearing and visual impairments; provides catering for assistance dogs; provides wheelchairs, scooters and other mobility aids; and provides wheelchair-accessible excursions.

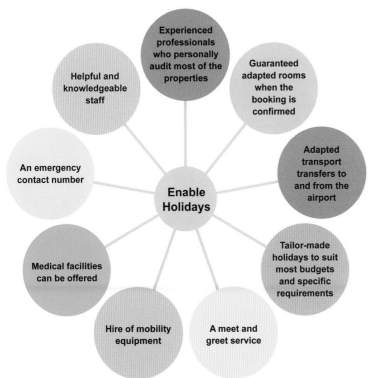

■ Figure 3.13: Do you think people with a disability feel more secure booking a holiday with a specialist company like Enable Holidays?

ACTIVITY

Different customer groups may need some assistance to meet their needs.

- Families with young children under the age of 5 would benefit from priority boarding on an aircraft, being seated together and keeping their pushchair until the last possible minute before boarding.
- Business travellers would need access to Wi-Fi and quiet working areas at the airport.
- Passengers with accessibility needs would need assistance with boarding and luggage and access to facilities, including accessible toilets, on board the aircraft.

Working in small groups, discuss how flexibility and assistance can improve the customer experience when taking a trip overseas, with reference to the three examples above and one more that you create.

ACTIVITY

Think about the customer types which would find a cruise ship holiday appealing and consider why accessibility is key. Consider life stages and disposable income.

CHECK MY LEARNING

Working in pairs, describe to your partner two different types of disability people may have.

Explain the practical assistance that each would require and why flexibility would be important in each case.

Lifestyle factors that influence choice

GETTING STARTED

Think of all the reasons people might go on holiday more when they have a full-time job.

Can you think of some reasons why they might not?

There are various lifestyle factors that influence choice when it comes to making decisions about what we do with our leisure time and when we take holidays.

Paid holidays

People who work in the UK are entitled to paid holiday. The amount of paid holiday entitlement depends on the number of days a week worked. The Holiday Pay Act was passed in 1938 and this had a major impact on the travel and tourism industry.

- Almost all workers are entitled to paid holiday, it is a legal right that employers must provide.
- Those that work a five-day week are usually entitled to 28 paid days' holiday a year.
- Part-time workers receive a **pro rata** amount of days' holiday.
- Employers may include bank holidays within the 28 days, or in addition to them.
- Employers may provide more than the statutory 28 days if they wish.

As a result of the act, holidays became accessible to everyone, including the working classes. How and when people take holidays will depend on the type of work they do. Not all full-time work means working nine to five at your place of work. Many employers allow working from home, flexi-time and shift work.

DID YOU KNOW?

Some employees increase the number of paid days' holiday with length of service: e.g. 28 days to start, 29 days after three years, 30 days after another three years and so on. Others allow employees to roll over unused days from one year to the next, or to be paid for the days not used.

Working patterns

Recent years have seen a growth in flexible working patterns (Table 3.9). Work–life balance is a key phrase used and employers are encouraged to allow employees to work more flexible hours to allow them to balance their life more evenly between work and spending time with family and friends. Job share and flexi-time positions are popular and these allow flexible working patterns to help balance work and family life.

KEY TERM

Pro rata means a proportional amount of something. For example, a worker working three days a week would receive three-fifths of the holiday a full-time worker working a five-day week would receive.

▣   Table 3.9: Common work options in the UK

Option	Detail
Full-time	Usually between 30 and 40 hours per week
Part-time	Usually less than 30 hours per week
Job share	Two employees share the work and pay of a full-time job
Compressed hours	A week's working hours are squeezed into a shorter working week. For example, 40 hours completed in four ten-hour days
Flexi-time	Allows flexible start and finish times to fit with other commitments, such as school drop-off or pick-up times
Shift work	Used when companies need 24-hour support, for example hospitals and emergency services. Shifts usually operate on a rota basis
Zero-hours contract	The employer does not have to offer a minimum number of hours and the employee does not have to accept the hours offered. In other words, there are no guaranteed hours

ACTIVITY

VisitBritain reported in 2017 that 26 per cent of adults living in Britain 'definitely' planned to take an overnight trip in the UK during Christmas and the New Year and that 61 per cent of adults living in Britain planned to visit friends or relatives over the Christmas and New Year period 2018.

1 Think about working patterns, including shift patterns, and consider how this can affect holiday planning and visits over the Christmas and New Year period.

2 What type of professions might have holiday restrictions at this time of year?

Disposable income

Holidays and travel are now much more accessible and affordable. Whatever the household income, many working people will now prioritise spending their disposable income on an experience, such as a holiday or a short trip or visit.

Each year, the average British family spends one-quarter of their annual disposable income on holidays:
- British families holiday, on average, twice a year and spend £855 per person
- Scottish nationals spend more than £850 per person on a holiday
- for every £10 of household income, more than £2 goes towards a holiday.

Amount of leisure time

Holiday trends would suggest that many people take more than one holiday a year. Paid holiday and flexible working patterns lead to increased leisure time. People are living longer and although the retirement age has increased, many people strive to retire earlier and enjoy their leisure time. The travel market for **baby boomers** and older people is growing. This is good news for the travel and tourism industry which is developing products and services to meet the needs and preferences of this market segment. More people seem to be focusing on creating memories rather than having possessions, and that means spending more on holidays and less on material goods.

Baby boomers

Many baby boomers have money to spend. Their children have grown up and left home, they are in their mid to late 60s and 70s and many have retired and have savings in the bank. They may travel as couples, but many are solo travellers. They seek adventure and luxury and have the budget to be able to meet these preferences.

According to a recent article in *Travel Weekly*, baby boomers spend almost three times as much on holiday accommodation (£890) when compared with their children's generation. This means that they are a valuable market segment to the travel and tourism industry, when considering target markets.

ACTIVITY

1 Why do you think baby boomers are taking more holidays?

2 What type of holidays do you think would appeal to the baby boomer market?

3 What time of year do you think baby boomers would prefer to travel and why?

LINK IT UP

We have already looked at disposable income and what it means for the travel and tourism industry, both in Component 2 and in this component earlier.

KEY TERM

Baby boomers are those born after the Second World War during a marked upswing in the birth rate (1945–1964), a socio-economic term.

CHECK MY LEARNING

Working individually, write a summary of how the four lifestyle factors (paid holidays, working patterns, disposable income and leisure time) can influence a customer's choice of when to book holidays, where to go and the type of holiday that they may choose. Give some examples of customer types where this will support your summary.

Other customer considerations

GETTING STARTED

Look back at your notes from Component 2 and recap on these topics. Working in pairs, discuss how the following might influence customer decisions to travel:
- personal safety and security in unfamiliar destinations
- health risks, including outbreaks of infectious diseases.

When selecting travel and tourism products or booking a holiday, there are other things that people may consider. We all have access to information from various sources, including online, and so it is easy to carry out our own research before making decisions about where to go on holiday. Choice will often be affected by what is in the media. For example, media coverage of an outbreak of illness in a destination or a terrorist attack will discourage some people from visiting a destination, even if it is an isolated incident in a destination otherwise considered safe.

Image of the destination

The image of a destination is often based on what we see in the media. This could be a TV news story because something good or bad has happened in a destination or a news article. Social media is another platform used by customers to give opinions and views on things, including holidays and experiences that they have had. From this information, we build up a picture of a destination and this informs the choices that are made about whether to go there.

LINK IT UP

In Component 2 you investigated safety and security in destinations, the effect of natural disasters and the impact of tourism on destinations. This knowledge and understanding will help you within this component.

Destination and tourism agencies are keen to promote a positive image to encourage tourism to their country or region as this is a main source of income for the national and local economy, by increasing employment and spending. Media coverage can very quickly influence people's perception of a country and whether or not they want to visit.

Tunisia

In June 2015, a lone terrorist attacker in the resort of Sousse in Tunisia resulted in the Foreign and Commonwealth Office (FCO) advising against all but essential travel to Tunisia. All UK tour operators withdrew their package holidays. Advice against travel was lifted in 2017 but the FCO still warns that terrorists are 'very likely to try to carry out attacks in Tunisia, including against UK and Western interests'. While tour operators and tourists are returning, numbers of visitors to Tunisia are still far lower than in the years leading up to and including 2014. The image of this country is still linked to the massacre and that damage will take time to repair.

ACTIVITY

Working in pairs, make a list of factors that could affect the image of a destination. Think of incidents and events that have occurred in destinations recently and discuss the impacts that these had on the destinations in terms of image and popularity.

Safety and security

In the light of incidents over recent years regarding safety and security across the world, this is a prominent consideration for consumers when deciding on where to travel and take holidays. Personal safety is a consideration, particularly if travelling alone or to a country where this has been highlighted as an issue. Terrorist attacks are becoming more unpredictable and common across the globe and people are aware more than ever before that these could happen anywhere and at any time. However, when a terrorist attack happens it tends to put people off visiting that destination. Political factors such as the threat or end of a civil war, change of leadership or a decision affecting entry requirements to a country are also a consideration.

DID YOU KNOW?

Each year British people make around 50 million trips abroad. Almost all of these trips are trouble-free. But every year the FCO helps tens of thousands of British nationals who have got into difficulty overseas.

The 2016 attempted political coup in Turkey resulted in a state of emergency being declared. The FCO advised against travel to Turkey at that time. The state of emergency has now been lifted and the FCO currently only advises against travelling to areas in the south-east of the country. However, the effect on tourist confidence is evident; tourist and traveller online forums still contain many questions and discussions about whether Turkey is a safe destination for a holiday.

Natural disasters

Fires, tsunamis, floods and earthquakes are becoming more common. Extreme weather conditions are influencing where people choose to go on holiday and tour operators are changing the programmes that they operate to reflect this.

Research conducted by VISA following the tsunami in the Indian Ocean in 2004 reported that one in five UK travellers who had committed to visit Asia had revised their destinations. Furthermore, those destinations not affected by the tsunami, but in the wider area, such as Hong Kong and Singapore were less likely to be chosen by UK tourists in 2005.

Health and outbreaks of infectious diseases

Vaccinations are required when travelling to certain countries across the world. However, there are some health outbreaks and infectious diseases that can close a resort or hotel and result in UK holidaymakers being **repatriated** back to the UK. An outbreak is something that affects a group of people. This could be diarrhoea and vomiting, rashes or respiratory problems. Common infectious diseases could be chickenpox or measles.

When major incidents occur in overseas destinations it may be necessary to repatriate customers back to their home country.

In 2016, the World Health Organization (WHO) declared a Zika virus outbreak that spread across countries in the Americas, including Latin America and the Caribbean. The outbreak of the virus and subsequent media attention had a negative effect on holidays to destinations across the region and cruise bookings.

Impact of tourism on a destination

As people become more socially and environmentally aware, they are conscious of the impact that tourism is having on destinations and this may influence their decision on whether to travel there. A destination known for **sex tourism**, **dark tourism** or **animal exploitation** may cause some people to reconsider booking a holiday and travel organisers need to consider these concerns when planning and marketing their products and services.

Over-tourism

Over-tourism is another consideration where a destination is overrun by tourists and this starts to have a negative effect on the local community, culture and daily life.

Machu Picchu is a 15th-century Inca site in Peru. It is a historical World Heritage Site visited by over half a million visitors a year. As visitor numbers increase so do the negative impacts on the local people and the environment. Local people are employed as porters, and the local souvenir trade also provides economic benefits to the local community. However, this can cause local people to become more westernised diluting traditional, local culture. The number of visitors to Machu Picchu is also causing erosion by wearing away the Inca Trail and surrounding area. Tourism does, of course, bring money to the area and this can be invested in preserving the site. These positive and negative impacts need to be balanced and this brings its own challenges. Tourism authorities have decided to restrict access to Machu Picchu to try and minimise the negative impacts.

KEY TERMS

Repatriate means to return someone back to their home country.

Sex tourism is travel planned for the purpose of sex, often in countries where prostitution is legal.

Dark tourism means travelling to places associated with death or suffering.

Animal exploitation is abusing animals to entertain tourists.

ACTIVITY

Think about the benefits and disadvantages of the initiative to limit and control visitor numbers to Machu Picchu.

1 How will this help to minimise negative impacts on the environment?

2 What issues could this create for tourists?

3 Do you think this is a good idea?

CHECK MY LEARNING

Working in pairs, think of another example that has occurred in a destination for each of these considerations: safety and security of destination, natural disasters, outbreaks of infectious diseases and impact of tourism on a destination.

Join with another pair and share your examples.

Learning aim A: assessment practice

How you will be assessed

In this component, you will be assessed by completing an internally assessed assignment. You may be required to complete several tasks, including producing reports, presentations or posters, for example.

Your teacher will set the assignment. They will provide you with an assignment brief that outlines what you will need to do as well as a date by which the assignment should be completed and submitted. The teacher will mark the assignment and tell you what grade you have achieved.

For Learning aim A, you will be expected to show that you know about the different types of market research and how organisations use this to identify trends and understand customer needs, preferences and considerations. This will include the following.

- Explaining how a selected travel and tourism organisation uses market research to identify customer trends and how it has responded to customer trends to meet their needs, preferences and considerations, with relevant examples.
- Assessing how effectively the travel and tourism organisation has responded to information about customer trends to adapt its products and services to meet customer needs, preferences and considerations, with detailed relevant examples.

CHECKPOINT

Review your learning of this component by answering the following questions; this will help you prepare for your assignment.

Strengthen
- Identify a named organisation that has easy access to relevant information.
- Identify how the organisation has used market research to identify customer trends.
- Describe how the organisation has responded to these trends by making changes to an existing product or by introducing a new product to meet identified customer needs and preferences.

Challenge
- Give at least two detailed examples of how the organisation has adapted products to meet the changing needs of specific target segments.
- Assess the effectiveness of the organisation in responding to customer trends.

ASSESSMENT ACTIVITY 1 | LEARNING AIM | A

Choose a specific travel and tourism organisation and:

- describe the organisation type
- explain the types of market research it uses and how these uses it to identify trends
- explain and assess its effectiveness in adapting products or services in response to customer trends identified through market research
- assess how this meets customer needs, preferences and considerations.

Present your findings in a PowerPoint® presentation with notes and images.

ASSESSMENT ACTIVITY 2 | LEARNING AIM | A

You have secured an apprenticeship at a local independent travel agent. A recent report in a travel newspaper has suggested that travellers are becoming more socially and environmentally aware and prefer to book holidays with tour operators which have a strong responsible tourism policy in place. Your manager has asked you to carry out some research to broaden your knowledge on this subject and put together a presentation.

You will need to choose a named travel and tourism organisation.

Your presentation should:

- identify an organisation with a responsible tourism policy in place
- explain the market research methods it used to identify trends in responsible tourism
- assess how development of this policy has met the needs, preferences and considerations of its customers.

Deliver your findings as a presentation.

TAKE IT FURTHER

Have you used very specific examples and are these examples detailed? Your work should not simply be a description. It should tell the reader why, who and how.

TIPS

Many organisations have a corporate website that gives access to company information. This is different from the main website used by the public.

Travel newspapers and trade organisations publish articles and reports making direct reference to specific organisations and product development.

TIP

Select an organisation that provides easy access to information on why their responsible tourism policy is in place, making reference to customer preferences, needs and considerations.

Providing products and services that meet needs and preferences

GETTING STARTED

Let's start by re-capping on your knowledge to date about holiday types and accommodation types. Think about as many different holiday types and accommodation types as you can.

LINK IT UP

In Component 1, you explored both the strategic and financial aims of travel and tourism organisations and looked in detail at the different types of holiday and accommodation.

In order to meet their financial and strategic aims, travel and tourism organisations need to offer a range of products to satisfy the requirements and preferences of different types of customers.

Holidays and accommodation

You have already explored market segments. In this lesson, you will identify the customer needs and preferences that are met by the range of different holidays and accommodation that are available.

Holiday types

Package holidays

A package holiday is put together by a tour operator and sold at an inclusive price. They make booking a holiday easier for customers by providing all of the components at one, inclusive price. They are ATOL protected, providing customers with security, and come with resort services, including company representatives. These types of holidays meet the needs of customers by providing security and are often at a cheaper price.

All-inclusive holidays

All-inclusive holidays, including all food, drinks and entertainment, can meet the needs of families looking for value for money as there are no extra costs once the holiday is paid for. Although the initial cost of the holiday may be more expensive, there is no additional cost once on holiday. These holidays also suit those looking for convenience.

Tailor-made holidays

Tailor-made holidays are made to order for each customer. A customer can decide where they want to go, how long they want to stay in each place, where they want to stay and what they want to do and the tour operator will put together an itinerary. This type of holiday suits those looking for something a little different. Customers may have more money to spend and want to explore.

Special interest holidays

Special interest holidays cater for people with a special interest or hobby; for example, bird watching or wine tasting. They meet the needs of people who want a little more from their holiday. They can mix with like-minded people who have similar interests and hobbies.

Multi-centre holidays

Multi-centre holidays combine two or more destinations into one holiday. Sometimes people may simply want to visit different resorts within a destination, so this type of holiday meets the needs of customers who want to explore.

Cruise holidays

Cruise holidays are perfect for people who like an all-inclusive holiday while also having the opportunity to visit different countries all on one holiday. They are suitable for people who like a sociable holiday, meeting new people, with entertainment, food and drink. Cruise ships are developing to cater for different markets and can range from sophisticated river cruises to full-on family entertainment with activities, clubs and water parks to keep children entertained.

Responsible holidays

Responsible holidays focus on the positive impact tourism can have. This is a growing market that appeals to customers with a focus on reducing the negative impact of tourism on destinations and promoting positive impacts. It will appeal to people who have an awareness of how travel can negatively impact on the environment and who want to travel with organisations that are actively doing something to minimise this.

Accommodation types

Budget hotels

Budget hotels provide basic rooms, facilities and, usually, meals at a cheap cost. Rooms are often small. Budget hotels are becoming more competitive in a growing market. This type of accommodation will appeal to people who are on a tight budget or do not focus on the accommodation as part of their holiday. People who are planning on sightseeing or activities that take them away from their accommodation for most of their stay may not want to spend a lot of money on accommodation that they are not going to spend much time in.

Luxury hotels

Luxury hotels often have a four- or five-star rating and include extras. They appeal to customers who enjoy luxury during their stay or who are celebrating a special occasion, such as an anniversary or a wedding. In these cases, the choice of accommodation will be an important aspect of the holiday.

Youth hostels

Youth hostels provide cheap accommodation, usually aimed at young people, travellers or those on some sort or walking or cycling holiday. Youth hostels are ideal for student groups or families who are looking for basic accommodation that can cater for groups and travellers who perhaps want to meet like-minded people. People who book this type of accommodation will usually be out for most of the day and are happy to use communal facilities to cater for their needs. Youth hostels are developing facilities to cater for families, with family rooms and en-suite facilities, although these types of rooms are limited and rooms are often dorms, with multiple beds. Youth hostels cater well for people who like the outdoors or who like to explore and sightsee but who are on a budget. They are often in rural areas or centrally based in cities.

Holiday parks

Holiday parks offer different types of accommodation, usually caravans and lodges. They mostly attract families, as on-site entertainment and facilities are provided. They can be independent or owned by holiday park organisations, such as Haven.

Camping and glamping sites

Campsites appeal to people who love the outdoors and are very popular with families who want to spend time together away from technology.

Glamping is luxury camping with tents or yurts that are already set up. This type of accommodation appeals to people who like the idea of being outdoors but who prefer more luxury. This is a growing market with families and couples alike as it provides time away from modern-day life, but also with an element of luxury, such as real beds, wood burners and running water.

ACTIVITY

Working individually, select a tour operator that can provide suitable holidays for each of the following and explain how the products and services will meet the customers' needs and preferences.

- A family with young teenage children would like some sporting activities that they can do together. The parents would also like some time to relax with some health and wellbeing options.
- A same-sex couple would like a beach holiday in an LGBT-friendly, long-haul destination.
- A retired couple in their 60s would like a split centre holiday in Europe to experience a contrast within the destination. They enjoy culture and exploration.
- A family with children, aged 7 and 10, would like an all-inclusive holiday in a European destination. They would like children's clubs, daytime activities and evening entertainment.

CHECK MY LEARNING

Pair up with another class member to discuss and compare your findings. Write down key points to explain how well the organisations do or do not provide adequate provision for these customer types.

Providing a range of activities

GETTING STARTED

Make a list of activities that you might like to do on holiday. These could be activities you have done before or ones you would like to try; for example, activities that you have done while on holiday or seen on television or YouTube.

Discuss your list with another student. Are there similarities?

What are the implications for travel organisations in trying to provide for long customer wish lists?

Trends would suggest that the beach holiday is changing, with people looking to do more than lie on a beach or by the pool. Family activities are growing in popularity and people tend to be taking more of an interest in culture. According to the ABTA Holiday Habits Report 2018, beach holidays are the second most popular holiday type taken by 40 per cent of people in 2018.

Holiday activities

Activity and adventure tourism is a growing market in its own right with many tour operators specialising in activity and adventure holidays. Many of these holidays are combined with responsible tourism to ensure the negative impact on the environment and local community is minimised and positive impacts are maximised.

Excursions

Just as the package holiday is being re-invented to cater for changing needs of customers, so too is the excursion package offered by tour operators. Bar crawls and island tours have been replaced by cultural days out led by local guides and horse riding through mountains. In certain destinations, customers will still find days out to a water park or a themed evening of entertainment but there is no longer a one-size-fits-all approach and excursions will differ depending on the destination and the market segment.

TUI Travel offers a service, gotui.com, where customers can access the website, click on their holiday destination and explore the excursions and activities suitable for them ahead of time. The website uses filters so that customers can categorise by price, suitability and theme, if desired.

Sporting activities

Health and wellness holidays are another growing market. People seem to be more aware of their own fitness and health and want to bring an element of this into their holiday. Many tour operators will offer hotels and packages that offer sporting activities or incorporate them into the holiday package. All-inclusive holidays include a range of activities from pool activities, such as volley ball and pool Zumba, to swimming lessons and football coaching for children. Certain destinations attract people with a special interest, such as walking or cycling. Majorca is very popular with cyclists and walkers. The south coast of England attracts people interested in surfing and this is often the reason that people take holidays there.

According to Neilson Holidays, holidays that include an activity, such as hiking, cycling or water sports are growing in popularity. Their research shows that it is mainly the younger market that is driving this growing trend. They asked 2000 people whether they would book a holiday that involved lots of activities, or a holiday with minimum activity involved. One in three millennials said they would choose an active holiday compared with less than one in ten (7.9 per cent) of baby boomers.

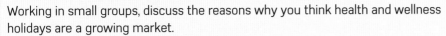

ACTIVITY

Working in small groups, discuss the reasons why you think health and wellness holidays are a growing market.

Visit the websites for TUI, Thomas Cook and Jet2 Holidays. Look at the type of excursions they offer in different resorts and see if you can see differences or common themes between the three tour operators.

Learning a new skill

Activities on holiday can also include those that provide people with the opportunity to develop a new skill. TV programmes at home can be the inspiration for people to want to learn to do something new, such as learning to dance or to cook exotic food. Tour operators may offer these classes as an activity on holiday.

Responsibletravel.com offers a product called Learn Something New Holidays. These holidays allow holidaymakers to combine a holiday experience with developing knowledge and skills. This can be learning music or salsa in Cuba, learning to speak Spanish and dance the tango in Spain, or learning traditional crafts in Scotland.

Special events

Holidays and travel services will often centre around special events. The World Cup and the Olympics are good news for travel operators and for the destination. Cultural events are also a reason why people may go on holidays or visit a destination. The Blackpool Illuminations can attract up to four million visitors a year. Holidays based around music festivals is a growing market and is expanding and developing across Europe, becoming popular with the younger market.

Families on the go

Families are changing and so are their needs and expectations. They now often want more choice and facilities when it comes to holidays and travel and tourism organisations must cater for these needs in order to grow their market and meet their business goals and objectives.

Families Worldwide is a tour operator which specialises in providing activity and adventure holidays for families looking for more from their holiday. These include: activity and adventure, cultural discovery, wildlife and nature, multi-activity, winter fun, water adventure, safari and camping adventures.

ACTIVITY

Working in pairs, discuss and list the reasons why you think this type of family holiday is a growing market.

How will developing products and services to meet this growing market help mainstream tour operators meet their business goals and objectives?

CHECK MY LEARNING

Return to the list you made in the Getting started activity. Would the examples on this page provide for your needs?

If not, then think about how they could be provided.

If so, then add two new things to do that are not included and think about how they might be provided.

▢ Do the products and services available meet the needs and preferences of the family market segment?

Tailor-made facilities and amenities

GETTING STARTED

Working in pairs, discuss the term 'tailor-made holidays' and come up with your own definition based on knowledge from earlier lessons in Component 1.

Give reasons why you think tailor-made holidays are appealing to customers and why it is beneficial to use a tour operator to plan and book this type of holiday.

Tailor-made holidays come with an element of exclusivity that make the customer feel special. These types of holiday are seen as a little more special than the average package holiday and mass market operators are starting to adapt their travel products and services to cater for this market to compete with specialist tour operators.

Tailor-made facilities and amenities

So, you know what tailor-made holidays are, but what about the customer needs, preferences and considerations when it comes to the facilities and amenities that these customers expect to come with this type of holiday?

Tailor-made holidays can offer good value for money but that doesn't mean that they are cheap. The value comes with the extra touches and personal service that customers pay extra for. Tailor-made holidays offer organisations a good opportunity to meet their financial aims. Chargeable options and extras give the customer choice, while at the same time bringing in extra revenue. The air of exclusivity will draw in customers with higher disposable incomes and therefore have the potential to bring in increased revenue.

Accommodation booked for a tailor-made holiday will usually be comfortable with a touch of luxury. Customers may expect that all needs are met when it comes to facilities, although this expectation may be different depending on the market segment; for example, couples or families. Facilities and amenities may include the following.

Spa and leisure

With the likely high standard of hotel booked, customers may well expect free use of a well-equipped gym and pool with spa facilities. They may want to indulge in beauty treatments to relax during their stay, have a sauna and a swim or participate in a fitness or wellness class. These needs and expectations may be unstated. By providing these facilities as standard, the travel organisation is striving to meet these customer expectations to cater for this target market.

Sport

Facilities such as tennis courts, a five-aside football pitch and water-sports facilities may also be an expectation of some customer types booking a tailor-made holiday, so that they can keep active and mix with like-minded people.

With the increase in popularity of holidays that provide activities, these facilities may well be expected by the customers who are booking this type of holiday. It is likely that tour operators who provide tailor-made holidays will arrange hotel accommodation that offers these facilities as standard.

ACTIVITY

1 What are the advantages of tailor-made holidays?

2 What customer types would these holidays appeal to and why?

Families

Families with young children will expect services and facilities to provide entertainment and care for babies and young children so that the adults can have some time to themselves and relax. This could include creche facilities, children's clubs and activities and communal areas where families can mix, with early-dining facilities. Some tour operators offer babysitting services by qualified staff.

A family who book a tailor-made holiday will have an expectation that there will be facilities to cater for their children that are appropriate to their age group. Some of these needs will be stated and others unstated. Travel companies which organise tailor-made holidays will offer products and facilities specifically matched to the needs of families and these will need to be established when putting together the tailored package.

Specialist tour operators

According to Mintel, 59 per cent of millennials would pay extra for a holiday tailor-made to their preferences. The travel industry has changed and continues to change. Natural disasters and political events have impacted on the way people feel about travelling. It may deter them from travelling to a destination because they feel unsafe or insecure about visiting for fear of the reoccurrence of an event. Customers are now more likely to complete their own research and expect much more from their holiday: they want experiences that feel unique to them. They also want to feel safe and secure and there is an increasing demand for the services of expert travel professionals. Tour operators need to develop the products and services that they offer to meet these needs and expectations.

Specialist operators, such as Exodus and Kuoni, have expert teams that can provide their customers expert travel advice on destinations, many of them new, that offer authentic experiences. These specialist operators can customise every element of the holiday experience including flights, hotels, extra nights, regional departures, beach extensions and stop-overs.

Mainstream tour operators

It isn't just specialist tour operators which need to keep up with evolving trends towards personalised travel. Mainstream tour operators, such as Thomas Cook and TUI, are offering customers different options in the way that they book and plan their package holidays. Changing customer needs and preferences have prompted holiday companies to innovate beyond just offering a wide choice of destinations and flight times. Thomas Cook has an obligation to its shareholders and its customers to provide products and services that will meet expectations and make a profit.

To achieve this, Thomas Cook is offering customers more choice to personalise their holidays. Segmentation is no longer enough, customers want personalisation. Mainstream operators like Thomas Cook may not yet offer the standard and choice that specialist operators can offer but they are developing their products and services to meet customer demand for personalisation. These holidays are growing in demand and different tailor-made holidays can cater for different lifestyles, work patterns and budgets.

ACTIVITY

Working independently, consider these two customer examples.
- Mr and Mrs A are a retired couple and would like to book an all-inclusive holiday in Cuba. They would like a 12-night stay and can fly from any airport in the North West of the UK.
- Mr and Mr B would like to travel with their children, aged 12 and 14 years. They would like an activity and adventure holiday in Europe and can fly from any airport in the London region.

Carry out research to find tour operators that offer tailor-made services to match the needs of these customers. Consider the holiday and the facilities and amenities that would meet the customers' needs and expectations.

Create a PowerPoint® presentation to deliver to the rest of the class. This must include:
- an outline of the travel and tourism organisation
- the holiday package and what it includes
- the tailor-made facilities and amenities that are included and/or are optional.

CHECK MY LEARNING

Practise your presentation ready to deliver to the rest of the class. Present your findings and give reasons why you think your chosen organisation is a suitable choice for your customer profile.

Meeting other customer needs and preferences

GETTING STARTED

In small groups, discuss green tourism and environmental concerns. Think about them from the point of view of the customer, the organisation and the destination. Consider the main issues and possible solutions. Is this a subject that you think will become more or less important in the future?

LINK IT UP

In Component 1, you investigated different types of holiday and the reasons why people travel. Use your notes and knowledge from this component to help you with this lesson.

KEY TERM

Sustainable means minimising the damage to something so that it can continue for a long time.

Two common recent themes in customer needs and preferences are wanting something different and a preference towards holidays that incorporate responsible tourism.

Green tourism

Green tourism considers the needs of the environment, local communities, businesses and tourists. The terms 'responsible tourism', 'eco-tourism', or '**sustainable** tourism' are all used interchangeably and they all mean pretty much the same, with the aim of making tourism sustainable. Customers increasingly feel that it is the travel organisation's responsibility to be environmentally responsible, so organisations need to incorporate this into policies to meet their organisational aims as well as meeting customer needs and expectations.

Conservation volunteering

This is becoming increasingly popular, especially with younger people who are perhaps taking a gap year or want to volunteer abroad between terms when they are studying. Organisations carry out project work focusing on the preservation of wildlife and the environment. They will work with local communities on projects to help with things such as education and building facilities like schools. Conservation volunteering holidays appeal to people who are looking for an experience and an adventure. They satisfy a customer need to travel with a purpose and to give something back.

Cultural activities

Cultural tourism is a market that is growing in popularity. Cultural activities can be to do with art, heritage, food and drink, crafts, music or history. People who are interested in cultural tourism and activities are interested in the history and culture of a destination. Cultural tourism can help to have a positive impact on destinations by helping to preserve traditions and communities. Travel organisations have an obligation to their customers to ensure that their products provide customers with a cultural experience that is authentic. Customers will expect expert advice and information from well-informed or local people.

Adventure tourism

Adventure tourism can involve anything from hill walking to extreme sports and everything in between. It can involve water sports, snow sports and activities on land. It is generally physically challenging in some way and often takes place in quite remote places. There are certain destinations that are popular with adventure tourism, such as the Lake District in the UK and New Zealand.

This type of tourism appeals to people with a preference for a challenge and who want to make a positive contribution to the destination they visit. They tend to be socially and environmentally aware and will tread carefully in their quest for discovery and adventure.

Adventure Alternative

Adventure Alternative is an independent adventure travel company based in Northern Ireland. It caters for people who want to go on hiking and walking expeditions around the world, with a focus on responsible tourism. It sets up local companies and employs local staff, training these staff members so that they can have a long-term career. It believes that this gives the customer a better experience. It is a profit-making organisation but believes that it also has a responsibility for the protection and promotion of the destinations and for the communities and local people that it employs. It values the people that it employs and the destinations that it works in.

ACTIVITY

Some Adventure Alternative customer reviews are shown below.

- Borneo – a wonderful and unforgettable experience with so many fantastic memories. Did so much in three weeks. This trip will be with me for a long time to come. Would not hesitate using AA again (this was my second time) as feel safe and secure with such a responsible company and for all what they stand for.
- I have just returned from Everest Base Camp with two friends. I just wanted to say that we all had a fantastic time – it was truly an amazing journey and a wonderful experience. The staff that Adventure Alternative employ are second to none – happy, helpful caring and informative. We were fortunate to have Tshring and Lopsang: both truly amazing guys, together with five porters, one for each of us. It's nice to know and reassuring that the company pay above 'normal wages' and that each porter carries one bag. We all saw too often how much other porters carry and for much less. It was hard enough doing the trek with our day sacks let alone having to carry around 20kg each step of the way.

Read these reviews and then discuss how these reviews reflect the company ethos of Adventure Alternative.

1 How does Adventure Alternative cater for the needs of its customers and how does this benefit the organisation?

2 Why would customers choose to book a holiday with Adventure Alternative?

ACTIVITY

Working in small groups, use your notes from previous lessons and the internet to access travel trend reports. Review travel trends in green or responsible tourism.

Your task is to find a tour operator with a holiday that matches the needs and preferences of the customer profiles below.

- A multi-generational family of six would like a package holiday in Europe. They would like all-inclusive accommodation with daytime facilities that can be both relaxing and active. They would like to be in a quiet resort with access to bars and restaurants and some evening entertainment.
- A female solo traveller in her 30s would like to travel to Europe for a 'wellness' holiday. She would like to stay in a relaxing hotel with meals included and have a range of relaxing activities and treatments available.
- A small group of students is looking for a volunteering holiday in Thailand. They can be away for up to four weeks.
- A same-sex couple would like to get married in Malta. They are looking for a hotel that can accommodate wedding guests, conduct the ceremony and host the reception with a beach location.

CHECK MY LEARNING

Working individually, write up an explanation of how the selected holidays match the needs of the customers. Don't forget to reference the organisation that you use.

Prepare your written summary for discussion and review with your teacher. Make sure that you can give a clear explanation for your selections.

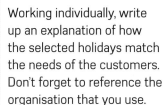

Planning a holiday to meet customer needs and preferences

GETTING STARTED

Imagine you are booking a holiday of a lifetime. How important is it that the travel organiser listens to you to find out exactly what you want before they start to look for holidays for you? What happens if this part of the process goes wrong?

LINK IT UP

To be successful at discovering customers' needs, you will need questioning skills. Refer back to earlier lessons in this component on market research and review your notes about the use of open and closed questions. Using the right questioning techniques and asking the right questions is key to obtaining the best information to cater for the needs and preferences of customers.

DID YOU KNOW?

A study suggests that in face-to-face communication, the majority of what is actually communicated is portrayed through non- verbal communication:

- words account for 7 per cent of the overall message
- tone of voice accounts for 38 per cent of the overall message
- body language accounts for 55 per cent of the overall message.

(Albert Mehrabian, Professor of Psychology, UCLA, USA)

Good tour operators will put together holiday packages that meet the needs and preferences of their customers. To do this they must first assess those needs and preferences and then research suitable options.

According to the ABTA Holiday Habits Report 2018, over one-third (36 per cent) of people booked a holiday with a travel professional in the past year. The main reasons people use a travel professional to book are the ease of booking (58 per cent), because it saves them time (51 per cent) and the fact that they feel more confident booking through a professional (45 per cent). There is a growing demand once again for travel professionals. Travel is becoming more complicated and travel professionals have the expertise to know what is new and exciting, they save people time and stress and can often find their customers a bargain. Whether it is for a business trip or a leisure trip, travel professionals will have greater access to the information needed to plan and organise the trip that is personalised to meet the individual needs of the customers. They are there as a point of contact from the beginning to the end of the journey, offering security and peace of mind to the customer.

Assessing general and specific needs

When tour operators put together a holiday or an itinerary for a customer, it is important that they use the information that the customer gives them and that they question appropriately to establish the customer's needs.

Some customers will know exactly where they want to go on holiday, some may have some ideas and others will have no idea at all. A travel agent will need to ask a range of questions to help the customer decide on the destination by finding out what type of holiday they want and what they want to get out of it.

General needs

Whatever the holiday type and whatever the destination, all customers need transport to get to their destination and so this is considered a general need. It is crucial that the correct type of transport is selected by listening to the customer and establishing what they want. Customers may want to travel by air, road, rail or sea and once that is established, there are then further preferences that have to be established. For example, what type of airline and class would they prefer?

Accommodation is another general need that needs to be established. The general type of accommodation preferred by the customer needs to be established. For example, do they want self-catering or serviced accommodation?

Specific needs

There are a number of factors to consider when it comes to identifying a customer's specific needs.

- **Time:** People who have more free leisure time can go further and may be interested in traveling to multiple destinations. People who are restricted for time may only consider destinations that are closer to home.

- **Travelling with other people:** Think about how travelling as a family, alone or as a couple can influence a choice of destination.
- **Weather:** People who want a city break to explore will probably not want extreme heat. Sun-seekers who want a beach holiday will want hot weather.
- **Budget:** It is important to establish a customer's budget and decide whether they are a budget or a luxury traveller.
- **The experience that a customer is looking for:** Understanding their motivation and reasons for travel based on the experience they are looking for is important.

Listening

Putting together a package to suit customer needs and preferences means getting as much information as possible. Effective communication skills are key to getting accurate information from customers and this means listening.

Active listening can be easy in some situations (Figure 3.14); for example, gossiping with friends. However, other situations demand a level of skill. It requires concentration, understanding and responses. People who listen actively will demonstrate positive body language and responsive facial expressions. They will repeat information back and check that they are clear about what they have heard.

Figure 3.14: We tend to listen actively to things we are interested in. Can you think of people in your life that you listening actively to?

ACTIVITY

Working in groups of three, take it in turns to play the following roles.
- Customer.
- Travel agent.
- Observer and note taker.

The goal is to practise gathering information and assessing needs. As a customer, you will enquire about some options for a holiday for you and your partner.

As a travel agent, you will listen to the customer and ask questions to identify their needs, what type of accommodation they want, location, facilities etc.

As the observer, you will listen and take notes about the type of questions being asked. Are they listening to the customer and identifying their needs to match them to the right products and services?

Once you have completed the role play, rotate so that you each play each role.

Review the notes you have from when you were the travel agent. Add to them from those made by the observer. You will build on these notes in the next few lessons, so it is important that they are detailed.

CHECK MY LEARNING

Working individually, write down what you have learned from the role play about what you would need to know and ask as an agent. Is it difficult to get sufficient information from the customer? If so, why? Think about how you could get around this and improve the way you gather information and assess needs.

Researching suitable destinations (sources of information)

GETTING STARTED

Think about researching suitable holiday destinations. What sources of information could you use to locate different holiday destinations for customers? Write down as many different sources of information as you can.

◘ In an age where information is just a click away online, how useful do you think other resources are?

Once the customer's general needs and preferences have been established, agents can begin to create holiday plans by looking at potential holiday destinations. In order to satisfy those needs and preferences, agents will need to know where to find suitable information.

Websites

Using the internet to access websites is a quick and useful way to find out information on just about anything. This is perfect when carrying out research on holiday destinations. Not all websites are reliable, so they must be used with caution. Official industry-linked websites that are professional and ethical are a great source of information.

Guidebooks

Guidebooks are a great source of information for travellers and for people organising holidays. They are often tried and tested and based on information gathered from experience and first-hand information. Guidebooks such as *Lonely Planet* and *Rough Guide* are popular and updated frequently.

Tourist leaflets

We may live in a digital world with information at our fingertips but leaflets about local attractions and the local area are still popular with visitors. They are commonly used at visitor attractions and in tourist information centres, both in the UK and overseas. Tour operators use them to promote excursions to people on holiday as a visual way of engaging people and creating an interest in things to see and do in holiday destinations. There are people who still prefer to read things in print and leaflets can be a great resource to use when planning a trip as they can be used as a reference and people can take them away to read at their leisure.

Atlases

Atlases can be used in different ways and can be a valuable resource when planning and organising a holiday. Maps can be used to locate different countries, but they can also be used to identify other geographical areas, such as rivers or national parks around the world. They include graphs and tables that give information about climate or populations. They also include information about transport routes and services and provide information about the history, culture and religion of a destination.

Holiday brochures

Holiday brochures may be less visible in a travel agency than they once were, but they are still an available resource. In a steadily growing paperless society, a tour operator may print fewer brochures but there is still a market for them, particularly with an older market segment. Some people still like to have something that they can take away; something that they can make notes in to mark resorts and itineraries. They like to have something to show other people and discuss.

 What purpose do you think brochures serve and who do you think would be more likely to use these?

Tourist information centres

Tourists information centres are a great resource for people who are new to an area and like to have face-to-face contact to gather information about an area without having to carry out their own research. They can be found across the world in popular tourist destinations. They can offer expert advice face to face, on the telephone and by email. They can also sell tourism products and services and make bookings for accommodation, events and transport.

ACTIVITY

Working individually, return to your notes from the role play, when you were the travel agent.

1 Review the information you gathered from the customer.

2 Using the information sources suggested here and from your own knowledge, research possible destinations to meet the needs and preferences of your customer.

3 Prepare a list of three potential destinations and holiday types, the first being the best fit (option 1), and the other two (options 2 and 3) being alternatives that still fit the customer's needs but offer something a little different. Spend about two-thirds of your time on option 1 and make sure it is detailed, use the other third to roughly plan out the alternative options 2 and 3.

4 Are you missing any key pieces of information? If so, make a list of things you still need to find out from the customer.

CHECK MY LEARNING

Review your notes from this and the previous lesson and put together a list of questions and points for discussion to help you gather useful information in preparation for a visit to a travel agency or to your class by a guest speaker.

Information to plan a holiday

GETTING STARTED

Working in pairs, consider the importance of travel itineraries. Can you list three purposes they might fulfil? Are they more relevant to certain types of holiday or types of customer?

Putting together a holiday **itinerary** can be a complex process that needs careful planning to make sure that it provides the customer with a seamless experience that meets their specific needs and preferences.

Travel itineraries

A good itinerary makes for a seamless trip (Figure 3.15). An itinerary is a detailed plan for a journey and should include details of:

- customer details
- dates
- transport
- accommodation
- activities and excursions
- health risks and precautions
- safety and security concerns
- total and itemised breakdown of costs.

KEY TERM

An **itinerary** is a detailed plan for a journey, that includes all essential travel details that a customer needs to reach the destination, such as dates, times, transport provider, and for when at the destination, such as details of accommodation and excursions, and relevant information about the destination in general.

Travel itineraries benefit the customer and the travel organiser by helping to:

- manage time by planning travel times, connections, check in and admission times
- budget and manage money
- make travel between one place and another quicker and easier
- prioritise and make sure that all the essentials are included
- make sure that everything is included, and that nothing has been forgotten.

LINK IT UP

In Component 1, you explored tourist destinations, reasons for travel, types of holiday and types of accommodation. Use your knowledge and notes from this to help you when you are planning a holiday.

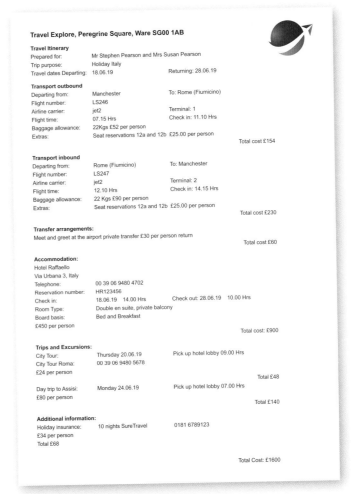

Figure 3.15: This sample itinerary is missing two key sections, what are they? Make sure you cover these in your plan.

Customer details

Names and contact details of principal traveller/organiser, number and names of people travelling (including ages and birth dates of those under 18).

Destination(s) and dates

Name of the destination, or destinations if a multi-centre trip. Dates and times of departure and arrival in local time. Dates and times of departure and arrival between destinations if a multi-centre trip.

Transport

Dates, times and connections with details of the transport provider for all transport. Include flight numbers for planes and ship names for ferry trips. Details of car hire, if included, such as the name and contact details of the provider, details of the pick-up and drop-off points.

Accommodation

Name, star rating, check-in dates and check-out dates and times and the board basis, along with the full address, telephone number and website.

Activities and excursions

Name and date of the excursion, name of the provider with their contact details and whether the excursion is included in the overall price or optional to be paid at the destination.

Health risks and precautions

Although personal health is the responsibility of the individual, a travel organiser has a responsibility to direct a customer to sources of information so that they can make themselves aware of any health risks or precautions. For example, seeking medical advice about any vaccinations that are necessary is advisable before visiting a destination. Include relevant information from recognised authorities, such as the NHS and FCO. Include details of any recommended/necessary vaccinations.

Safety and security concerns

Include relevant information from the FCO for the destination, but ensure you advise the customer to check this information closer to the time of travel. Situations change and the FCO updates its advice regularly.

Total and itemised breakdown of costs

A clearly identified total cost and an itemised breakdown of costs. Itemised costs could be included under the above sections or gathered together in one section. Include details of any payments not included, such as those to be made locally on arrival; for example, any tourist taxes or resort fees.

LINK IT UP

Component 2 looked at safety and security concerns in detail. What safety information should you include in a holiday itinerary?

ACTIVITY

Working independently, devise an itinerary template (ensure you include the two areas missing from the sample in Figure 3.15) that can be used for planning a holiday, to include all necessary information, including a breakdown of costs and total price. This should be in a format of your choice.

Your teacher will review this template with you and give you feedback to develop this into a working document.

CHECK MY LEARNING

Review your template and then swap it with a classmate for a peer review. Give each other constructive feedback and highlight any good practice and parts that you think could be developed.

Providing accurate information

GETTING STARTED

Why do you think producing professional written plans is important? Think about how a travel organisation would portray a positive image.

LINK IT UP

In Component 1, you investigated organisational, strategic and financial aims and objectives. Review these notes and think about how producing accurate, professional information can link to these aims and objectives.

ACTIVITY

Bearing in mind the checklist for written communication, return to the itinerary template you created in the previous lesson.

Review the notes you have from the role play a few lessons back when you were acting as the travel agent.

Put together a written itinerary for the customer's holiday, option 1, using your template from the last lesson and destination research from before that.

Pay attention to detail and make sure that the information matches the customer's needs and preferences as outlined in the customer profile.

Documentation produced by staff on behalf of a travel organisation must be produced to a professional standard to provide accurate information and promote the organisation in a positive way.

Clear written communication

Electronic written communication is becoming more commonly used in the travel and tourism industry. However, there may still be times when handwritten communication is required. For example, working for a small independent travel agent using a template for a handwritten itinerary or working overseas for a small independent tour operator as a holiday representative using handwritten reports.

Whether written communication is by hand or is electronic there are some basic guidelines that should be followed (Figure 3.16).

> ### Checklist for written communication:
>
> ✔ Clearly legible
> ✔ Checked to make sure there are no mistakes with spelling, grammar and punctuation
> ✔ Appropriate language for the intended audience; for example, a customer or a colleague
> ✔ Made clear who it is to and who it is from
> ✔ The content makes sense
> ✔ The information is accurate and up to date

▣ **Figure 3.16: Would you add anything to this checklist?**

Accurate information

Written communication needs to be accurate and professional. The customer will take away a written itinerary and will depend on this information being clear and precise. Attention to detail is essential. It must be presented in a professional format to reflect the company image in a positive way.

The itinerary must be checked against the customer's requests, needs and preferences with alternatives given if it cannot meet these exact needs.

Accurate information within an itinerary will instil confidence and trust in the organisation. When the customer receives high levels of service with attention to detail and accurate information, they are more likely to return and become loyal to the business. An itinerary should outline a timetable of events that provides a seamless journey and a great experience.

There are many benefits for the customer of using a travel agent to put together their travel itinerary, as shown in Figure 3.17.

However, it must be right. It is important that all the travel arrangements in the itinerary are booked and checked to ensure that the customer does not encounter any problems or issues during their trip.

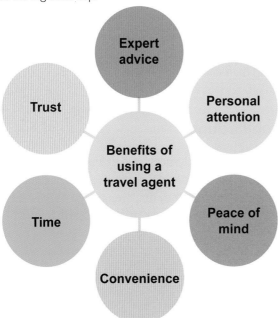

🔲 **Figure 3.17: For the customer to benefit, things must be done correctly. What could the consequences be of a mistake on an itinerary?**

Consequences of inaccurate information

Accurate information regarding personal details, spellings of names, flight times and connections are crucial if the customer is to have the seamless experience that they expect when they use a travel agent to book a trip or a holiday.

Under The Package Travel and Linked Travel Arrangements Regulations 2018, a travel agent has a legal obligation to provide accurate information and this includes information about an itinerary. If there is incorrect or misleading information on the itinerary, then the travel organiser is responsible. While the customer has a responsibility to check the itinerary, the implications of an itinerary containing information that is incorrect or inaccurate can be, at the least, stressful for the customer and can even lead to legal action against the organisation. This can damage the company's reputation by attracting bad press and more complaints and losing future business from the customer affected and those they tell about their bad experience.

ACTIVITY

Back in your role-playing groups of three from before, you will again each take turns to play the part of the customer, travel agent and observer; switching roles so you all take a turn at each – you must follow the same pattern so the same customer is with the same agent.

As the customer, discuss the holiday itinerary with the travel agent.

As the travel agent, you must clearly explain to the customer why the holiday and itinerary you have selected (option 1) meets their requirements. Keep options 2 and 3 in reserve. If you had a list of additional questions, after reviewing the previous role play, make sure you remember to ask them.

As the observer, you will again listen and take notes about how the agent presents their itinerary and the type of further questions the agent is asking. Are they listening to the customer's feedback on their suggestion? You should then provide feedback to the other two people in your group and help them expand their own notes.

CHECK MY LEARNING

Carry out a review of the role-play activity. Makes some notes about how the customer reacted to your holiday itinerary. Was the customer satisfied that the plan met their needs and preferences?

How could you improve things? Is there anything that you could adapt or change to make the plan fit even better? If so, write these changes down.

Overcoming objections and understanding customers

GETTING STARTED

Why do you think it is important to show understanding to customers?

How would you go about doing so in the following situation: a holidaymaker objecting to a late flight in their itinerary.

Meeting customers' needs and preferences can be quite demanding. Customers will always have objections and it is important to show understanding towards different types of customer and their needs and preferences and respond to these objections in an appropriate manner.

Overcoming objections

Objections are the reasons that customers have for not buying a product or service (Figure 3.18). They are barriers that prevent closing a sale. For example, selling a boat BBQ excursion. A customer may say they don't want to go as they are vegetarian. This objection can be overcome by offering vegetarian options that form part of the package.

DID YOU KNOW?

Sir Richard Branson, the founder of Virgin Holidays, believes that 'solving problems means listening'. Objections are simply a problem or a reason for not buying a product. By listening, these objections can be overcome.

■ Figure 3.18: Common objections – how would you respond to these?

It is important to read your customers and not be too pushy. At the same time, it is important to try to overcome objections as you develop your relationship with your customers in the consultation and planning stage.

Cost

Cost is possibly the most common objection. Establishing a budget at the start of the process is crucial to prevent this from becoming an objection. Come up with alternatives so that you can give the customer choices if they decide the first option is too expensive.

Cheaper elsewhere

The product being cheaper somewhere else may also be a common objection that can be pre-empted by asking customers if they are looking at other options online or with other agents. Sell your service and make sure that there are no hidden costs with the product you are selling.

Need to consult with others or need time

Customers may often say that they don't want to purchase a product or make a booking until they have consulted with their travel companion or until they have time to think about it. This can be pre-empted by encouraging them to come in together when it comes to making plans and booking. If this is not possible, try to get the other person on the phone. Book in a time or make a note of when to follow up with a customer to encourage them to have that conversation and try to keep your sale.

Bad experience in the past

When people have used the company before or bought a similar product and had a bad experience, they may be reluctant to commit. This can be overcome by showing empathy with the customer and identifying exactly what the issue was. Tell the customer what has been done or what you can do to make sure that this doesn't happen again.

◘ How would you avoid a meeting becoming confrontational?

Showing understanding

It is important to show customers that you understand their individual needs and preferences. There are different ways that you can do this:

- listen – this is the first stage in understanding what they are saying and showing them that you care
- empathise – this is the ability to put yourselves in their shoes and show an awareness of how they feel about things
- give options – this is crucial to show that you can adapt things to meet the needs of the customer and don't have your own agenda
- reassurance – when customers are buying holidays, they are often buying dreams and they can't try before they buy. They are spending a lot of money and, on some occasions, this will be their once-in-a-lifetime holiday. It is important that you reassure customers that you will meet their expectations so that they trust you.

CHECK MY LEARNING

Working individually, review the role-play exercise and make notes about how, when you were the agent, you overcame the customer's objections and what you could have done differently. Include notes about what went well and what you did to show understanding.

ACTIVITY

Back in your role-playing groups of three from before, you will again each take turns to play the part of the customer, travel agent and observer. Switch roles so you all take a turn at each – you must follow the same pattern so the same customer is with the same agent.

As the customer, raise first a minor objection about the holiday plan presented to you in the last role play (perhaps the flight is too late in the day) and allow the agent to try to resolve it. Then raise a major objection, one that might mean the holiday presented won't work for you.

As the travel agent, you should listen to the customer and try to work out a change to resolve the minor objection. Then, in response to the major objection, try to convince them that option 1 could be adapted to resolve their issue. If you do not think it can be adapted, you could present your alternative options 2 or 3.

As the observer, you will again listen and take notes about how the agent handles the objections and complaints. Are they listening to the customer's feedback on their suggestion? You should then provide feedback to the other two people in your group and help them expand their own notes.

Learning aim B: assessment practice

How you will be assessed

In this component, you will be assessed by completing an internally assessed assignment set by your teacher. They will provide you with an assignment brief that outlines what you will need to do as well as a date by which the assignment should be completed and submitted. You may be required to complete a number of tasks, including producing reports, presentations or posters, for example. The teacher will mark the assignment and tell you what grade you have achieved.

For Learning aim B, you will be expected to show that you can meet the needs and preferences of travel and tourism customers. This will include:

- explaining how selected products or services meet customer needs and preferences of customers in given scenarios, with valid examples
- assessing customer needs and preferences to select appropriate products and services and producing a considered holiday plan that meets all customer needs and preferences, justifying decisions made.

CHECKPOINT

Review your learning of this component by answering the following questions; this will help you prepare for your assignment.

Strengthen

- Identify two different customer types.
- Identify the general needs and preferences of each customer type.
- Match travel and tourism products that may be suitable for these customer types.
- Explain why these tourism products are suitable.

Challenge

- Consider relevant factors that could influence the needs and preferences of these customer types.
- Make detailed recommendations for suitable travel products and services and justify why these recommendations are suitable.

ASSESSMENT ACTIVITY 1   LEARNING AIM   **B**

Below are two customer profiles; read them carefully.

- Mr and Mrs A and their children, aged 10 and 12 years, would like a holiday in the sun. Mrs A enjoys sunbathing and relaxing, her children enjoy water sports and spending time in the swimming pool and Mr A enjoys playing golf. They would like a short flight time, flying from Manchester airport. They would like a three- or four-star rated self-catering accommodation near to bars and restaurants. They like English food.

- Miss C and her friend, both in their early 20s, would like a holiday in the Greek Islands. They would like to fly from their regional airport of Newcastle. They are on a limited budget. They would like to spend their days on a beach or by the pool but would also like to spend a couple of days sightseeing. They would like some nightlife but also want to experience Greek food and culture.

For each of the customer profiles, you should:

- describe their needs and preferences
- match suitable products and services to meet their needs and preferences
- explain how the products and services you have selected meet the needs and preference of the customers.

Present your findings in a PowerPoint® presentation with speaker notes and images.

TIP

You may benefit from consulting holiday brochures and online holidays to get some ideas for your holiday plan.

ASSESSMENT ACTIVITY 2   LEARNING AIM   **B**

You are working as an apprentice in a local travel agent. A member of staff has asked you to work with her to put together a travel itinerary for a customer. Choose one of the following customer profiles:

- Mr and Mrs P are in their 60s and have recently retired. They would like a two-week holiday in Italy. The would like a multi-centre holiday with a week in the Lakes and a week in a city but have no preference which. They would like warm weather but not too hot and would like to avoid school holidays. A high standard of hotel accommodation with breakfast included is important to them. They would like to fly from Manchester. Budget is not an issue.

- Mr and Mrs E would like a seven to ten nights' beach holiday in Cuba. They would like to stay in an all-inclusive, four- or five-star hotel that is adults only. Their budget is £2,500. They would like to fly from London Gatwick. They would also like to visit Havana. Their dates of travel are flexible.

For each of the customer profiles, you should:

- analyse the needs and preferences of your selected customer
- plan a holiday to meet the needs and preferences of the customer
- explain how the planned holiday meets the needs of the customer.

Present your findings as a formal written travel plan and an information pack for the customer.

TIP

Research similar holidays, products and services to get some ideas for your travel plan.

TAKE IT FURTHER

Think of reasons why the travel plan meets the needs of your customer type. How well does it match what they want? How closely does it match their requirements?

Glossary

Ancillary services are services which support the main travel and tourism components and organisations. For example, when taking a flight, ancillary services could include travel insurance, airport lounge access and transfers.

Animal exploitation is abusing animals to entertain tourists.

Baby boomers are those born after the Second World War during a marked upswing in the birth rate (1945–1964), a socio-economic term.

Biodegrade means the breakdown of an object by bacteria and other living organisms.

Bleisure is a way of combining business with leisure travel.

A **brownfield site** is an area of land that has previously been built on.

Carbon footprint is a measure of the amount of carbon dioxide released by an individual or organisation.

A **city break** is usually defined as a short trip with overnight accommodation, of three nights or fewer.

Competition is companies selling similar products and services to the same target groups.

A **concierge** is a member of staff, usually in a hotel, who helps guests by providing directions, recommendations and advice, booking tours, and making reservations at theatres and restaurants.

Connectivity is the ability to link and communicate with other electronic devices, computer systems and the internet.

The **customer journey** is the full experience a customer has using an organisation's products and services, viewed holistically, but made up of each individual interaction: booking, airport, transfer to hotel and so on.

Dark tourism means travelling to places associated with death or suffering.

Destination management is the coordinated management of the different elements that make up a tourist destination, including visitor attractions, infrastructure, marketing and pricing.

Destination management organisations are generally inbound organisations that promote, manage and help to develop tourism in their area.

Differentiation is distinguishing between the needs and expectations of two or more groups of people.

Disposable income is the amount of money a person has left after the deduction of taxes and basic living costs. Income spent on the things that a person wants rather than needs, such as a holiday.

Eco-tourism is sustainable tourism that has as little impact as possible on the natural locations offered; it often also encompasses support of local conservation work.

An **ecosystem** is a community of interactions between the living and non-living environment.

An **epidemic** is when a disease or virus affects a particular region or large area of the world.

Ethical means something that is morally right or correct.

Flexibility means opportunities for and ease of arranging changes to the standard provision, sometimes at short notice.

A **gateway** is a place where visitors enter or exit the UK and continue their journey, for example a large international airport, such as London Heathrow, or seaport, such as the Port of Dover. Travellers often change from one mode of transport to another at the gateway.

A **government subsidy** is a form of financial aid provided with the aim of promoting a particular policy, such as stimulating tourism growth.

Gross domestic product (GDP) is the value of a country's economy. GDP measures the value of all goods and services over a specific time period (usually one year).

Ground transport moves visitors and travellers when they are not flying between destinations, for example a transfer from the airport to a hotel.

High season is those periods of the year when destinations attract the most visitors and the cost of travel and holiday accommodation rise.

A **hub** is a central location in a transport system with a number of inbound and outbound connections that use the same mode of transport; for example, a major railway station such as Euston in London.

Infrastructure is the structures and facilities, such as roads, buildings and power supplies, that enable a tourist destination to function properly.

Intellectual property (IP) means intangible property, the results of human creativity, encompassing copyrights, patents, literary and artistic works.

An **itinerary** is a detailed plan for a journey, that includes all essential travel details that a customer needs to reach the destination, such as dates, times, transport provider, and for when at the destination, such as details of accommodation and excursions, and relevant information about the destination in general.

Jobseeker's Allowance is an unemployment benefit that people can claim when they are looking for work.

Legislation means laws made by a government, e.g. UK Health and Safety at Work etc. Act 1974.

Local government refers to an administrative body for a small area such as a parish, town or county.

Low season is those periods of the year when destinations attract fewer visitors and the cost of travel and holiday accommodation falls.

Market segmentation is dividing a market into groups (segments) by characteristics; the segments comprise potential customers with similar characteristics and who are likely to respond to the same type of marketing and buy the same type of products and services.

National government is responsible for the whole country and has the power to set laws.

A **niche market** is a small or specialised market for a particular tourism product.

Package holidays are holidays where the price includes at least two components, for example air, rail or coach transport to get you to your destination, plus at least one night's accommodation.

A **pandemic** is the worldwide spread of a disease.

Practical assistance is help, often physical, to enable travellers to do something, be that moving from an airport lounge to departures and on to a plane, or negotiating selfservice technology.

Primary research is research that directly collects new data or facts to address a certain problem, validate a decision taken or answer specific questions.

Pro rata means a proportional amount of something. For example, a worker working three days a week would receive three-fifths of the holiday a full-time, five-day a week worker would receive.

Qualitative research seeks to understand the reasons, opinions and motivations of respondents and their behaviour. It targets why people do a certain thing. It is sometimes used to identify ideas for follow-up quantitative research.

Quantitative research – collects objective, measurable data, that can be used for statistical analysis. It targets how many people do a certain thing.

Questionnaires have a predefined set of questions, designed to collect data about specific things, most often in the form of a customer satisfaction questionnaire. Sometimes confused with a survey.

Regional government is responsible for the administration of larger geographical areas including collections of counties, in the UK, or states in larger countries such as Australia.

Regulations are rules set and monitored by an administrative body, such as the UK Trading Standards Institute.

Rejuvenation means restoring to a previous, better state or revitalising, improving the appearance of something.

Repatriate means to return someone back to their home country.

Repatriation is the return of a person to their country of origin.

A **resource** is a consumable item or supply, such as water, metal or fish. Can also be applied to people; for example, staff and labour.

A **rickshaw** is a light, usually two-wheeled, passenger vehicle that is usually pulled by a person either on foot or a bicycle.

Screen tourism is a type of tourism where people visit destinations and locations made popular in films and television series.

Seasonal variations are the changes in weather, temperature and climate at different times of the year, for example in summer or in winter.

Secondary research is research that builds on and uses existing primary research, sometimes by bringing together similar data from different sources or analysing their findings.

Self-catering apartments, holiday chalets and villas are offered to customers on a self-catering basis, where kitchen and cooking facilities are provided for customers to buy and prepare their own meals.

Sex tourism is travel planned for the purpose of sex, often in countries where prostitution is legal.

Social impacts are the effects on the surrounding society, in the case of tourism the people and social structures in host destinations.

Socio-demographics is a combination of the social and demographic characteristics of a population.

A **stakeholder** is a person or organisation that has an interest in the business or project. This can include the local community, customers, suppliers and businesses. Stakeholders can include organisations from the public, private and voluntary sectors.

A **staycation** is a holiday spent in a person's home country rather than abroad, quite often at home with day trips out to visit local attractions.

Surveys include the whole process of collecting data, through the use of questionnaires among other means, and then analysing the returned data to work out the significance of the responses and to draw conclusions from them. Sometimes confused with a questionnaire.

Sustainable means minimising the damage to something so that it can continue for a long time.

Tax credits are extra payments from the government paid to people in lower-paid work and/ or who have children that may require paid childcare.

A **terminal** is a location where transport journeys start or end, for example Liverpool Lime Street Station.

Tourists are people travelling for leisure.

A **trade union** is an organisation of workers from a particular profession that protects and furthers their rights and interests.

A **trend** – something that changes or develops in a general direction over time.

Visitors are people making a visit to a main destination outside their usual environment and for less than a year, for any main purpose, including holidays, leisure, business, health and education.

Water stress is when an area does not have enough water to meet the needs of the population.

World Heritage Sites are landmarks or areas selected by the United Nations Educational, Scientific and Cultural Organization (UNESCO) as having significance (cultural, historical or scientific) and are legally protected by international treaties.

The **WWF** (The World Wide Fund for Nature) is an international organisation dedicated to wildlife conservation.

Zero-hours contracts are a type of contract between a worker and employer, where the employer is not obliged to provide any minimum hours of work.

Appendix

Command words

The following lists key words that may be used in your assessments, with a definition.

- **Analyse** – Examine (something) methodically (e.g. break down into its component parts) and in detail, typically in order to explain, interpret or communicate something.
- **Assess** – Give careful consideration to the factors or events that apply and identify which are the most important or relevant. Make a judgement on the importance of something, and come to a conclusion where needed.
- **Complete** – Complete a table to categorise/classify.
- **Define** – Give the meaning of a term or phrase.
- **Describe** – Give an account of something, such as steps in a process or characteristics of something. The response should be developed, but does not require justification or reasoning.
- **Discuss** – Consider the different aspects in detail of an issue, situation, problem or argument and how they interrelate.
- **Explain** – Provide reasoning to justify or exemplify a point. The response should be developed using linked points providing reasoning/justification.
- **Evaluate** – Consider various aspects of a subject's qualities in relation to its context, such as strengths or weaknesses, advantages or disadvantages, pros or cons. Come to a judgment supported by evidence, which will often be in the form of a conclusion.
- **Give/Name/State** – Provide an accurate piece of information.
- **Identify** – Provide or select an answer from information given in the question.
- **Match** – Learners match between two sets of options.
- **What/When/Which/Why** – Learners identify which option is correct from the given options.

Index